CLEANLINESS AND CULTURE

VERHANDELINGEN
VAN HET KONINKLIJK INSTITUUT
VOOR TAAL-, LAND- EN VOLKENKUNDE

272

CLEANLINESS AND CULTURE

Indonesian histories

Edited by

KEES VAN DIJK and JEAN GELMAN TAYLOR

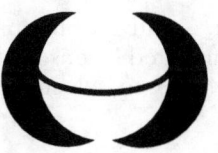

KITLV Press
Leiden
2011

Published by:
KITLV Press
Koninklijk Instituut voor Taal-, Land- en Volkenkunde
(Royal Netherlands Institute of Southeast Asian and Caribbean Studies)
P.O. Box 9515
2300 RA Leiden
The Netherlands
website: www.kitlv.nl
e-mail: kitlvpress@kitlv.nl

KITLV is an institute of the Royal Netherlands Academy of Arts and Sciences (KNAW)

KONINKLIJKE NEDERLANDSE
AKADEMIE VAN WETENSCHAPPEN

Cover: Creja ontwerpen, Leiderdorp

ISBN 978 90 6718 375 8

© 2011 Koninklijk Instituut voor Taal-, Land- en Volkenkunde

KITLV Press applies the Creative Commons Attribution-NonCommercial-NoDerivs 3.0 Unported License (http://creativecommons.org/licenses/by-nc-nd/3.0/) to selected books, published in or after January 2011.

Authors retain ownership of the copyright for their articles, but they permit anyone unrestricted use and distribution within the terms of this license.

Printed editions manufactured in the Netherlands

Contents

	INTRODUCTION	VII
1	SOAP IS THE ONSET OF CIVILIZATION *Kees van Dijk*	1
2	BATHING AND HYGIENE HISTORIES FROM THE KITLV IMAGES ARCHIVE *Jean Gelman Taylor*	41
3	THE EPIDEMIC THAT WASN'T BERIBERI IN BANGKA AND THE NETHERLANDS INDIES *Mary Somers Heidhues*	61
4	HYGIENE, HOUSING AND HEALTH IN COLONIAL SULAWESI *David Henley*	95
5	BEING CLEAN IS BEING STRONG POLICING CLEANLINESS AND GAY VICES IN THE NETHERLANDS INDIES IN THE 1930S *Marieke Bloembergen*	117
6	WASHING YOUR HAIR IN JAVA *George Quinn*	147
7	TROPICAL SPA CULTURES, ECO-CHIC, AND THE COMPLEXITIES OF NEW ASIANISM *Bart Barendregt*	159
	CONTRIBUTORS	193
	INDEX	195

Introduction

Perceptions of cleanliness and dirtiness have been used to describe, praise and denounce individuals and groups subscribing to different social, economic, religious or ethnic backgrounds. Villages, urban quarters, cities, even whole nations have been declared clean or filthy. Some colonial travellers even succeeded in projecting their dislike of other cultures onto the natural environment. As they traversed a country, they would decide that it was as dirty as its inhabitants, even though nowadays such landscapes may be renowned for their beauty, and the population might not have been as unclean as they presumed. Apparently blind to all evidence which might lead to a different conclusion, being clean was and is one of the yardsticks by which people declare themselves superior to others who differ from them in social and economic status, nationality, religion, and, as we all are sadly well aware, the colour of their skin. The consequence was that in propagating health and cleanliness, misled by feelings of superiority, some of the movements went terribly wrong, only to be damned and discredited for generations to come. Nowadays the German Hygiene Museum, founded in 1930 by the manufacturer of Odol mouthwash, is a Museum vom Menschen, a Museum of the Body, distancing itself from a past in which the Nazis high-jacked a perfectly comprehensible global movement promoting hygiene and health, in which Germany had been one of the forerunners (*Deutsches Hygiene-Museum* 2005:5-9).

Roughly since the middle of the nineteenth century, cleanliness has also become inextricably linked to the combating of epidemics and contagious diseases; sometimes leading to the enforcement of drastic sanitary measures by governments, health authorities, and colonial civil servants. In Europe slums and their inhabitants – the proverbial 'great unwashed' – had to be cleaned up in the name of progress. In Asia and Africa the indigenous population and non-white immigrants, who were viewed in more or less a similar way, were subjected to hygiene campaigns and sanitation projects. Needless to say, a great deal was accomplished, but ignorance, misconceptions about the causes of diseases, prejudices – not least about being or not being clean – and mutual distrust fostered by nationalist sentiments or personal dislikes influenced the research, the precautionary measures taken, and the efficacy of combating epidemics.

The efforts to combat contagious diseases both in Europe and the tropics produced an impressive array of socio-medical studies about personal and public hygiene in the Western and non-Western world. A dazzling Dutch example is a study by the pharmacist H.F. Tillema, published between 1915 and 1923, in which he analysed the sanitary conditions in the Netherlands Indies: six volumes, in quarto format, over 2000 pages in total, with hundreds of black-and-white photographs. In recent years, a number of books of another nature have been published. These deal with how attitudes towards cleanliness, towards taking a bath, washing clothes, and changing underwear have shifted over time. Some are simply entitled 'clean' (Smith 2007; Ashenburg 2008), others stress the 'dirt' at a particular moment in history (Cockayne 2007). The bulk of this literature refers to Europe. The non-Western world and the 'cleanliness superiority' Westerners outside Europe and the United States claimed receives scant attention. This book focuses on cleanliness in Indonesia. It contains a selection of the papers read at a conference about cleanliness sponsored by the Koninklijk Instituut voor Taal-, Land- en Volkenkunde (KITLV, Royal Netherlands Institute of Southeast Asian and Caribbean Studies) in Leiden in August 2007 organized by Kees van Dijk.

The first two chapters deal with physical hygiene and the everyday environment; taking a bath or not, the washing of clothes, and keeping houses, yards and streets spick and span. This is followed by two contributions about cleanliness and the battle against such diseases as beriberi and skin complaints in a tropical environment. In a fifth chapter the attention shifts from the physical to the immaterial, to the sensitive topic of social and political cleanliness. The final two chapters turn away from the past; dealing with body care in present-day Indonesia.

In his well-known study, Schama (1988) has drawn attention to the fame of seventeenth-century Dutch housewives and their maids who were renowned for their scrupulous cleansing of their streets and homes. The Dutch even transported this habit to their colonies, where as Kees van Dijk relates, by enforcing city cleanliness regulations in Malacca autocratically, a certain Mr Sweep even entered the realm of Malay literature. When personal hygiene was concerned it was a different story. Bodies were not scrubbed as vigorously as the streets. In the first chapter Kees van Dijk traces the change in the cleanliness of Europeans in Europe and in the tropics. One of the questions he tackles is how in an age in which both Westerners and Asians frequently washed their bodies Europeans in their colonies succeeded in convincing themselves that they and only they had claim to be really clean, and that Malays, Javanese, Indians and other such peoples fell short of the proper qualifications to be referred to as such. For a brief period in history one answer found was that the former used soap and the latter did not, making soap one of the markers of civilization. Another way of maintaining Western cleanliness superiority was to concede that Asian bodies might be clean, but that their clothes and houses were filthy; obviously blotting out all the assiduous washing of clothes which took place in full public view, and indeed of which many pictures and photos have been preserved.

One vast collection of such pictures and photos is in the possession of the KITLV. What it can tell us about the topic of cleanliness is analysed by Jean Gelman Taylor. As it did in Europe, the change in favour of taking a bath among Europeans in the tropics commenced in the middle of the nineteenth century. Before that moment, Europeans must been a conspicuously smelly minority amid a wider indigenous society whose members took a bath more than once a day. Later the Europeans in the tropics did wash themselves frequently, but striking differences remained entrenched. Europeans had transported to the tropics their sense of privacy regarding such acts as washing. As Jean Gelman Taylor writes in her chapter, the colonial and Indonesian elite washed their bodies in the bathroom and away from the public gaze. Hence there are no pictures of Europeans or sultans and princes taking a bath, but an abundance of photos of Indonesians bathing in canals and rivers.

The next section, cleanliness and the battle against diseases, opens with Mary Somers Heidhues tracing the search for the cause of beriberi, a vitamin deficiency, at the end of the nineteenth century. The story told resembles that of other contemporaneous medical breakthroughs. Racist notions, rivalries among medical researchers, and the strong belief that a disease from which so many people suffer must have something to do with a filthy environment and poor hygiene – or with germs – spurred scientists and policy makers on in the wrong direction. They ignored, indeed even ridiculed findings indicating what really did cause beriberi. Or, as she writes: 'For years, however, ideas of cleanliness or contagion turned out to be enemies of appropriate treatment for the victims'. One community where beriberi struck in the Netherlands Indies was among Chinese coolies mining tin in Bangka. It would be the second decade of the twentieth century before the cheap, industrially milled and vitamin denuded white rice the coolies ate was replaced by healthy brown rice. Thereafter beriberi no longer posed much of a problem.

| *Introduction*

Changing medical knowledge also features in David Henley's treatise on hygiene and health in the Minahasa in North Sulawesi. Nineteenth-century literature depicts the its inhabitants as extremely filthy and given to unhygienic habits. The conclusion was easy to draw. Because access to water for washing and drinking was then limited in many parts of North Sulawesi, various kinds of chronic skin disease were rampant. In contrast, nowadays such afflictions are rare, as are cholera, dysentery and a number of the other diseases which used to plague the population. In explaining the significant improvement in health conditions during the last century, Henley turns to changing housing patterns, the outcome of a combination of colonial health policy measures and a spontaneous reaction to new economic opportunities and the establishment of peace. Houses were built closer to roads and streams; big, multiple-hearth houses were replaced by smaller ones; supervisory measures were taken to keep dwellings and their immediate surroundings clean; and children were taught how to clean themselves. Soap and footwear were introduced. As Henley concludes, such changes were important, but it is difficult to weigh up their effects on general health against those of administering medicines and improved nutrition.

The colonial section ends with a contribution by Marieke Bloembergen. So far attention has centred on European images of the other, with an occasional insight into how these Europeans preferred to depict themselves. In this chapter the ideal self-image of a particular group of Europeans, the police force, is presented. It also highlights the gruesome consequences the use of cleanliness and related words can have when used in a metaphorical sense, especially when being clean is linked to being pure and, as a further step, to strength. In Indonesia between 1965 and 1998 the authorities succeeded in giving the term clean environment their own special metaphorical meaning. The way they used the term had nothing to do with the tidiness of cities or nature, but had all to do with the barring of people who had or had had communist relatives, friends, or tutors from government positions. Marieke Bloembergen describes something similar but in the colonial setting: the sudden pursuit of European homosexuals and the arrest of around 225 men, among them senior colonial civil servants, in the Netherlands Indies in 1938 and 1939. Commenting on the investigation colonial newspapers, the authors of letters to the editor, the police, and colonial authorities all spoke in terms of cleanliness and hygiene, using terms such as a spring-clean and a cleansing process; a vocabulary all too familiar to present-day newspaper readers. As the title of her chapter suggests, the police campaign

Introduction

against homosexuals was intended to show that European society and the police in the Netherlands Indies were clean and hence strong in a time of growing political problems in the colony itself and in the world.

The last two chapters focus on bodily hygiene and religion. George Quinn discusses traditional Javanese bathing-places as centres of communal life and religious ritual and the ceremonial washing of hair. In Java, the ritual washing of hair is performed in public and *en masse* at holy places during religious holidays and as a private ceremony in the family sphere at important transition points in human life, such as in the preparations for marriages, during and after pregnancy, and after death. In these ceremonies, the hair is cleansed with lye made by burning dry rice stalks. Traditional shampoo is still widely used in rural villages but commercial brands, some still based on the rice stalks extract of the past, have stolen a march in the cities. Social and economic changes have inevitably left their mark, resulting in complaints that the hair-washing ceremonies at holy places have been robbed of much of their original meaning and have become more of a tourist attraction. Even so, tradition lives on, albeit it in a different form. The option of wearing of a headscarf taken by an increasing number of Muslim women requires frequent washing of the hair, imbuing the action with an element of piety. As its members move up in the world socially and are proud to show it, the burgeoning middle class copies many features of the traditional Javanese wedding ceremony, including the washing of the hair.

An image of the East contrasting with that described by Kees van Dijk in which Westerners claimed to be standard-bearers of cleanliness is discussed by Bart Barendregt. His contribution examines the world of the tropical spas, a fast-growing sector of the leisure industry in Southeast Asia, frequented by well-to-do Europeans and Asians. An analysis of coffee-table books and magazines reveals that owners and managers of such spas show a distinct propensity to link up with a romanticized Asia of the past: extolling the healing qualities of rivers and springs, the beauty of the human body and the natural environment. Ancient goddesses, queens, princesses and palaces, and spirituality, are all pivotal elements. Hence, the concomitant stress on traditional Asian beauty and health treatments. Such spas come in various forms. There are luxurious spa resorts where rich tourists and wealthy Southeast Asians can stay overnight, but also Muslim day spas. In Indonesia, clients can also engage the service of a spa to prepare for a marriage in traditional style and the bathing ceremonies required by such a marriage ceremony, a practice which George Quinn also notes has gained popularity in

| *Introduction*

Indonesia. The spas are an integral part of a New Asian Lifestyle of the local well-to-do, emphatically proclaiming the virtues of slow traditional food, the natural and the authentic.

The topic of cleanliness presented in this book is part of a new trend in bringing sensory history to the field of Southeast Asian Studies. The sources are manifold. They include travel books old and new, anthropological and medical studies, ego-documents, Southeast Asian traditional and modern literature, brochures, eye-witness accounts, laws, newspaper stories, advertisements, images, and song texts. It shows how cleanliness of body and spirit is integral to individual and group identity and the conception of the other.

REFERENCES

Ashenburg, Katherine
2008 *Clean; An unsanitised history of washing*. London: Profile Books.
Cockayne, Emily
2007 *Hubbub; Filth, noise & stench in England 1600-1770*. New Haven, CT/London: Yale University Press.
Deutsches Hygiene-Museum
2005 *Deutsches Hygiene-Museum Dresden*. München: Prestel.
Schama, Simon
1988 *The embarrassment of riches; An interpretation of Dutch culture in the Golden Age*. N.p.: Fontana Press.
Smith, Virginia
2007 *Clean; A history of personal hygiene and purity*. Oxford: Oxford University Press.
Tillema, H.F.
1915-23 *'Kromoblanda'; Over 't vraagstuk van 'het wonen' in Kromo's groote land*. 's-Gravenhage: Uden Masman. Six vols.

1

Soap is the onset of civilization

Kees van Dijk

'We are dirty, We are dirty. We do not know how to wash ourselves. We have not acquired education.' These were just some of the lines children in colonial Rhodesia had to sing early in the twentieth century on their first day at school at the St Faith Mission while they were being marched to a stream (Burke 1996:196). Were those children dirty? Besides washing, they may have smeared their bodies with a mixture of soil and oil or fat to repel the dirt, but I am sure they were not dirty. Smearing oneself with soil and oil may sound strange but in sixteenth-century England dirt was removed from clothes by smearing them 'with mud or scouring them with dung' (Cunnington and Cunnington 1992:47). Why then did the St Faith missionaries force these children to sing that they did not know how to wash themselves? The answer probably is that they did not use soap.

In the course of the nineteenth century soap was appropriated in certain European and American circles, of which Christian revivalists were in the vanguard, to emphasize cultural superiority. Soap was presented as the talisman to modernization. A Unilever slogan even exults that 'Soap is civilization' (McClintock 1995:207) (Figure 1.) In a 1890 advertisement for one particular brand, Pears' Soap, the washing ashore of a soapbox somewhere along the coast of Equatorial Africa was hailed as 'The birth of civilization'. The consumption of soap was 'a Measure of the Wealth, Civilisation, Health and Purity of the People' (Richards 1990:140-1). The person portrayed in the advertisement does not look like an inhabitant of Africa; he looks much more like a fantasy of a South Sea Islander. This gives the message conveyed an additionally nasty flavour. From the 1840s coconut oil extracted from copra had been in great demand as an ingredient of soap. As copra became a much sought-after commodity – 'the glory and the wealth of the South Sea islands' (Forbes 1875:52) – it led to an influx of ruthless Western businessmen and adventurers. The aftermath on Hawai'i, Samoa and other Pacific islands was civil war, alienation of land,

Figure 1. 'The birth of civilization'. A Pears' Soap advertisement.

forced labour recruitment and migration, and the destruction of the local social structure and culture.[1]

Soap was not the only reference point on the scale of civilization. There were many: dress, language, and even the toilet. The man who was most adamant about the glorious function of our loo was George Jennings, the successful designer of a wash-down closet. He proudly displayed his patented flushed water-closet at the 1851 Great Exhibition in London, the supreme opportunity to show off the accomplishments of Western technology, and the first in a long series of World Exhibitions. His contraption was a great success. It conquered the world and at the Great Exhibition over 827,280 visitors paid a penny to use Jennings' 'monkey-closet'.[2] Jennings once observed that 'the civilization of a people can be measured by their domestic and sanitary appliances,' although he may have had monetary considerations and the domestic or Western market rather than a civilizing mission in the forefront of his mind (Horan 1996:85, 88). It is too good an opportunity to fail to point out that Jennings' yardstick would have placed the European colonial community in British India rather low on the scale of civilization. In 1856 there still were no water-closets in Government House in Calcutta, the official residence of the Governor-General (Dalrymple 2006:122).

Water closets had been known since the end of the sixteenth century, but had not enjoyed great success. There was always the risk they could cause cesspits to overflow and consequently needed an expensive sewage system. Other drawbacks were that they could leak and, most importantly, that the waste-pipe went straight down. The goose neck had not yet been invented to isolate the smell of the sewer from the house. Rather than being hailed as a blessing, water closets were even considered decadent and wasteful. Nevertheless, it was an invention greatly esteemed by the English. It was a marker of their advanced level of civilization. Water closets created a way of relieving oneself far superior to the way the Dutch, or for that matter any other nationality abroad. It made the Dutch, among other nations, look very backward. Dutchmen in need sought the waters of a lake, as the drawing of James Gilray from 1796 'Dutch convenience – the lake' shows (Cockayne 2007:144; Horan 1996:72-5). Later, for instance in Siam during the reign of King Rama V (r. 1868-1910), one of those modernizing monarchs at the turn of

---

1 About a decade later copra would become an important ingredient for the manufacture of candles. Because of the American Civil War the South Pacific also became an important producer of cotton, giving an additional impetus to the exploitation of the Islanders.
2 See also: http://home.netlinc.org.uk/ContentStore/__Public/Documents/0019400/19478/cdrom/East%20Midlands/victorian/timeline.htm (accessed 10-6-2011).

the last century, toilets did indeed become one of the symbols of the drive towards civilization. Shitting around had become a sign of backwardness. Not everybody agreed. There were advantages in selecting a nice place in a field with a good view and a cool breeze as a Thai farmer told an American doctor somewhat later: 'You Americans are strange. Before you came here, if I felt like relieving myself, I found a quiet spot in the open with gentle breezes and often a pleasant vista. Then you came along and convinced me that this material that comes from me is one of the most dangerous things with which people can have contact. In other words I should stay away from it as far as possible. Then the next thing you told me was that I should dig a hole, and not only I, but many other people should concentrate this dangerous material in that hole. So now I have even closer contact not only with my own but everyone else's, and in a dark, smelly place with no view at that.' (Hanlon 1969:67.)

The flush toilets developed by Jennings and others turned out to be a dubious contribution to civilization, not to speak of cleanliness. Though for many who used the Jennings' water closet at the Great Exhibitions this was a novel experience, the middle of the nineteenth century was the moment at which WCs were being installed in increasingly more houses in London and in other European cities. In London water now entered the city's drainage system in abundance, and enriched with what it had flushed away ended up in the River Thames. The amount of faecal matter daily dispensed in this way was enormous: in the 1840s some 250 tons, in the 1860 thousands of tons (Smith 2007:279). In 1858, seven years after the Great Exhibition, during an exceptionally hot summer London endured its Great Stink.[3]

The water closet conquered only part of the world. In 1943, when Ibn Saud, King of Saudi Arabia, met President Roosevelt aboard the *USS Quincy*, the way in which his sixty-men entourage answered nature's call by simply leaning over the rail upset American sailors, as they probably had to clean the mess on the deck (Oren 2007:472). And even nowadays modern tourists in Paris may go to McDonalds not to eat but in search of a decent toilet and not a simple hole in the ground (Lagarde 2005).

Nevertheless, it was soap which emerged as the pre-eminent marker of personal hygiene and civilization in European eyes. Soap ensured people were physically clean and helped them meet one of the criteria of being civilized.

---

3 Halliday 1999:42-7. Because of this problem, some British cities discouraged the use of water closets (Halliday 1999:45). For similar problems in France, see Barnes 2006.

1 Soap is the onset of civilization

THE FLIGHT FROM THE BATH

At this point it must be remembered that bodily hygiene had disappeared from Europe after the Middle Ages. In the Renaissance people had still found pleasure in taking a bath (Roche 2000:158-9). They had also detested body odours, preferring to smell sweet (Smith 2007:158). Italians especially had 'cared deeply about being clean and keeping their environment clean' (Biow 2006:xii). In Northern Europe it may have been thought that the way they did so was a little excessive. In one story recounted around 900 by the Swiss monk Notker of St Gall (840-912), also known as Notker the Stammerer, entitled *The deacon who washed too much* readers are warned not to embrace the grooming 'habits of the Italians'. The over-hygienic deacon 'used to take baths, he had his head very closely shaved, he polished his skin, he cleaned his nails, he had his hair cut sort as if it had been turned on a lathe, and he wore linen underclothes and a snow-white shirt' (Smith 2007:148).

Washing was part of this Italian lifestyle, but the sensation of being clean was above all evoked by putting on fresh, pleasant-smelling clothes. Washing with water was not especially essential. Wiping off dirt or rubbing one's body clean and changing clothes could suffice, both then and later in European history. Consequently, in those days soap was more important as a means to clean clothes than it was to clean bodies (Biow 2006:15, 99; Cockayne 2007:60; Ashenburg 2008:106-7). Such emphasis on changing clothes indicates that the persons whose bodily hygiene is described here must have had money. It goes without saying that region, social class and wealth all can cause differences in the use of water and also of soap. Soap was available, but even when it was not excessively greasy and did not act as an irritant to the skin when cleaning the body, it was too expensive to be affordable to many (Cockayne 2007:60).

Whatever the case and with the exception of such countries with a strong sauna tradition as Finland, Russia, and Ireland (Aaland 1978:72, 115, 122-5, 132-3), there was, what one author described, a 'flight of the elites from the bath' after the Renaissance (Roche 2000:159). To bathe it was usually necessary to undress (though as we can observe nowadays among some strict Muslim women using swimming pools or going to the beach, not necessarily so) and the growing influence of Christianity and its rejection of nudity certainly had something to do with this. A variety of saints, male and female, had for centuries decided that a sound and devout mind should be housed in a filthy body and had stopped washing themselves and their clothes.⁴ Still, exceptions were made. In his *Règles de la bienséance et de la civilité chrétienne* from 1695, the seventeenth-century French Saint Jean-Baptiste de la Salle (1651-1719) urged people to wash their ears in order to hear better what was said in church (Perrot 1987).

For a long time such a saint may have belonged to 'a vociferous minority of religious puritans' (Smith 2007:140) and did indeed at first form an exception but in the end their repulsion to cleanliness prevailed. In the sixteenth and seventeenth centuries, the popular medieval communal bathhouses, a continuation of Greek, Roman and local traditions, were considered all the more offensive as in some people of both sexes mingled. They began to be looked on as dens of iniquity and disappeared from the cities and villages. Steam baths which Crusaders had discovered in the Middle East suffered a similar fate (Perrot 1987:13). The Church condemned such worldly pleasures as taking a bath and enjoying it. Even anti-Islamic sentiments played a role. In Spain the situation did not improve when Christianity prevailed over the Peninsula. Ashenburg (2008:111) argues that because 'the Moor was clean, the Spanish decided that Christians should be dirty'. Bathing was considered to be a Muslim, Moorish custom. Bath houses were banned in 1576 and the Inquisition considered taking a bath an indication that converted Muslims and Jews were reverting to their old ways. Temporal authorities also may have found the sight of the lower classes bathing in rivers morally offensive. Church and Government fought a losing battle. The habit of swimming in rivers was very difficult to eradicate, also as it was a popular pastime even among the elite.⁵

At least in France, but probably all over Europe, smelling foul became associated with strength, health, and wealth. At least up to the end of the eighteenth century, some medical doctors believed

---

4   Smith 2007:134-9; Ashenburg 2008:58-62. The unwashed saint emerged early in Christianity. The most famous perhaps is Saint Francis of Assisi (1181-1226), who, as it is observed with some astonishment on a website devoted to him (Bonacorsi n.d.), 'went on behaving more and more strangely, up to when he start walking around Assisi dressed in rags and very dirty'. To Francis of Assisi a dirty body was 'a stinking badge of piety' (Ashenburg 2008:60). The examples Virginia Smith (2007:138-9) mentions include St Melania (383-439) and St Anthony (1195-1231). A more recent example is Benedictus Labre (1748-1783) who ate the vermin which covered him and believed in the virtues of excreta (Corbin 1986:274), a fact which now tends to be glossed over in any mentions of this saint. Equally old is the lashing out at bath-houses. St Jerome (340-420) regarded public baths as 'evil' and St Athanasius (296-373), considering a basin 'sufficient [...] to wash away your dirt', fulminated against 'the women who bathe [...]. And have dragged others down into corruption.' (Smith 2007:139.)
5   Roche 2000:163-4; Smith 2007:201, 219. Until the beginning of the nineteenth century, precautions were taken at the Dutch bathing resort of Scheveningen to spare the well-to-do seaside visitors the sight of ordinary villagers bathing naked in the sea (Kuus 2007:16).

in the medicinal merit of stench to combat the plague, while others thought that a bath in excreta could even cure that pestilence. Labourers engaged in smelly jobs were also convinced of the benefits to their health of noxious odours (Corbin 1986:267-8). Some people even feared that frequent bathing would rob them of their strength. Others, and this was a widely held notion, considered bathing a health hazard (Soo and Stevenson 2007:37; Roche 2000:158, 163; Corbin 1986:59-62). Carl Linnaeus (1707-1778), the famous eighteenth-century botanist whose profession was medical doctor, also did his bit to promote rankness, warning that washing one's hair might cause epilepsy (Koerner 1996:158). And, for the sake of honesty, it has to be admitted that the fear of catching syphilis (a new disease in Europe around 1500) and the plague certainly also played a role in the disappearance of bathhouses (Smith 2007:179-82).

Elsewhere in the world people did not stop bathing Europeans noted. Emily Cockayne (2007:60) observes that such minor routines as cleaning the body are hardly mentioned in diaries, travel reports and other literature. Although this is generally true, the exception is when something unexpected is observed. Maybe this is why frequent bathing and the washing of hair are often mentioned by late-sixteenth- and early-seventeenth-century Europeans visiting Asia. One of them, Jan Huygen van Linschoten, observed in his famous *Itinerario* that villagers near Goa in India and the indigenous wives of the Portuguese living in that city washed their bodies daily, a habit he dismisses as a useless ritual (Van den Boogaart 2000:20-2; Rouffaer and IJzerman 1925:29, 306-7; Breet 2003:446-7). Such travellers could also observe that taking a bath might even have a social and ceremonial function. When the commander of a small English fleet, Thomas Best, visited Aceh in 1613 he noted in his diary that the 'King invighted me to his founteyne to swime [...]. And having washed and bathed ourselves in the water, the Kinge presented us with an exceedinge greate bankett, with two much rack [arak]; all to be eaten and druncke as wee sett in the water; all his nobles and greate captaynes beinge presente.' (Foster 1934:55.) It is an early reference to the water palaces of the rulers in the region. Called by the Dutch *waterkastelen* (water castles) or *lusthoven* (gardens of delight), they were built in such places as Cirebon (Sungaragih) and Yogyakarta (built by Sultan Hamengkubuwono I between 1758 and 1765).[6] Elsewhere in the East the same fondness for taking a

---

[6] In Yogyakarta there were two such bathing palaces: Taman Sari (Garden of Delight) and Taman Ledok (Lower Garden). How beautiful and imposing the Yogyakarta 'water palace' may once have been can be surmised from its depiction in Thorn (1815, 2004: Plate XXV). See also Dumarçay 1978, Groneman 1885 and Bosboom 1902.

bath was observed. In retrospect, some authors who acknowledge the 'Hindu love of washing' are even sure that the Indian bathing habits contributed to the spread of new notions of hygiene in Great Britain (Spear 1998:146; Smith 2007:235).

SWEEPING THE STREETS

Europe and Europeans must have stunk – in some regions more than in others - in the seventeenth, eighteenth, and nineteenth centuries. One small contribution to this was that there were no inhibitions about breaking wind. And when farting was disapproved of, we can conclude from morality books, such as an early sixteenth-century work by Erasmus (1530, and still reprinted in the eighteenth century), which bear a strong resemblance to a collection of fatwas, and an early eighteenth-century treatise by La Salle (1729), it was the noise which was considered offensive not the stench.[7] Nevertheless not all was dirt. Clothes, furniture, except for beds which were hardly ever aired and stank, floors, and streets were cleaned (Cockayne 2007:58-9). In France and England this did not perhaps occur as fanatically as in the Netherlands. In Schama's description (1988:375-85) in his *The embarrassment of riches*, Dutch housewives and maids of the seventeenth century so absorbed in scrubbing and polishing emerge as members of a weird Calvinist sect, not fully understood and appreciated by contemporaries abroad.

The overwhelming Dutch passion for cleanliness in cities also made a lasting impression on the Malays. One of the persons who figures in Abdullah bin Abdul Kadir's autobiography *Hikayat Abdullah* (finished in 1843) is Mr Bamgoor. His real name must have been Van Goor, Secretary to the Dutch Governor of Malacca in 1818. Bamgoor, also known as Mr. Sweep, is portrayed as being obsessed with urban cleanliness. Each night he inspects the streets and hands out fines to inhabitants when rubbish is left lying in front of their houses. Abdullah bin Abdul Kadir calls him 'a leech, drinking the blood of Allah's servants'. Consequently: 'When Bamgoor came out of the Fort riding his horse there was everywhere a general rush for home to get brooms and to start sweeping in front of the houses, until the noise of sweeping rent the air. Because people were afraid of being fined...' But revenge was sweet. God inter-

---

7   Perrot 1987:15; Elias 2001:90, 196-7, 199. The term morality books I borrow from the field of Chinese Studies and the discussions of shansu (morality books) literature. See, for instance, King (2007)

vened and 'before three months were out Mr. Sweep became ill and demented, crying out constantly in fear and declaring that people had struck him' (Abdullah bin Abdul Kadir1970:148-9).

Differences between European countries have to be taken into consideration. The Dutch cleaning mania was not unique in its sort. Around 1400 one of its prominent citizens of Florence, Leonardo Bruni, praised the city as being 'so clear and neat that no other city could be cleaner'. In Florence nothing was to be found that was 'disgusting to the eye, offensive to the nose, or filthy under foot' (Kohl 1978:138). Later, in the sixteenth and seventeenth century Swiss and German cities enjoyed a similar reputation to those in the Netherlands (Ashenburg 2008:4, 103), but in the same period it is not difficult to find descriptions of foul-smelling French and English cities, especially in the summer. In the 1650s the Common Council of London concluded that the city's streets were 'extreme offensive to the Inhabitants and Passengers, with ashes, dust, dirt, rubbish and filth, and with noysome and unwholsome smels' (Cockayne 2007:184-5). One century later it was decided that the streets of the city were so filthy that it might have been inhabited by 'a herd of barbarians, or a colony of hottentots' (Cockayne 2007:181). In 1777 a high official of the Russian Ministry of Foreign Affairs, Denis Fonvizin (2006:46, 120) admittedly no friend of the French, wrote home to his sister that he had arrived in France and that there was no doubt about that: the awful stench in the very first French city he had entered. It was the same in all towns and villages in France. It was essential to pinch one's nose. There was nothing for the Russians to borrow from the notion of cleanliness of the French, of their moral behaviour still less.

REDISCOVERING THE CLEAN BODY

Bathrooms or the pleasure people found in bathing had not completely disappeared, but the idea that washing might actually be healthy only gained ground in the second half of the eighteenth century (Roche 2000:162-5). Concurrently, what Corbin (1986:85) calls a decrease in the tolerance of smells began to evolve among the elite. The passion for smelling sweet and pleasant returned (Corbin 1986:106). It was the period in which the aristocracy and the elites returned to their bathrooms, which eventually became essential elements in their houses (Smith 2007:230, 234-5). Consequently, bodily hygiene became a characteristic of the rich, and well into the twentieth century stinking was presented as a marker of social backwardness and of the lower orders, the working class and the poor, who had no option but to live in dismal circumstances (Soo and Stevenson 2007:36-7; Perrot 1987:108; Corbin 1986:158-206). It was a period in which well-off British people could still speak of the masses as 'the great unwashed', a term coined by the English writer William Makepeace Thackeray in his 1849 novel *Pendennis* (Ashenburg 2008:170). The unwashed masses may have taken offence at this qualification, but, initially at least, had no problem with their bodies and environments smelling less than fresh (Corbin 1986:83). A great social distance separated the elite from those who, when all is said and done, can be termed the domestic natives, being treated and viewed in a manner very similar to the way inhabitants of the British and other colonies were. Language testifies to this. Savages was one of the terms used to denote the 'very poorest' in Great Britain (Smith 2007:280); taking its place alongside those as 'rabble, mob, caste, mass, sheep and herd' (Kildea 2006:11-2).

In the early nineteenth century the well-to-do also discovered shampoo, not for the hair but for the body. Shampoo must be mentioned here because it is a Hindi loan word, meaning massage, and is one of the contributions of the non-Western world to Western hygiene. In the 1810s shampoo entered Great Britain when an Indian immigrant, Sake Dean Mahomed, set himself up in Brighton as a 'shampooing surgeon'. A few years later he opened his Indian Vapour Baths and Shampooing Establishment in the city. Sake Dean Mahomed claimed that the massage and sweating baths he offered cured his clientele, members of the nobility and gentry, from rheumatism and other diseases. His business did not enjoy a promising start. People talked about 'a cheat and a Hindoo juggler'. Whatever the odds he encountered, Sake Dean Mahomed would eventually rise to the position of Shampooing Surgeon to both King George IV and King William IV. He advertised in a book his medical successes, *Shampooing, or benefits resulting from the Indian medicated vapour bath, as introduced into this country, by S.D. Mahomed (A native of India)*, of which the first edition was published in 1822.[8]

Taking their vapour baths and having declared bathing healthy, the elite began to promote washing and hygiene in general, not

---

8 See www.fathom.com/course/21701766/session5.html (accessed June 2011). Another non-European bathing habit the Turkish bath or hammam was introduced into Great Britain and the rest of Europe in the middle of the nineteenth century (Aaland 1978:5). In Great Britain, it became popular in the Victorian Era (http://en.wikipedia.org/wiki/Hammam accessed June 2011) and others attribute its introduction to the Scottish diplomat David Urquhart and his travelogue *The Pillars of Hercules* (1850). Urquhart was indeed an enthusiastic advocate of the hammam, suggesting the building of a 1000 Turkish baths in London to 'wage war against drunkenness, immorality, and filth in every shape' (Aaland 1978:48). It may, however, well be that the first Turkish baths in Great Britain were of an earlier date (Smith 2007:206).

least because they were confronted with among other horrors outbreaks of cholera in European cities. Public bathhouses reappeared, initially to cater to the middle classes. Later industrialists built bathhouses for their labourers, while municipalities took care of the bodies of the poor, probably as was the case in the Netherlands first in the cities and later on in the countryside (Smith 2007:243, 281-2; Perrot 1987:18-20, 118; De Leeuw 1993:176, 262, 464). But it was only around the middle of the nineteenth century, when the upper and middle classes could no longer stand the stench emanating from the others, that the idea that washing was hygienic and healthy gradually gained ground in wider society.[9] Personal cleanliness developed into a real mania in Europe and the United States in the early twentieth century;[10] almost inevitably also resulting in a fair amount of scholarly studies about cleanliness and about how people reacted to smelly armpits, bad breath, and other bodily odours (Soo and Stevenson 2007). The rise of such attention is recent. Norbert Elias, who writes about spitting, farting, blowing one's nose and other such things in his study of 1939 *Über den Prozess der Zivilisation*, hardly mentions bathing except for one lengthy footnote. When he does, it is to illustrate changing European attitudes towards nakedness. He is sure that up to the second half of the eighteenth century, hygiene enters the picture only as a *post-factum* discovered justification for changing social habits (Elias 201:176, 178, 783). There is no word in *Über den Prozess der Zivilisation* about such core elements of personal cleanliness as the use of soap and the changing of underwear.

THE ANGLICIZATION OF THE BRITISH RULING CLASS IN INDIA

In the colonies another process was taking place. At the end of the eighteenth century a campaign was launched by the newly emerging colonial elite to 'Anglicize' the British ruling class in its colonies, allowing for all kind of prejudices, among them those about cleanliness to gain force. In India the advance of the new elite spelled the

---

9 Of course this was a gradual process. The idea that bathing could endanger one's health or bordered on immorality took a long time to die (De Leeuw 1992:354). Another point still stressed by some was that the wearing of clean underwear was more important than a frequently washed body (Perrot 1987:113).
10 Ideas of personal hygiene spread over the world. In the colonies hygiene campaigns to combat diseases became almost endemic. As the story of the Thai farmer and his struggle with a modern, Western toilet indicates, such campaigns did not leaving independent countries like Thailand and China unaffected (Hell 2007:133-73; Dikötter 2007:205-9).

end to generations of British men who had happily and comfortably adjusted to the local high-life in the seventeenth and the eighteenth century; some of whom are so vividly described in studies by William Dalrymple (2002) and Maya Jasanoff (2005). Such people, then on their way out, had had a keen interest in local culture and did not speak of Indians or the natural environment being dirty. The Asians with whom these men mingled had taught them to bathe and to enjoy it. They had also made them familiar with smoking a waterpipe (hookah) and other local pleasures. Dalrymple (2002:36) writes that it was Indian women who had introduced British men to 'the delights of regular bathing'. Others among their compatriots had not yet come so far. On their return home, such bath-taking British were 'scolded by their less hygienic compatriots' and were considered to have become 'effeminate' (Dalrymple 2002:36).

Initially, such European bath lovers may only have been a happy few. In Southeast Asia, other Europeans had almost certainly also been shown the way to the bath by native women, but in the seventeenth and the eighteenth century it probably took at least one generation before Europeans in the tropics could shed what the Dutch historian De Haan (1922, II:80) has called their hydrophobia. Describing life in Batavia in the middle of the eighteenth century, he writes that 'born Dutchmen' detested bathing as did the Portuguese. They left this to the ladies, who were of local or mixed descent (De Haan 1922, II:80). Jean Gelman Taylor (1983:1010) also notes that European men in Batavia 'refused to adapt to the Asian custom of frequent bathing'. What Europeans did was to put on clean clothes regularly. A group which certainly did not like bathing were European soldiers. Around 1750 it was deemed necessary for health reasons that soldiers in Batavia took a bath once every eight or ten days. The order to bathe must have led to some grumbling and unrest. Whatever the reason may have been, and of this we cannot be sure – perhaps the explanation is that their officers also suffered from De Haan's hydrophobia – in 1775 it was decreed that soldiers should not be forced to take a weekly bath (De Haan 1922, II:80-1).

As in Europe the change in favour of taking a bath among Europeans in the tropics came in the middle of the nineteenth century. For Batavia we have an observation by the German author of travel books, Friedrich Gerstäcker (1855:420-2), to substantiate this. In the 1870s male Europeans, including those staying in hotels, in Levuka in Fiji took a bath before breakfast and before dinner in water pools or in the river. 'On they came, young and old, planters, merchants and sailors; in a word, all the white men in the place – sometimes single, sometimes in twos or threes, carrying soap and towels, till there could not have been fewer than forty to fifty round the largest pool.' (Forbes 1875:26.) About European females the author remains silent. Not everybody was suddenly converted and access to water was a factor that could make a difference. In the southern part of nearby Taveuni Island, where people were dependent on rain for their water supply, settlers did not bathe; as the owner of the local hotel explained, 'we don't do much washing here' (Forbes 1875:50).

In Fiji the Islanders – using their own soap made of the rind of a fruit species or of alkaline earth – had their own bathing places, separate from those of the Europeans (Forbes 1875:26). This is indicative of another change which had set in earlier. At the close of the eighteenth century and early in the nineteenth century, Europeans in British India who had adjusted themselves to Indian life and their Eurasian offspring fell victim to a change in the British attitude towards the East and its inhabitants. European men who did not conform to the new standards of Britishness were being eased out of the colonial elite. Often European women are blamed for this, but one of the decisive factors which made this change in attitude possible was the growing influence of Evangelicals, or what we nowadays would call the religious right. The Evangelical Movement was born of a reaction to the Enlightenment and, in their dealings with other religions and cultures, its protagonists often usually showed a rigid and uncompromising attitude. They thought that conversion to Christianity, read Protestantism, and the expansion of Western civilization would free the non-Western world from its backwardness. This also meant that Evangelicals were adamant that young impressionable British minds should be shielded from the harmful influence of native society. At home, leading members carried great weight in British politics and in the Court of Directors of the East India Company. In India Evangelicals were well established in the top positions of the East India Company administration and its army. Their disdain for what we nowadays call Orientalism (Fry 2001:202), the preponderance of power they gained in ruling British India, and the harm they did to the training of aspirant employees of the East India Company and to the study and appreciation of local society and culture are well documented (Fry 2001; Kopf 1995; Trautmann 1997). Celebrating temperance and cultural superiority, Evangelicals and their kindred spirits were, as are many others who think that they can save mankind, in the habit of banning things. It did not take long for the consequences of their influence to become visible. European East India Company servants were no longer allowed to don Indian dress and by the 1820s it had become 'the extremity of bad taste to appear in anything of Indian manufacture' in European circles. Army officers were forbidden to participate in Indian festivals. (Dalrymple 2002:50; Spear 1998:142).

Evangelicals were not the only group responsible for the shunning of native society, but they were a major driving force. Nevertheless, this does not preclude the fact that they had some sensible ideas. William Wilberforce, the great abolitionist, was a prominent Evangelical. Unfortunately Wilberforce's views about India were less laudable. He was among those – and his words carried weight – who argued that 'the Indian family was a source of moral decay' (Trautmann 1997:17). He also made no secret that he believed that the conversion to Christianity of the Indian population was more important than the abolition of slavery (Gilmour 2005:12, 102). Being a man of authority, he was one of the persons responsible for the opening up of India to missionary activities.

RAFFLES'S CIVILIZATION MISSION

During the British Interregnum between 1811 and 1816, the new British notion of European superiority was disseminated to the Netherlands Indies. One of the persons responsible for this, the British Lieutenant-Governor of the Island of Java and its Dependencies, Sir Thomas Stamford Raffles (1817, I:353-4), certainly did not consider the Javanese dirty. He praises them for their cleanliness, significantly mentioning as an exception: 'the higher classes, and especially those who mix with Europeans'. It is one of the rare indications of the fact that acculturation can work both ways and that it cannot be precluded that contact with a European lifestyle caused at least some members of the non-European elites to lower their standard of personal cleanliness. These exceptions apart, the Javanese took meticulous care of their physical hygiene. The common Javanese who bathed, Raffles wrote, once a day or once in the two or three days were 'more clean than the Chinese and even the European', although 'he would suffer by a comparison in that particular with the natives of Western India'.[11] The one thing Raffles did not like was the way Javanese groomed their hair. Javanese 'abundantly oil their hair, which among the common people, on account of its length, is too often filthy in the extreme' (Raffles 1817, I:353-4).

11   Not everywhere in India was frequent bathing the norm. An English lady, Mrs Meer Hassan Ali, who had married an Indian Muslim, reported about life in Lucknow in Northern India in the 1830s that the local women might not change their clothes and underwear for a week, and usually would also bathe once a week. Around the same time, a Muslim scholar, Jafar Sharif, discussed the pros and cons of bathing each day, concluding that taking a bath on Friday removed all sins (Tillotson 1998:22, 47-8).

During his lifetime Raffles was hailed as the epitome of enlightenment. Nowadays he still is and Raffles certainly worked within the tradition of an illustrious group of late- eighteenth-century East India Company administrators-cum-scholars who included the Governors-General Warren Hastings and the Marquis of Wellesley, and above all Sir William Jones, the founder of the Asiatick Society of Bengal. Nevertheless, he was a different breed from those British who preferred an Indian way of life. He is always portrayed wearing respectable Western garb. Among other things, Raffles' attitude towards religion was much less relaxed (Dalrymple 2006:64-6). Though in his early years not a very religious person, in later life, probably succumbing to Evangelical influences – he and Wilberforce became close friends and after Raffles had settled in England even next-door neighbours – and perhaps to those of his wife, Olivia Mariamne, who was a devout Christian, Raffles began to take religion seriously (Aljunied 2005:55-7; Miller 1966:118-202). He was transformed into an advocate of missionary work, sure in the conviction that Western civilization was superior to that of other cultures (Aljunied 2005:60-4).

Another characteristic of Raffles was that he was very British, or maybe it was his wife, Olivia Mariamne, who was. A publication from 1930 praises her for having rid the European ruling class in the Netherlands Indies of 'a number of less reputable customs and peculiar imitations of native ways' (Van de Wall 1930:3). Before the British Interregnum the British fashion of 'distancing' themselves from local society and culture had not yet reached the Dutch possessions in Asia. Writing about Malacca in 1811, Collis (1966:50) concludes that the 'Dutch mixed more with local inhabitants and met them on a greater social equality than the English at this period and later'.

In Java the Dutch administrators with whom the British had to co-operate whether they liked it or not had to be converted. Olivia Mariamne Raffles appears to have been the motor of a British campaign to civilize the Indo-European wives of the most senior Dutch civil servants who happily chewed betel and dressed in what the British though resembled underwear, namely sarong and kebaya. The fact that these women were not white but Indo-Europeans only added to the dismay with which the British officers and their British wives regarded them.[12] Somehow, in about a year and in spite

---

12   Taylor 1983:96-100. In Malacca, the British had encountered a similar situation. Reaction there had been different. The Earl of Minto, Governor-General of India, described the Eurasian girls he met here during a ball in 1811 as 'intensely and beautifully brown', and admired their flirting (Collis 1966:49-50). Some of the younger ladies were dressed in 'English' fashion, but also present were some older ladies dressed in the 'Malay loose gown' and chewed betel. In Bogor, Minto was less flattering, the reason being that most of the Eurasian ladies he saw there at a ball were fat (Collis 1966:65; see also Taylor 1983:97).

of great opposition, Olivia Mariamne Raffles succeeded in her aim or, as it was recorded in the not impartial *Java Government Gazette* in 1812: great 'improvement has been introduced in respect to the attire of the Dutch ladies since the British authority has been established. The *cabaya* appears now generally disused and the more elegant English costume adopted.' (Van de Wall 1930:5.) The same opinion was expressed by Major William Thorn (1815:248) who noted down that the Batavian women 'adopted the fashionable habiliments of our countrywomen, and in their manner as well as dress they are improving wonderfully'.

After a few years the British left Java again. English dress and the idea of Western superiority, of which soap was later to become a small and insignificant element, were there to stay, and probably even without the British Interregnum would have been embraced by the Dutch in the Netherlands Indies. Differences remained. The change in the British attitude towards the local population in their colonies, which was gaining momentum at the turn of the nineteenth century, as said, owed much to Evangelicals and their intemperate religious zeal. In the Netherlands, this form of Christian pressure group failed to muster the same amount of influence it had in Great Britain. Missionaries were not allowed to work in Muslim regions, where anyway as everybody knew, perhaps with the exception of the missionaries themselves, their rate of success would be minimal and fierce and violent discontent could easily be the result. So, the observation made in the 1850s by Friedrich Gerstäcker (1855:440), that the Dutch in the Netherlands Indies stood out for their 'tolerant and sensible freedom of religion' may not have been an unsubstantiated remark.

SOAP AS THE MARKER OF CIVILIZATION

Oblivious of their own recent history of tending to wallow in dirt and enthusiastically embracing the newly rediscovered notion of cleanliness, Europeans and Americans began to use taking a bath as a yardstick to judge others. Nevertheless, it was soap, not bathing, which made a person civilized. There is some logic in this. As the first Europeans who sailed to Southeast Asia did not fail to notice the Malays, the Javanese and other people in Southeast Asia did bathe, and this more times a day than a Westerner would do. All this was inessential. It did not count. By the end of the nineteenth century the belief in the dirty native and the dirty servant seems

1 Soap is the onset of civilization

to have become widespread, at least among the colonial British.[13] Imagine the bewilderment of a three-year-old girl in India in 1880 who had been told by her parents that she should not talk to one of the servants, the poor man who kept the punkah, the fan, moving, because he was dirty. After a while she returned to her mother saying 'He has bathed' (Buettner 2004:53). And, some forty years later it is recorded in a manual about *The home and health in India and tropical colonies* that Indian servants differ from the British in their 'standard of personal cleanliness' (Platt cited in Buettner 2004:39).

Soap may have made the difference. In Malaya, *The Straits Independent and Penang Chronicle* of 23 May 1894 contains a report by George C. Bellamy, the District Officer of Kuala Selangor about his trip to Ceylon. In Colombo he visited a government milk factory. What he saw impressed him. Penang should also have such an enterprise. With its 'abundant rainfall, and the consequent richness of its pastures', it was actually 'much better situated for such an industry' than Colombo. Away, he wrote, with the '[f]ever and other diseases [which] lurk in our milk cans'. And think about the spin-offs: the production of cheese and butter! Health and profits loomed, but this could only be realized under European management. When such a statement is made, it might have been expected that a discussion of the managerial qualities of Europeans, Chinese, Indians, and Malays, the usual procedure when non-Europeans were considered for the first time for a profession which up to then had been closed to them. Such a debate would often end with the conclusion that non-Europeans lacked the right mentality, muscular strength, or proper education to qualify them for the job. This time there was nothing of the sort. Management of such an enterprise should be in the hands of 'people to whom cleanliness is a virtue'. This assessment disqualified all non-European residents: 'Chinese, Klings [Indians] and natives will bathe, sometimes as many as three times a day, but they are none the cleaner, they smell none the sweeter for all that. The few buckets of water they throw over themselves on these occasions does not wash their dirt away.'

Is this because they did not use soap? Bellamy does not mention it. Nor does the story about the Indian servant give any indication. Bellamy does give other reasons the natives were denied their cleanliness. The clothes they put on after they had taken a bath were 'as filthy as ever'. In their houses 'the accumulated dirt of twenty years may be

---

13 There is a very good chance that the idea of the unclean servant was constructed upon an older European tradition about domestics being dirty. In the second half of the eighteenth century and well into the nineteenth century, the well-to-do in France and Germany considered their domestic servants dirty and complained about their smell (forcing some of them to take a bath). Some contemporary authors suggest their readers should keep domestics out of the children's nursery or bedroom and to air the rooms they lived in (Corbin 1986:189, 192, 203, 214).

scraped off the walls, to say nothing of the floors on which they sleep'. Evidently, Bellamy does not agree with his contemporaries, who – it must be admitted – did exist, who considered Malays to be personally clean because they washed themselves. He exclaims: 'Away with this delusion; cleanliness, like its neighbour godliness, is a different thing altogether, a thing which only a white man can appreciate at its proper value'. His conclusion is clear. A European should be appointed the manager of the milk factory. Once this had become reality 'our stinking Kling milkman would then become a thing of the past'.

We can expand the story. Bellamy was not alone in his observations. Howard Malcolm (1839:192-3), travelling through Southeast Asia in 1837 as representative of one of the larger American missionary societies, observed that in Burma people could always be seen bathing, but he continues by writing that '[v]ery little is accomplished towards removing the filth from their bodies by their daily ablutions, as they seldom use soap...'. Malcolm (1839:192-3) also informs us that those bathing were a very small proportion of the whole population and that the washing of clothes was 'done only at very distant intervals'. It is as if he is taking pains to assure his readers that those Burmese were actually a filthy lot. Malcolm's words are a remarkably early denunciation of the soap-less. Mass-produced soap, we must remember, is a relatively new commodity in Europe and the United States. It appeared on the market only in the second half of the nineteenth century. When Malcolm wrote down these words only a very select group of rich Europeans and Americans could afford to wash themselves with soap.

Linking soap and civilization only really began to pick up in the 1880s when advertising in newspapers and magazines took off. Here the history of soap and that of advertising meet. The person who brings them together is Thomas J. Barratt who had fortuitously married the great-granddaughter of the founder of the Pears' Soap Company. Barratt is hailed as 'the father of advertising'. He was also responsible for many of the advertisements depicting cleanliness and soap as the embodiment of civilization.

Among the people who, it was suggested, might benefit from the introduction of soap were the inhabitants of the Philippines, or rather the Americans who had just taken over the colony from Spain. In 1899 Pears' Soap had a piece of advice for the American administration in Manila. Teaching the virtues of cleanliness was the first step towards lightening 'The White Man's Burden' (the title of the poem written by Rudyard Kipling to persuade the United States to take possession of the island group and prevent a Filipino-run independent state from coming into being). How better could this be done than by distributing soap? The 1899 'Admiral Dewey' advertisement leaves no doubt about this (Figure 2). In

Figure 2. 'The white man's burden'. A Pears' Soap advertisement, 1899.

the bottom-right corner a person can be seen presenting soap to a figure, and I suspect it is a Moro, a Muslim from the South, who, to make the contrast the greater, has a Neanderthal appearance.

In contemporary British eyes, Boers were no better than uncivilized natives, and suffered a similar fate. Boers even shared the misfortune of being put on display with non-Western people. In May 1899 an exhibition in London presented 'a horde of savages direct from their kraals, comprising 200 Matabeles, Basutos, Zwazis, Hottentots, Malays, Cape and Transvaal Boers' (Shephard 1992:97). In an account of the Boer War dating from 1900, the Boers, who inflicted a number of humiliating defeats on the British, are not only portrayed as cowards – they are also dirty: 'The Boer cannot stand steel. He has as great a horror of it as he has of soap and water and a change of clothing.' (Neilly cited in MacDonald 1994:39.) Unfortunately for the British, in the rest of Europe, the United States and in what one Dutch author rather enigmatically described as 'the civilized non-British part of Asia', the Boers were hailed as heroes (Andriessen 1904:490). As such they were eligible to appear in advertisements, including those for soap (Figure 3). Nevertheless, it has to be admitted that in the case of the Boers there may be some truth in the observations that they were not exactly clean. Maurice Nyagumbo, a politician from Zimbabwe, one of those who in their youth had had to sing that they were dirty, recalls a visit to the Orange Free State in the 1930s. He notes that the Boers were 'completely oblivious to' cleanliness: 'The whole building was infested with swarms of flies. Women came into the dining-room with hair falling everywhere. People blew their noses and spat everywhere in the dining-room.' (Burke 1996:197.)

But did the Boers deserve soap? The answer is ambiguous. Emily Hobhouse, one of those British ladies determined to do something about the plight of Boer women and children interned in concentration camps during the Boer War, was appalled at what she saw there. One of the matters which especially offended her, and she took pains to emphasize this, was that there 'was no *soap* provided' (italics hers; cited in Pakenham 1992:506). Initially the authorities refused her request to send soap to the camps, arguing that 'soap is an article of luxury'.[14] In the end, the women and children were allowed one ounce of soap a week per head (Pakenham 1992:506).

The British elite and those Britons who ventured to the East or to Africa, as may have become evident by now, nurtured their own peculiar worldview. The Boers were not the only Europeans who were low on the scale of British appreciation. They shared this fate with the Italians and the Irish. In 1846 a young British Roman Catholic man found Italians 'a people of dirty habits, offensive

14 http://www.anglo-boer.co.za (accessed June 2011).

Figure 3. 'Kruger'. A Schichts Seifen advertisement, 1904.

those who came from a nation that valued cleanliness' (Newsome 1997:96). In 1880 a Belgian economist, Gustave de Molinari, observed that British newspapers 'treated the Irish as an inferior race – as a kind of white negroes' (McClintock 1995:52). In fact, it could be even worse. The qualification of the Irish by the novelist Charles Kingsley has become notorious. In 1860, in a letter from Ireland to his wife, he called them human or white chimpanzees (Curtis 1968:84). Being branded inferior, the Irish were also considered to lack hygiene (Maxwell 1999:31). In this respect the British valued the Dutch and the Swiss and above all the Germans more (Newsome 1997:94). That is why while *The Malay Daily Chronicle* stated on 14 October 1912 that Great Britain could 'claim the pioneer's honour' in the study of hygiene, the newspaper had to add that Germany had 'introduced more method into its administration of a Department of Public Health'. Competing for political, economic and cultural supremacy, Germany and Great Britain were also each other's rivals in the field of the promotion of hygiene. Victorian Britain and Wilhelmine Germany produced the most beautifully ornamented and decorated lavatory pans (Corbin 1986:222).

Of course, Anglo-Saxons were not alone in stating that natives were dirty. Frenchmen were very apt to make sweeping statements about the inhabitants of Indochina. In 1886, it was observed that an Indochinese was 'of disgusting dirtiness, devoured by vermin and eaten away by skin diseases, covered in stinking rags ...[he] sweats filth and ignoble wretchedness through his very pores' (Aldrich 1966:202). In a similar vein, in *Le Figaro* a French naval officer described the inhabitants of Vietnam as 'apelike' and smelling of 'yellow sweat, incense and filth' (Spence 1998:149). In the Netherlands Indies washing and the use of soap also became part and parcel of civilization. In August 1914, just after the outbreak of the World War One, a number of native policemen from German New Guinea, their uniform consisting of a cap and a loincloth, fled to Hollandia. In the newspaper *De Locomotief* (24-8-1914) there is a report of what happened to them. After being properly dressed in a jacket (*jas toetoep*), trousers, and a planter's hat – one of them even donned boots – they visited the Assistant-Resident and asked him to give their 'naked wives' a make-over. Subsequently, the women were given a 'thorough bath with a piece of soap' and were dressed in sarong and kebaya. What had been done was once 'again a masterly example of civilization work', the report concluded.

CLEANLINESS AND GODLINESS

These examples indicate that real cleanliness was becoming the preserve of Europeans, and, it has to be added, of Christianity. Soap became an attribute of God – or rather the Protestant conception of Him. Natives and Muslims were either less clean or definitely dirty.

Cleanliness and godliness were presented as the two sides of the same coin. 'Cleanliness is next to godliness' became the slogan in the Anglo-Saxon world in its attempts to induce those poor souls at home and abroad who had not yet discovered the virtues of the new standards of hygiene to wash their bodies and their clothes. This Jewish saying was first made popular among British Methodist by one of the founders of this movement, the Englishman John Wesley (1703-1791).[15] It is a far cry from the idea that a filthy body was a sign of religious devotion advocated by the mediaeval saints.

Instead of quoting from Jewish sources, John Wesley may have also turned to Islamic tradition according to which the Prophet Muhammad said that 'cleanliness is half of faith'. Muslims performed their very visible ritual ablutions before prayers; and were required to wash the whole of their body after sexual intercourse, though the latter stipulation was probably not known by the Europeans and Americans visiting Muslim regions. Such religious commands to observe cleanliness did nothing to save Muslims from being regarded as dirty by Christian travellers. The British poet and traveller, James Elroy Flecker (1884-1916), wrote that he hated the Orient and that thank God the Lebanon was Christian (Kabbani 1991:28). Flecker's lamentation is akin to the observations made in the 1830s by the American John Lloyd Stephens. He hailed the 'privileges of civilization' after having encountered 'an utter lack of hygiene' in the Middle East (Oren 2007:159). Stephens's observation encapsulated the American experience in the Middle East. Many of his fellow Americans who visited the region were missionaries or pilgrims with a Christian background. Their reaction, especially to what they saw in Palestine, the Christian Holy Land, was, as Oren (2007:140) captured this in words, 'a blend of aesthetic disgust and spiritual elation'.

Being Americans, they, and Mark Twain and Theodore Roosevelt were among those who did, thought nothing of the River Jordan of which, reading the Bible and listening to sermons, they had formed their own grand image. The river was simply too small (Oren 2007:134, 242, 310). Another, the explorer William Francis Lynch, exclaimed that the 'curse of God' had surely fallen upon the Dead Sea (Oren 2007:139). Mark Twain, whose description of Syrian men includes the words rags, dirt, and sores (Oren 2007:242)

---

15 It is certainly possible that Wesley's cleanliness was still a spiritual cleanliness. He uses the phrase one of the first times in his sermon 'On Dress' he gave on 30 December 1786. In it he fulminates against the wearing of jewellery and costly clothing. Attire should be cheap and plain. Wesley speaks about neatness of apparel, but may have meant this in the sense of being without adornments.

must be counted among those explorers, travellers, and missionaries about whom the first question which enters one's mind is: why did they do it? He wrote that a death sentence was preferable to residence in the Middle East (Oren 2007:240). By World War Two the American outlook did not seem to have changed much. General Dwight D. Eisenhower liked Algiers, it was a 'beautiful and picturesque' city, but he did complain about the Arabs who seemed 'to have very little regard for personal cleanliness' (Oren 2007:464).

Some Dutch persons were guilty of similar perceptions. Describing a journey into the interior of South Sulawesi in 1856 B.F. Matthes (1857:13) writes: 'I did not like the trip at all. Lake Tempe, which is so highly praised [and is nowadays a tourist attraction], was completely as are indeed the land and people – as it were, strikingly squalid'. Other regions where the elite and the 'advanced', the new intelligentsia, had begun to assimilate some parts of the European way of life suited such persons better; especially when the change implied a turning away from the culture of Islam. Around 1900, writing about North Sulawesi another Dutchman, N. Graafland (1898, I:3) complained that while 'the Minahassa may already be counted among the countries where Christianity and civilization have obtained a firm footing [...] in Gorontalo one is transported back into a totally Mohammedan world, with much that revolts'.

Soap, Christianity, and civilization became intertwined, they merged into one entity. In the 1880s in a Pears' Soap advertisement the Reverend Henry Ward Beecher, a famous American Evangelical clergyman and a brother of Harriet Beecher Stowe, the author of *Uncle Tom's Cabin*, exclaimed that 'if cleanliness is next to Godliness, Soap must be considered a Means of Grace, and a Clergyman who recommends moral things should be willing to recommend Soap'. Not insignificantly in view of the expanding Evangelical flock in America, and in an example of denominational shopping in the material sense of the word, he adds in the advertisement that he had been told that his 'recommendation of Pears' Soap has opened for it a large sale in the United States'. The link is clear. In the 1930s, in its campaign 'instructing Natives in Hygiene', the Southern Rhodesian Missionary Conference concluded that the natives should be taught that 'cleanliness is next to Godliness' (Burke 1996:194-5).

Another region featuring in the Pears' Soap advertisement was China. (Figure 4) Missionaries may have 'adopted native dress, "pigtail" and all, to avoid undesirable attention among the vast hordes of interior China', but, an advertisement from 1910 informs us the 'exceedingly neat and cleanly appearance of these white people in the native dress' could be attributed to the use of Pears' Soap. Always rely on Pears' Soap: 'If anything can civilize and Christianize China, Pears' Soap and the missionaries will'.

Figure 4. 'Christian missionaries in China'. A Pears' Soap advertisement, 1910.

In the Netherlands Indies, the association of soap with Western cleanliness was more muted. The link connecting the two in this case is that icon of cleanliness, the proverbial Dutch housewife (Figure 5). What better image to sell soap, in this case Sunlight soap, than that of a Dutch lady carrying a laundry basket filled with freshly washed clothes climbing a ladder? The advertisement in the Malay-language *Bintang Soerabaia* of 9 January 1918 urges its readers, who must have been Indonesians, Eurasians, and assimilated peranakan Chinese, to buy Sunlight soap, not least because, as we read, it makes a heavy task lighter and easier. Why the Dutch housewife had to climb a ladder remains a mystery, and what exactly she is wearing on her head also gives some cause for conjecture, but the advertisement is also peculiar in another respect. In the Netherlands Indies Dutch women did not do their own washing. They had their native servants to perform this task. But, on second thoughts, again with the exception of the ladder and the headdress, is the advertisement as odd as it appears at first glance? It responds to the association of European habits with a modern way of life which was then gaining ground in Indonesian society. An indication that this was indeed the case and that soap was indubitably considered to be one of the material artefacts of modernity is that, among the many pen-names used by Indonesian contributors to Malay-language newspapers, we also find the English name 'Sunlight Soap' alongside that of *Nieuwe Pakkendrager* (New Wearer of Suits), and admittedly also *Steeds Lijder* (Eternal Sufferer) and *Bin Troelala*.

Some authors have stressed the racial message of soap advertisements in the colonial era. Anne McClintock (1995:209) discusses the advertisements within the wider context of 'commodity racism' and 'commodity jingoism'. Garvey (1996:203) argues that 'black characters appeared in contemporary soap advertisements only as a racist joke, to demonstrate the claim made in the advertisement that black skin could be scrubbed white by the product'. Others have drawn a similar conclusion; and it has to be admitted there were indeed some very dubious advertisements (see also Prabasmoro 2003) (Figure 6). Nevertheless, we are faced with the fact that soap and taking a bath removes dirt and that a convenient way to visualize this is by turning a black person into a white one.

The *Bintang Soerabaia* advertisement with the Dutch housewife up the ladder indicates that the relationship between soap and race is more complex. Using soap made Indonesians white in the metaphorical sense. It was a tiny step on the road towards emancipation; just as was donning Western attire in the first decades of the twentieth century. The colour of the skin was less important. Dressing in the Western fashion allowed Javanese to enter the European public sphere, which, in the context of the Netherlands Indies, meant

1 Soap is the onset of civilization

Figure 5. A Sunlight Soap advertisement, 1918

the European/Eurasian public sphere, from which a preference for Javanese clothing would have banned them. Dressed in a Western fashion, they also were treated in a much friendlier manner by Europeans than were they to have approached the latter in Javanese clothing. They could quite literally leave their native compartment and travel European class at the railways. There was one drawback – Indonesians in European garments were not allowed to buy the cheaper ticket reserved for 'Easterners' (Van Dijk 1997:58-71).

THE PORTRAYAL OF OTHERS AS DIRTY

Soap is not mentioned terribly often in their evaluations of the level of civilization of the other by Europeans and Americans. As Bellamy's statement about the milk factory and Malcolm's remarks about Indochina indicate, it is easier to ignore the body and concentrate on unwashed clothes and perceived slovenliness in houses in efforts to brand non-Europeans filthy. This seems to have been the ultimate technique which allowed Westerners to maintain the top position

Figure 6. Black turning white. A Pears' Soap advertisement.

on the global scale of cleanliness. When all is said and done, even Japanese, the nation certainly well-known, perhaps even famous for the frequent bathing of its inhabitants, could be disqualified. In 1863 *Harper's New Monthly Magazine* recorded a statement: 'As far as their persons are concerned the Japanese are certainly a very cleanly people. But this does not hold good of their garments. These are worn day and night, and rarely changed.'[16] (*Soap advertising* n.d.:1.)

This raises the question: how many times did contemporary Europeans and Americans change their clothes, especially their linen, in those days? In the mid-nineteenth century Europeans in the tropics, at least in Batavia, it has to be admitted, took a bath and changed clothes twice a day (Gerstäcker 1855:420-2). Judging from the advice to nineteenth-century Dutch boarding-school girls that they change their underwear at least once a week, people were not as keen on the daintiness of their garments in a cooler climate (De Leeuw 1992:177). Around 1900, once a week, or perhaps even once a fortnight, may indeed have been the norm among the middle classes in the Netherlands. In rural areas, farmers washed their clothes and themselves much less frequently (De Leeuw 1992:215, 326, 328). Incidentally, changing underwear once a week also was promoted in a fatwa issued by the Russian State-appointed mufti, Gabdulvakhid Suleimanov, on the instigation of the Russian authorities in their campaign to combat diseases in the Ural Mountains in 1849. It was coupled with the suggestion to 'wash once a week in warm water' (Crews 2006:80).

Writing about the portrayal of others as dirty, in one of his books MacDonald (1994:35) observes that the harshest qualifications are reserved for people of a mixed race. He suggests that the 'fear of the other may be expressed at its deepest in things sexual, for the most violent language is reserved to describe those who are thought to be the product of miscegenation'. MacDonald's conclusion is that the 'insistence on the "cleanliness" of the whites and the "dirtiness" of all other races seems in essence to express a fear of things sexual', indicative of 'a culture in which East and West, Light and Dark, were polarised.'

The examples I have mentioned about the attraction of the idea of modernity in the Netherlands Indies, and the possibility for Indonesians to enter the European sphere of life because it had become impossible to differentiate them from the Indo-Europeans indicate that something different was at play. Moreover, MacDonald's remarks concern a British colonial setting. Some members of the British upper and middle classes may have been especially sensitive to racial prejudices; for a long time opinions among the ordinary British were

---

16 http://www.clas.ufl.edu/users/jshoaf/Jdolls/jdollwestern/Ads/japrose.html (accessed April 2011).

remarkably broad-minded (See Fischer 2004). It may indeed well be as one author, Garvey (1996:203), suggests that the Pears' Soap advertisements with a racial connotation appeared primarily in Great Britain.

Contrary to what is sometimes assumed, the colour of the skin was much more important to Europeans in British India and Malaya than it was in the Netherlands Indies, where discrimination against Eurasians did take place, but on a lesser scale. Eurasians were legally discriminated against in Malaya and British India, a state of affairs made possible by the fact that formally they were not considered Europeans, but were listed as a separate category in population statistics (De Cock Buning 1916-1917:380). In 1904 and 1910 Eurasians and non-Europeans in Malaya were denied access to administrative positions in the civil service (Shennan 2000:70). In India, with the exception of the most humble positions, Indian-Europeans had already been barred from 'employment in the Civil, Military, or Marine Service of the [East India] Company' in the late eighteenth century; a fate they shared with respect to the Army and with Roman Catholics.[17]

Dutchmen could gloat over the way Indian-Europeans were treated in British India, which one Dutch author noted in the 1910s was 'shocking according to Dutch standards' (De Cock Buning 1916-1917:380). In India and Malaya the colonial elite was white and being white mattered, very much so also in mixed-race circles. Among mixed-race individuals having a fair complexion was definitely considered a blessing, paving the way for upward mobility. The British detested Indo-Europeans who hid their background in order to advance in society and turned to an investigation of marks on the body which could expose such persons, scrutinizing fingernails and eyes in a failed effort to identify Indo-Europeans who were pretending to be white; a failing which other Europeans and Americans also resorted to on occasion (Buettner 2004:69, 84-5) Even in the Malay Eurasian community 'skin discrimination' could be obtrusive. *De Locomotief* of 26 January 1917 calls attention to families in the Straits Settlements in which members who had a browner skin were ostracized by their fairer relatives. In the article it was also observed that in the Straits Settlements a marriage between a full-blood European boy and a Eurasian girl was rare and that when it did take place the girl had to have a fair complexion. This, the newspaper concluded, was a very different situation from that in Java, where Eurasian girls seemed to exert a great sexual attraction on European boys.

---

17 Fisher 2004:79, 201; Dalrymple 2002:50. The ban was formally lifted in 1833 when Parliament ruled 'that no "native" of the Company's territories or "natural born subject of His Majesty" would be excluded from any appointment in the Indian civil service or army on the basis of religion, place of birth, descent, or colour' (Fisher 2004:211).

1 Soap is the onset of civilization

CONCLUSION

What is described above seems to be a matter long dead and gone, but occasionally it comes to the surface again. The British, as Jeremy Clarkson not so long ago wrote with his usual sense of humour in his column in *The Sunday Times* (27-5-2007), still 'harbour a cheery notion that Britain and its people are a shining beacon of hope and goodness to the dirtier and less well educated'. Just how alive such sentiments remain became evident after *The Sunday Times* had paid attention to Hortense de Monplaisir's book *Le Dossier: How to survive the English.* In its next issue the paper (11-7-2007) published some reactions of its readers. They had written about Frenchwomen 'with questionable hygiene', a French girlfriend who 'only brushes her teeth every few days', women in France who turned up 'at the beauty salon and have what looks like camembert between their toes', and – a final blow to the French – that British women 'may all have huge bottoms' but that the British had proper toilets, unlike the French, 'who insist on going by the side of the road'.

In the Netherlands such ideas also persist. A striking example, and I must confess I am still not sure whether this meant to be irony or not, is a letter to the editor published some years ago in *De Volkskrant* (16-9-2006). Its sender wrote that it struck him that Muslim terrorists are 'so ugly' and that he 'has never seen an attractive Islamic fanatic, male or female'. His advice is simple: with 'a little more attention to the appearance – such as personal hygiene and pretty clothes – they will go further in the world', and, it is implied, keep them from committing acts of terrorism.

The concept of cleanliness is multifaceted. It concerns the body, attire, the house, the natural environment, and also what is now called the built environment. There are many factors which contribute to the way different people define cleanliness. Class, social status, ethnicity and nationality, religion and religious denomination, medical discourse, and place and time all play a role in shaping opinions about bathing and washing. Feelings of superiority should also not be overlooked. Those who think of themselves as belonging to The Clean may tend to consider cleanliness to be an exclusive characteristic of their own social environment, blinding them to any indications to the contrary. They can also promote their own ideas about cleanliness with religious zeal, without realizing those they see as less clean are not as dirty as they assume. At times such efforts even become inextricably linked to real missionary activities.

REFERENCES

Aaland, Mikkel
1978 *Sweat; The illustrated history and description of the Finnish sauna, Russian bania, Islamic hammam, Japanese mushi-buro, Mexican temescal and American Indian and Eskimo sweatlodge.* Santa Barbara, CA: Capra Press.

Abdullah bin Abdul Kadir
1970 *The Hikayat Abdullah; An annotated translation by A.H. Hill.* Kuala Lumpur: Oxford University Press. [Oxford in Asia Historical Reprints.]

Aldrich, Robert
1996 *Greater France; A history of French overseas expansion.* Basingstoke: Macmillan. [European Studies Series.]

Aljunied, Syed Muhd Khairudin
2005 *Rethinking Raffles; A study of Stamford Raffles' discourse on religions amongst Malays.* Singapore: Marshall Cavendish Academic.

Andriessen, W.F.
1904 *Gedenkboek van den oorlog in Zuid-Afrika.* Amsterdam: Hollandsch-Afrikaansche Uitgevers, v.h. Jacques-Dusseau.

Ashenburg, Katherine
2008 *Clean; An unsanitised history of washing.* London: Profile Books.

Barnes, David S.
2006 *The great stink of Paris and the nineteenth-century struggle against filth and germs.* Baltimore, MD: Johns Hopkins University Press.

Biow, Douglas
2006 *The culture of cleanliness in Renaissance Italy.* Ithaca, NY/London: Cornell University Press.

Bonacorsi, Paolo
n.d. *Saint Francis of Assisi* (English version by Elisa Fiolini) (http://www.assisiweb.com/vita_san_francesco_en.html)

Boogaart, Ernst van den
2000 *Het verheven en verdorven Azië; Woord en beeld in het Itinerario en de Icones van Jan Huygen van Linschoten.* Met een vertaling van de Latijnse teksten bij de *Icones* door C.L. Heesakkers. Amsterdam: Het Spinhuis, Leiden: KITLV Uitgeverij.

Bosboom, H.D.H.
1902 'Het verdwenen waterkasteel te Djokdjokarta (uit oude papieren)', *Tijdschrift voor Indische Taal-, Land- en Volkenkunde* (*TBG*) 45:518-29.

Buettner, Elizabeth
2004 *Empire families; Britons and late imperial India.* Oxford: Oxford University Press.

Burke, Timothy
1996 'Sunlight soap has changed my life; Hygiene, commodification, and the body in colonial Zimbabwe', in: Hildi Hendrickson (ed.), *Clothing and difference; Embodied identities in colonial and post-colonial Africa*, pp. 189-212. Durham, NC: Duke University Press. [Body, Commodity, Text.]

Breet, Michael
2003 *De Oost-Indische voyagie van Wouter Schouten.* Zutphen: Walburg Pers.

Bijl de Vroe, C.L.M.
1980 *Rondom de Buitenzorgse troon; Indisch dagboek van C.L.M. Bijl de Vroe.* Ingeleid en bewerkt door Marian Schouten. Met een woord vooraf door A. Alberts. Haarlem: Fibula Van Dishoeck.

Cock Buning, W. de
1916-1917 'De Indo-Europeaan', *Koloniale Studiën* 1:370-402.

Cockayne, Emily
2007 *Hubbub; Filth, noise & stench in England 1600-1770.* New Haven, CT/London: Yale University Press.

Collis, Maurice
1966 *Raffles.* London: Faber and Faber.

Corbin, Alain
1986 *Pestdamp en bloesemgeur; Een geschiedenis van de reuk.* Nijmegen: Sun. [Originally published as *Le miasme et la jonquille; L'odorat en l'imaginaire social, XVIIIe-XIXe siècles.* Paris: Aubier Montaigne, 1982.]

Crews, Robert D.
2006 *For prophet and tsar; Islam and empire in Russia and Central Asia.* Cambridge, MA/London: Harvard University Press.

Cunnington, C. Willett and Phillis Cunnington
1992 *The history of underclothes.* New York: Dover. [First edition 1951.]

Curtis, L.P.
1968   *Anglo-Saxons and Celts; A study of anti-Irish prejudice in Victorian England.* Bridgeport, CT: Conference on British Studies at the University of Bridgeport. [Studies in British History and Culture 2.]

Dalrymple, William
2002   *White Mughals; Love and betrayal in eighteenth-century India.* London: HarperCollins.
2006   *The last Mughal; The fall of a dynasty, Delhi, 1857.* London: Bloomsbury.

Dikötter, Frank
2007   *Things modern; Material culture and everyday life in China.* London: Hurst.

Dumarçay, J.
1978   'Le taman sari (Étude architecturale)', *Bulletin de l'École française d'Extrême-Orient* 65-2:589-625.

Dijk, Kees van
1997   'Sarong, jubbah and trousers; Appearances as a means of distinction and discrimination', in: Henk Schulte Nordholt (ed.), *Outward appearances; Dressing state and society in Indonesia*, pp. 39-83. Leiden: KITLV Press. [Proceedings 4.]

Elias, Norbert
2001   *Het civilisatie-proces; Sociogenetische en psychogenetische onderzoekingen.* Amsterdam: Boom. [Originally published as *Über den Prozess der Zivilisation; Soziogenetische und psychogenetische Untersuchungen.* Basel: Haus zum Falken, 1939.]

Fisher, Michael H.
2004   *Counterflows to colonialism; Indian travellers and settlers in Britain 1600-1857.* Delhi: Permanent Black.

Fonvizin, Denis
2006   *Brieven uit Frankrijk 1777-1778; Een Russische bojaar op grand tour aan de vooravond van de Franse Revolutie.* Vertaald, ingeleid en van commentaar voorzien door Emmanuel Waegemans. Antwerpen: Benerus.

Forbes, Litton
1875   *Two years in Fiji.* London: Longmans, Green, and Co..

Foster, William (ed.)
1934   *The voyage of Thomas Best to the East Indies.* London: Hakluyt Society. [Works issued by the Hakluyt Society, Second Series, 75.]

Fry, Michael
2001 *The Scottish empire*. East Lothian: Tuckwell Press, Edinburgh: Birlinn.
Garvey, Ellen Gruber
1996 *The adman in the parlor; Magazines and the gendering of consumer culture, 1880s to 1910s*. New York: Oxford University Press.
Gerstäcker, Fr.
1855 'Javaansche schetsen (naar het Hoogduitsch van Fr. Gerstäcker)', *Bijdragen tot de Taal-, Land- en Volkenkunde* 3:413-91.
Gilmour, David
2005 *The ruling caste; Imperial lives in the Victorian Raj*. London: Murray.
Graafland, N.
1898 *De Minahassa; Haar verleden en haar tegenwoordige toestand*. Tweede druk. Haarlem: Bohn. Two vols. [First edition 1867-69.]
Groneman, J.
1885 'Het waterkasteel te Jogjåkartå', *Tijdschrift voor Indische Taal-, Land- en Volkenkunde (TBG)* 30:412-34.
Haan, F. de
1922 *Oud Batavia; Gedenkboek uitgegeven door het Bataviaasch Genootschap van Kunsten en Wetenschappen naar aanleiding van het driehonderdjarig bestaan der stad in 1919*. Batavia: Kolff. Two vols.
Halliday, Stephen
1999 *The great stink of London; Sir Joseph Bazalgette and the cleansing of the Victorian metropolis*. Thrupp: Sutton Publishing.
Hell, Stephan
2007 *Siam and the League of Nations; Modernization, sovereignty, and multilateral diplomacy, 1920-1940*. PhD thesis, University of Leiden.
Horan, Julie L.
1996 *The porcelain God; A social history of the toilet*. London: Robson Books.
Jasanoff, May
2005 *Edge of empire; Lives, culture, and conquest in the East, 1750-1850*. New York: Knopf.
Kabbani, Rana
1991 *Europese mythen over de Oriënt*. Amsterdam: Contact.

Kildea, Paul
2006 'The proms; An industrious revolution', in: Jenny Doctor and David Wright (eds), *The Proms*, pp. 10-32. London: Thames & Hudson.

King, Michelle T.
2007 *'Drowning daughters'; Violence and the gendered body in nineteenth century Chinese morality books on infanticide*. Paper, Fifth International Convention of Asia Scholars (ICAS5), Kuala Lumpur, 2-5 August.

Koerner, Lisber
1996 'Carl Linnaeus in his time and place', in: N. Jardine, J.A. Secord and E.C. Spary (eds), *Cultures of natural history*, pp. 145-62. Cambridge: Cambridge University Press.

Kopf, David
1995 'The historiography of British Orientalism, 1772-1992', in: Garland Cannon and Kevin R. Brine (eds), *Objects of enquiry; The life, contributions, and influences of Sir William Jones (1746-1794)*, pp. 141-60. New York/London. New York University Press.

Kohl, Benjamin G.
1978 'Leonardo Bruni; Panegyric to the city of Florence'. Translated by Benjamin G. Kohl, in: Benjamin G. Kohl and Elizabeth B. Welles (eds), *The earthy republic; Italian humanists on government and society*, pp. 135-9, 149-54, 168-75. Philadelphia: University of Pennsylvania Press.

Kuus, Saskia
2007 *Baden en flaneren aan zee; Badcultuur en strandmode op Scheveningen sinds 1818*. Scheveningen: Muzee Scheveningen. [Historische Reeks 14.]

Lagarde, Riana
2005 'Where to pick a flower in Paris; Public restrooms'. http://www.slowtrav.com/france/paris/rl_restrooms.html.

Leeuw, Kitty de
1992 *Kleding in Nederland 1813-1920; Van een traditioneel bepaald kleedpatroon naar een begin van modern kleedgedrag*. Hilversum: Verloren.

McClintock, Anne
1995 *Imperial leather; Race, gender and sexuality in the colonial contest*. New York and London: Routledge.

MacDonald, Robert H.
1994   *The language of empire; Myths and metaphors of popular imperialism, 1880-1918.* Manchester and New York: Manchester University Press.

Malcom, Howard
1839   *Travels in South-East Asia embracing Hindustan, Malaya, Siam, and China with notices of numerous missionary stations and a full account of the Burman Empire; with dissertations, tables etc.* Vol. 1. Boston: Gould, Kendall, and Lincoln.

Matthes, B.F.
1857   'Beknopt verslag van een verblijf in de binnenlanden van Celebes, waar Boegineesch gesproken wordt, gedurende zes maanden, van 24 April tot 24 October 1856', *Verzameling van Berigten betreffende de Bijbelverspreiding* 91:1-28.

Maxwell, Anne
1999   *Colonial photography & exhibitions; Representations of the 'native' and the making of European identities.* London and New York: Leicester University Press.

Neilly, J. Emerson
1900   *Beseiged with B.-P; A complete record of the siege.* London: Pearson.

Newsome, David
1997   *The Victorian world picture; Perceptions and introspections in an age of change.* London: Murray.

Oren, Michael B.
2007   *Power, faith, and fantasy; America in the Middle East, 1776 to the present.* New York and London: Norton.

Pakenham, Thomas
1992   *The Boer War.* London: Abacus.

Perrot, Philippe
1987   *Werken aan de schijn; Veranderingen van het vrouwelijk lichaam in de achttiende en negentiende eeuw.* Nijmegen: SUN. [Originally published as *Le travail des apparences, ou les transformations du corps féminin XVIIIe-XIXe siècle.* Paris: Seuil, 1984.]

Platt, Kate
1923   *The home and health in India and the tropical colonies.* London: Baillière, Tindall and Cox.

Prabasmoro, Aquarini
2004   *Becoming white; Representasi ras, kelas, feminitas dan globalitas dalam iklan sabun.* Kata pengantar oleh Safrina Noorman. Bandung: Jalasustra.

Raffles, Thomas Stamford
1978 *The history of Java*. Reprint. With a new introduction by John Bastin. Kuala Lumpur: Oxford University Press. Two vols. [Oxford in Asia Historical Reprints.] [First edition 1817.]

Richards, Thomas
1990 *The commodity culture of Victorian England; Advertising and spectacle, 1851-1914*. London and New York: Verso.

Roche, Daniel
2000 *A history of everyday things; The birth of consumption in France, 1600-1800*. Translated by Brian Pierce. Cambridge: Cambridge University Press. [Originally published as *Histoire des choses banales*. Paris: Fayard, 1997.]

Rouffaer, G.P and J.W. IJzerman.
1925 *De eerste schipvaart der Nederlanders naar Oost-Indië onder Cornelis de Houtman 1595-1597. Journalen, documenten en andere bescheiden*. Uitgegeven en toegelicht door G.P. Rouffaer en J.W. IJzerman. 's-Gravenhage: Nijhoff. [Linschoten-Vereeniging.]

Schama, Simon
1988 *The embarrassment of riches; An interpretation of Dutch culture in the Golden Age*. N.p.: Fontana Press.

Shennan, Margaret
2000 *Out in the midday sun; The British in Malaya, 1880-1960*. London: Murray.

Shephard, Ben
1992 'Showbiz imperialism; The case of Peter Lobengula', in: John M. Mackenzie, *Imperialism and popular culture*, pp. 94-113. Manchester: Manchester University Press.

Smith, Virginia
2007 *Clean; A history of personal hygiene and purity*. Oxford: Oxford University Press.

Soo, May L.M. and Richard J. Stevenson
2007 'The moralisation of body odor', *The Mankind Quarterly* 47-3:25-56.

Spear, Percival
1998 *The nabobs; A study of the social life of the English in eighteenth century India*. Delhi: Oxford University Press. [Oxford India Paperbacks.]

Spence, Jonathan D.
1998 *The Chan's great continent; China in Western minds*. London: Penguin.

Taylor, Jean Gelman
1983   *The social world of Batavia; European and Eurasian in Dutch Asia.* Madison, WI: University of Wisconsin Press.

Thorn, William
1815   *Memoir of the conquest of Java; with the subsequent operations of the British forces, in the Oriental Archipelago, to which is subjoined, a statistical and historical sketch of Java; Being the result of observations made in a tour through the country; with an account of its dependencies.* London: Egerton.

2004   *The conquest of Java; Nineteenth century Java seen through the eyes of a soldier of the British Empire.* With an introduction by John Bastin. Singapore: Periplus.

Tillotson, Sarah
1998   *Indian mansions; A social history of the Haveli.* New Delhi: Orient Longman.

Trautmann, Thomas R.
1997   *Aryans* and *British India.* Berkeley, CA: University of California Press.

Wall, V.I. van de
[1930] *The influence of Olivia Mariamne Raffles on European society in Java (1812-1814).* [Batavia]: n.n.

2

Bathing and hygiene
Histories from the KITLV Images Archive

Jean Gelman Taylor

Studies of cleanliness in social histories of colonialism mirror the concerns of cultural and medical anthropologists in their attention to public health and to comparisons of European and Asian approaches to physical and mental well-being. Daniel Headrick (1981) and Philip Curtin (1989) have demonstrated that colonial rule was both an offshoot of advances in Western science and a sponsor of tropical medicine research. David Arnold (1993), Peter Boomgaard (1996), Lenore Manderson (1996) and the specialists working with Norman Owen (1987) document how 'colonization of the body' proceeded alongside colonization of territory in the late nineteenth and early twentieth centuries in Asia. They study the intrusive, and often resented, impact of Western medical practices such as vaccination, quarantine and autopsy, disinfection of private housing and slum clearance. Autobiographies of prominent Indonesians, such as Margono Djojohadikusumo (1973:17), contain painful memories of being labelled a 'dirty Native' at school by members of the colonial class. And yet the habit of frequent bathing by Indonesians is one of the most characteristic observations made by visitors to Indonesia since the first decades of the Verenigde Oost-Indische Compagnie (VOC, East India Company).

Bathing and cleanliness are the subjects of this chapter. In the first part I draw on studies of evolving Western concepts of cleanliness, developments in house design and household implements, and the visual record of Dutch paintings of the Golden Age. By the mid-nineteenth century, the handkerchief, fork and ceramic washbasin had spread widely amongst Dutch people of all social classes. Dutch people in the Indies brought these items in their travelling kits. Immigrants brought with them habits of personal fastidiousness that such everyday accessories fostered. In the second part of this paper I consider documentation by the Dutch of bathing and cleanliness in the Indonesian territories they were colonising from the 1850s. This is the era for which we have a photographic record. The inquiring eye of the camera fixed on Indonesians as well as on Dutch people in the course of their everyday life. My source material comes from the rich store of photographs in the online KITLV Images Archive.

DIRT, WASHING, STATUS AND POLLUTION IN WESTERN EUROPE

It is a commonplace that concern for cleanliness is typically Dutch. Simon Schama brings the weight of academic research to support this received idea in his discussion of seventeenth-century household manuals written for the Dutch housewife. They prescribed daily washing of the entryway to the home, set schedules for cleaning the front room, kitchen and cellar, required daily laundering of clothes, and laid down rules for scouring cooking pans and utensils, for making beds, folding linens, dusting and sweeping. From this evidence Schama argues that cleanliness was associated, in the minds of Dutch people, with pride and shame. A shared understanding of cleanliness fostered a sense of group solidarity. To be clean was to be patriotic, to defend hearth and homeland from dirty, unwanted invaders, whether vermin or aliens (Schama 1987:376-80).

Dutch paintings reinforced this message that dirt and moral failing go together. The ideal home and its occupants are neat and clean; human weakness takes place in scenes of domestic slovenliness.[1] Schama focuses on the cleaning of objects such as cooking pots and passageways. He has nothing to say of cleaning bodies, but clearly there were rules for personal hygiene too. In Leiden's Doelensteeg a plaque recording establishment in 1650 of an almshouse there for elderly women by the pious Eva van Hoogeveen states that residents were required to bathe themselves at least once each month. Yet, for a country so associated with cleanliness, seemingly few studies have yet been made of the history of personal hygiene in the Netherlands. Academic literature on cleanliness focuses on Italy, France and England. It covers concepts of the body and developments in material culture such as plumbing and the flushing toilet. Historians of ideas explore concepts of pollution and purity;

---

1 See, for example, 'Interior with two women beside a linen press' by Pieter de Hooch, Rijksmuseum Amsterdam, SK-C-1191 and 'The drunken pair' by Jan Steen, Rijksmuseum, Amsterdam, SK-C-232.

they argue that dirt and cleanliness are social constructs, or, in Terence McLaughlin's words (1971:1), matters of 'judgement'. Other scholars support investigations of concepts of privacy and sociability through their research into the history of the bath, bathroom and bathing practices. An important factor in all these studies is class, which directs attention to place. Studies focus, accordingly, on palace, drawing room, tavern or street.

Introducing Volume 3 of *A history of private life*, Philippe Ariès writes that in Europe's Middle Ages many acts of daily life were performed in public in the small confines of village, town and royal court. By contrast, nineteenth-century society was vast and anonymous. Middle class people sought refuge in private, family life; they left the street to the poor. Such social changes were reflected in the planning of grand houses, which now had rooms with designated functions in place of all-purpose spaces. Bedrooms and living rooms were separated from each other and from kitchen and scullery by hallways, front and back staircases (Ariès 1989:1-7).

Schama (1987:380) has observed how frequently the Dutch painted interior views of the households of commoners. He links this painterly trend to growing levels of prosperity in the United Provinces compared with other European states, and to the absence of royalty. In paintings of the living spaces of humbler folk we find the curtained bedstead as a prominent feature, but in paintings of the prosperous bedsteads are replaced by harpsichords and dining tables. Such interiors suggest larger residences and the allocation of personal functions, such as sleeping and lovemaking, to parts of the house to which viewers are not invited. Paintings seem to reflect trends towards privacy and value for the family that Ariès establishes. In many portraits the subject stands at the door or looks out from a window. Doorway and window stop observers at the threshold.

Interior views were being produced throughout the seventeenth century, which is the first century of global operations of the VOC. Dutch merchants hired by the Company were living and working in Asia far from the reach of those emblem books, manuals and paintings that were delivering to Dutch stay-at-homes messages about the proper domicile. The majority of all VOC employees, of course, were soldiers and sailors. Sailors were generally Dutchmen, but soldiers were recruited from the disadvantaged and drifters of Western Europe. For both, street, tavern, hovel and poorhouse were more likely the remembered home than the idealised interiors of instruction manual and painted record.

Historians of the senses tell us that the European body in the seventeenth century was wiped, not washed in water, to cleanse it.

Lawrence Wright (1960:138) quotes from advice manuals that cautioned against using water on the face, as it would rob the skin of its protective qualities against sun and cold; their authors recommended instead wiping face and hands with a piece of clean linen. Douglas Biow (2006:15) says that soap was first manufactured for washing clothes, not people. McLaughlin's description (1971:42-3) of soap-making and of soap's propensity to rapidly turn rancid explains why this was so. According to Georges Vigarello (1985), people cleaned themselves by washing the undergarments that touched their skin. He and Alain Corbin (1986) document the history of personal linens and changing attitudes to bodily smells. Dutch portraits of the seventeenth century make a show of the spotless linen their middle class subjects wore beneath heavy outer garments of velvet and wool. The white underwear visible at neck and wrists proclaims that the sitters are clean. Dress historians, such as Lou Taylor (2002), emphasize that silks and other expensive cloths were difficult to care for and hence were worn only by people who could afford servants. We can also consider the difficulties of drying clothing in a pre-industrial age and the threat of chills to uncovered bodies in poorly heated rooms.

Concepts of cleanliness are embedded in religious discourse and practice. The *mikvah*,[2] baptism and ritual ablution are not mediums for washing away dirt, but for preparing the individual for an altered state, whether recovery of ritual purity, entrance into a relationship with the divine, or readiness for prayers. Water is the element common to Jewish, Christian and Muslim rituals. Uncleanness represents a spiritual condition of sin or ritual impurity. The concept translates into popular wisdom in numerous English expressions: 'Cleanliness is next to godliness'; the ignorant or classes excluded from political power are the 'great unwashed'; cursing and swearing are language of the gutter; a 'filthy' mouth betrays the coarse person.

Biow argues that the topic of cleanliness obliges us to rethink issues such as self-respect, status and social distinction. He says that in Renaissance Italy personal cleanliness became a mark of social honour (Biow 2006:2). The different hygiene habits of others destabilise the viewer's sense of decorum. Such insights help us to understand why it was that travellers to Batavia in the seventeenth century recorded their disgust at the town's Asian inhabitants not only cleaning their entire bodies with water, but doing so in public view in Batavia's canals. Travellers do not speak of the refreshment

---

2   *Mikvah* refers to laws of purity in Judaism, to immersion in the ritual bath, and to the bath and bathhouse.

of bathing in a tropical climate, or of wishing to cool their own bodies. Theirs was a shocked reaction to the transgression of their own understanding of modesty.

Norbert Elias (1994) speaks of the 'advancing shame frontier' in his analysis of European manners. He marks Erasmus's etiquette manual of 1530 for boys as a milestone in this journey into the private, for Erasmus advises his young readers to make acts to do with the body, such as blowing the nose, private, and establishes conventions that restrain spitting and flatulence. Lawrence Wright traces the history of withdrawing personal functions from the public domain in his history of the bathroom and water closet. He begins by reminding us that the bathhouse makes its appearance in societies as a communal place for men. The bathhouses attached to the Greek gymnasium or constructed in Roman and Turkish cities were for sociable relaxation. The public baths and spas of eighteenth and nineteenth-century Europe offered medical cures, and were gathering places for high society to *drink* the water rather than to clean themselves in it. It is only in the industrial era with its pumps and pipes that the primary function of the bath became cleaning the body. Wright studies interior layouts of houses and the history of manufacturing washbasins, jugs, washstands and cabinets for concealing chamber pots. He discusses the portable hipbath that was used in the kitchen,[3] and the history of laying underground pipes for bringing water to individual households. He consults sales catalogues. By 1900 the model bathroom in England had a hand basin, bathtub, shower with waterproof curtain and heated towel rail, although most English people were unable to afford houses with a room dedicated to bathing until after World War II (Wright 1960:233, 258).

Personal cleanliness relies on more than tub and flushing toilet. The toothbrush is first mentioned in England in 1651 (Wright 1960:245). European museums display, among their Rococo porcelain collections, toiletry sets with containers for pomades, perfumes and ointments and matching accessories such as brushes, combs and mirrors. Delftware, which was manufactured in Holland as a cheap substitute for expensive porcelain imported from China, offered crockery that was easy to clean and aesthetically pleasing. Cottons imported from India or manufactured in Manchester provided clothing material that was easy to wash and dry. Global trade, forged first by the VOC, brought cotton textiles and china into Dutch households, changing habits and raising the general standard of living.

3 Viriginia Smith (2007:289) records that the mass-produced tin baths date from the 1850s.

| Jean Gelman Taylor

VIEWING HYGIENE IN THE INDIES

In 1870 the Netherlands Indies was opened to private enterprise and unrestricted immigration from Holland. Suez and steamer encouraged women to travel with their husbands to the Indies. Ideas of the age persuaded Hollanders to think about maintaining a Dutch lifestyle and culture, and to consider their practices as marks of superior civilization. By this time, Dutch men and women were accustomed to eating with knife, spoon and fork, rather than with their fingers; they washed their body on a weekly or daily schedule as a private act, and they were in the practice of changing their clothes regularly. Advice manuals prepared women for the task of maintaining a 'proper' Dutch home in the East. In them the link between personal habits and morality was made explicit. Sections were devoted to hygiene practices for preserving the health and energy of family members in the tropics, the necessity of avoiding certain foods, and other precautions to preserve moral character. Such information was also made available to female emigrants, before their departure from Holland, through the Colonial School for Women and Girls that was established in The Hague in 1920 (Locher-Scholten 1997, 2000). Dutch people who looked down on eating with their fingers and who had codes of privacy regarding bodily functions now took themselves off to the tropics with its fevers and heat.

So what does the KITLV Image Archive reveal?[4] Examples of paintings and photographs located by the keywords Bathing, Hygiene, Washing, Water, Sanitation, and Rivers yielded many images of Indonesians in the acts of washing their bodies, their clothes or their animals outdoors. Indonesians were also photographed at cisterns for ablutions at mosques, using public toilets along riverbanks and checking their companions' heads for lice.

To find the Indies Dutch in relation to water, I had to use other keywords, such as Swimming and Swimming Pools. Photographs and drawings of the colonial house sometimes showed bathrooms, but not adult Dutch in the act of washing themselves. Mostly the pictorial evidence is of the Dutch at play. A preliminary observation regarding documentation in the KITLV Images Archive is that race and class and absence must be built into our analysis of cleanliness, for there is an abundance of material on Indonesians of the poorer classes and almost nothing on Indonesians of the middle and upper classes or of the Dutch.

---

4   Images in the KITLV online archive are identified here by their reference number. I refer also to several photographs from private collections published in two of Rob Nieuwenhuys's *Tempo doeloe* volumes.

The dominant impression from the images is of life lived outdoors. Early camera technology is partly responsible for this conclusion, for the imperatives of lighting caused photographers to bring their subjects into the garden or street. Adaptation to tropical climate perhaps also produced a greater use of the outdoors for work and leisure. Consequently, those areas of daily life that were invisible in Holland in the late nineteenth century, because they took place in the privacy of the home or workplace, were conducted in public view in the colony and hence visible to the newly arrived immigrant as well as to the photographer. For example, immigrants found, not the closed Dutch house built on to the street, but the colonial bungalow set back in a garden filled with potted plants. Instead of a private domestic life hidden in the cosy interior, Indies home life took place in public view on the front veranda. Photographs of colonial houses show that the Dutch overseas attempted to recreate cosiness in verandas cluttered with round tables, easy chairs, hanging lamps, framed photographs and pot plants. It is as if the veranda is a room with three sides missing.

Everywhere the immigrants came up against evidence of a long history of intermarriage between Dutch men and Indonesian women, of cultural borrowing and adaptation. Indies Dutch ladies, in full view of their indigenous household personnel, walked out on to the back veranda to bathe in a room equipped with a tub of water (4441), or, if their property bordered one of the canals, they went to water's edge to a bathhouse. Eurasian ladies spent the morning hours in *kain kebaya*;[5] they sat in full view of passers-by or took a morning walk in what seemed, to newcomers, to be their underwear, their long hair unbound and uncovered (Nieuwenhuys 1961:126). It was not only the Indies Dutch who transgressed Dutch boundaries. A huge Indonesian underclass spent their lives in the street, being shaved, having their hair cut or searching for head lice (30456), eating at stalls, washing their bodies and their clothes in canals (53649, 26384), and performing toilet functions (35435). Here were people performing shameful acts without shame in public.

Hygiene practices and class are inextricably linked. For the colony's elites, the proper place for washing the body was behind walls in the bathroom. When Dutch people in the Indies bathed in public, it was for pleasure in the ocean (18014) or the municipal swimming pool (13238). They were fittingly clothed in bathing costumes and removed from the gaze of the masses. Within their leisure complex the only 'Natives' admitted were the swimming pool attendants.

---

5   A variant of Javanese women's dress consisting of a length of batik wrapped around the waist and falling to the ankles (the *kain*) and a long-sleeved blouse fastened with ornamental pins or brooches (the *kebaya*).

Figure 1. KITLV 4441, Mevrouw Tolk and her bathroom, Ambon, 1914

Figure 2. KITLV 53649, Javanese bathing in a stream, Lampung, circa 1940

Figure 3. KITLV 35435, Public bathing and toilet facilities for Indonesians, Palembang, circa 1932

Figure 4. KITLV 13238, Foltynski family at a swimming pool, Bandung, 1925

Figure 5. KITLV 4161, Royal bathing place, Ambarwinangun, Yogyakarta, 1895

Historians of bathing and cleanliness learn from the KITLV Images Archive that Java's sultans had bathing places at scenic spots for pleasure. There are photographs of these royal bathing places (4161, 40222), but no photographs of sultans relaxing in the water with their wives or with male and female entertainers.[6] Nor did members of the courts wash themselves in Java's rivers. The aura surrounding Java's sultans discouraged private acts in public view.

Class prerogatives allowed Dutch and Indonesian elites to conceal pastimes and personal hygiene from the public, but their class status prevented them from enjoying their pleasures and maintaining their personal standards of hygiene unaided. Servants and washerwomen, drawn from lower classes that conducted their personal body functions in public, moved freely in the private quarters of bungalow and palace as they maintained the cleanliness of their employers. A favourite subject of the colonial camera was the

---

6   Anthony Reid (1989), however, draws on accounts of European visitors to Aceh to describe how rulers of the seventeenth-century sultanate enjoyed river bathing and ate feasts while standing in the water.

faithful Javanese nursemaid carrying her young European charge in a *slendang* (long scarf) (15285; see also Nieuwenhuys 1982:135). European children apparently did not lose status by being naked and bathed by the Javanese nursemaid. I have found no photographs in the KITLV on-line archive of a Dutch mother washing her own child. In the tropics, that seems to have been the work of servants.

Colonial sensibilities allowed photographers to show Dutch children being washed by Indonesian nursemaids, but I have not found in the KITLV archive contemporary photographs of Indonesian servants washing the children of their royal or aristocratic employers. The Javanese photographer, Kassian Cephas (1845-1912), apparently did not intrude into the middle class Indonesian home to photograph children being washed by their servants or their mothers.[7] In his long career, Cephas photographed many of the same subjects as his fellow European professional photographers: Java's antiquities, European and Indonesian dignitaries; colonial infrastructure and commercial enterprises; and colonial 'types'. As photographer to Sultan Hamengkubuwono VII of Yogyakarta, Cephas also took many photographs of the palace, members of the royal family and of palace performers (Knaap 1999), but he apparently did not record on film the private habits of his Javanese employers. Children of sultans and aristocrats are only seen posed stiffly in photographs with parents, never being washed. Clearly, then, there is a history to be written of Indonesian conceptions of public and private, of Indonesian taboos, with attention to class, status and change over time.

The colonial camera had varied roles, from which we can make some preliminary conclusions. There is the camera as historian, preserving a record of bathing sites linked to Java's antiquities. The camera as ethnographer documents royal spas and washing facilities for ritual purification at mosques, and records Indonesians going about their personal hygiene. As tourist, the camera brings us shots of bathing places at scenic spots in the islands. Sometimes, the camera is an obliterator of history. Many snapshots of rivers are emptied of human life: no boats transport goods or ferry people, there are no fishermen, no children at play, no one bathing. As documenter of the ordinary, the camera is of interest to labour historians, for it shows the gendered allocation of jobs. Washing the

---

7 He did go into the private parts of Indonesian houses, however. Photograph 34594, for example, is of Wahidin Soedirohoesoedoe and acquaintances taken, around 1902, on the back veranda of his house.

family's clothes appears to be the task of women (26384), but the work in commercial laundries on rivers and canals was performed by men (26479).

The camera is also the creator of rural idylls. Boys wash the family buffalo in the village stream (9721), reminding us of a common theme of painters in the *Mooi Indië* (Beautiful Indies) school. It is worth noting that the camera, which is a product of modern technology, presents images of Indonesians leading a rural, 'simple' life. Indonesians wash buffalo, but I did not find any photographs of Indonesians washing their employer's motorcar or any other modern object. The camera also contributes to the making of the exotic. The caption to photograph 35201 of Aceh's Gunungan identifies it improbably as the 'bathing place of the sultan's women in the neighbourhood of the sultans' graves near the Kroeëng Daroe at Kotta Goenoengan at Koetaradja'.

The colonial cameraman was ready to record the private acts of others for the Dutch at home in Holland to see. We can think of the camera as voyeur, creating titillating images of naked Balinese women (25964) and naked Balinese men (26154). Other photographs are more coy (40138). The styles are quite different from the wholesome images of Dutch and Eurasian families at the municipal swimming pool and water polo competitions. The only Javanese fully clothed who are posed near water are Javanese swimming pool attendants (55026).

A case can be made that the colonial camera degrades and shames by its intrusion into intensely private acts. In contrast with so much native flesh, the archive contains only a few photographs of adult Europeans washing their bodies or performing toilet functions in public. These Dutch men photographed are German sympathisers. The year is 1940, the month is May, and the site is a prison camp. Photograph 19063 shows a Dutch man from behind, his buttocks naked. More remarkable still is 19094 of Dutch internees seated on latrines. Taken in similar conditions, a photograph of Dutch women in a Japanese camp (2618) from 1945 following the collapse of Japanese power, draws attention to the misery of their conditions, the primitive washing facilities and the absence of servants. The intent seems to be to convey sympathy for the innocent, wrongfully imprisoned, not to debase them. Traitors, on the other hand, have no honour, self-defence or even a modicum of privacy. They have betrayed the nation, transgressed the boundaries of group solidarity and loyalty. They alone among Europeans deserve to be shown defecating. The camera puts such men below the indigenous majority.

Figure 6. KITLV 9721, Two boys bathing cattle in a river, Bali, circa 1920

| *Jean Gelman Taylor*

Figure 7. KITLV 19094, European men interned as Nazi sympathizers on latrines, Ngawi, 1940

We can analyse the interest in photographing Asians bathing in terms of the colonial voyeur, following Edward Said (1979), postcolonial and cultural studies, in order to discuss 'Othering' and Western gaze. Or we can be historians. To illustrate this argument we may consider the photographs and paintings in the KITLV online archive of stretches of water that evoke admiration for the beauty of nature in Indonesia. While the colonial camera tells us that rivers functioned as bathroom and laundry for the indigenous majority, in this landscape genre Indonesians do not interrupt or distract the viewer's contemplation of nature. Indonesians are absent altogether or else they are depicted at water's edge in miniature and seen from a great distance (47D-21). We can argue that such river views are contrived to belittle Indonesians, or, as historians, we can note conventions of Dutch landscape painting that depicted people (whether Dutch or Indonesian) fitting humbly and naturally into the physical universe.

TOWARDS INDONESIAN HISTORIES OF BATHING AND HYGIENE

In revisiting this issue of the camera as voyeur or instrument of oppression, we should place Indonesian bathing practices within the history of ideas and technology, as historians have done for Europeans and their bathing practices. People bathed and washed their clothes in Batavia's canals, not because they had no shame, but because they lived in houses that lacked bathrooms, laundries and light. Small structures of bamboo and thatch had little space; their windows were of insufficient size to admit the light necessary for many daily activities. Consequently, the majority of Indonesians conducted their everyday activities outdoors. The colony's municipal governments did not install pipes for running water and sewerage systems in most indigenous neighbourhoods. In circumstances where water could not be brought to the house, people had to walk to the water source and carry water back home for drinking and cooking. The *kendi* (water container) was the ubiquitous item of every household. Made from clay and produced by local potters, it was designed to hold the quantity of water that women could manage to carry (31789). There were no ready means of transporting water in the volumes needed to fill baths. Men could carry at most two water containers suspended from a pole over the shoulders. The abundance of rivers and warm temperatures in Indonesia made bathing outdoors practical, rather than construct public bathhouses that were the solution for cold climates or environments where water was scarce.

The encounter between Dutch and Indonesians occurred at a time when technologies were not comparable. The Dutch had withdrawn most of their personal activities from the street and made them private because they had the engineering technology, the appliances and the funds to enable them to do so. Municipal councils in Holland commissioned sewer systems; water engineers designed them; taxpayers financed the laying of pipes and safe disposal of wastewater; householders paid for the installation of flushing toilets. The Dutch could not have colonised the Indies until advances in Western science and their application through technology made colonies possible. The Dutch who had the water closet were the Dutch who colonised Indonesia. The Dutch who did not have running water and bathrooms, who wiped their face and hands on a piece of linen, were the Dutch of the VOC who lived a precarious existence on the fringes of Indonesian kingdoms. Schama sees dirt as forming a boundary between the Dutch of the seventeenth century and their enemies. Two centuries later the camera's viewpoint could help the Dutch to draw boundaries in foreign lands, preserve an identity, demarcate honour and shame.

Of course, the camera does not record what the photographed thought as they performed their private acts under its gaze. But

Nieuwenhuys (1961:27) prints a photograph that suggests in the separate groups of men and women in the river an Indigenous etiquette of public bathing. Clearly, the Dutch camera broke the rules of discretion and modesty; perhaps it reinforced for the photographed their sense of being powerless subjects.

In calling for an Indonesian history of cleanliness, we must include a section on the diffusion of Indonesian conceptions and practices to the Dutch. The bathroom, with its tiled water tank and dipper, became a fixture of the Dutch house in the Indies long before Dutch houses in the Netherlands acquired a separate room dedicated to personal bathing. In the Indies the Dutch adapted themselves to the indigenous practice of washing the whole body using this precursor of the shower and they took up the Indonesian habit of regular, daily bathing (36D-722). Newcomers and old-timers alike waxed sentimental about the morning *mandi* (bathing) and the steaming *kopi* (coffee) that followed. Here is a major cultural transfer. Europeans adopted Asian personal hygiene habits and values, Asians did not adopt theirs.[8] The colonized did not give up daily bathing for a wipe or an infrequent wash.

KITLV Images Archive offers material for beginning a history of bathrooms and hygiene in Indonesia. For example, under keywords 'Sanitation' and 'Water' there are numerous photographs of storage tanks, reservoirs and municipal sanitation works; there are also examples of neighbourhood improvement for the Indigenous such as newly built water closets lining the river and municipal street sweepers (30155). No middle class Indonesian washes body or clothes in the river. Middle class people today have a bathroom and they employ servants to wash their clothes. A tee shirt that becomes grubby in the course of the workday is the clothing of Indonesian labourers; the freshly laundered and ironed shirt is the uniform of the office employee. The middle class lady covers her mouth with a handkerchief when laughing; she carries the handkerchief prominently *outside* of her handbag, establishing status differences from village women who pull on cloth wrapped around the waist to blow their nose and wipe their brow. Nationalists and the Islamic-oriented sometimes prefer using fingers for eating in a now deliberate, conscious show of difference from Western manners and modernity. To European histories of religion and pollution may be added studies of Indonesian practices, such as the use of water transformed by the addition of flower petals for prepar-

---

8   Smith (2007:235) similarly refers to the influence of baths and showers on Englishmen in eighteenth-century India.

ing a bride or a corpse. Here water and bathing have the function of marking transitions. There is a history to be written of the rapid transfer of technology, such as bathtubs and flushing toilets in Indonesian hotel bathrooms (37006) and running water in Indonesian kitchens.

Drawing all these threads together, consider a final image. A Dutch man relaxes in a municipal swimming pool; on the wall someone has attached a poster of a man in a bathtub (13119). Water represents cleansing, leisure, status and difference. The KITLV Images Archive is an enormously rich source for social history. It is to be hoped that it may be able to borrow photograph albums in the possession of Indonesian families and make available online more visual documents for further explorations of daily life.

Figure 8. KITLV 13119, Swimming pool and poster, Bandung, 1925

REFERENCES

Ariès, Philippe
1989 'Introduction', in: Roger Chartier (ed.), *A history of private life; Vol. 3: Passions of the Renaissance.* Translated by Arthur Goldhammer. Cambridge, MA: Belknap Press of Harvard University Press.

Arnold, David
1993 *Colonizing the body; State medicine and epidemic disease in nineteenth-century India.* Berkeley, CA: University of California Press.

Biow, Douglas
2006 *The culture of cleanliness in Renaissance Italy.* Ithaca, NY: Cornell University Press.

Boomgaard, Peter, Rosalia Sciortino and Ines Smyth (eds)
1996 *Health care in Java, past and present.* Leiden: KITLV Press. [Proceedings 3.]

Corbin, Alain
1986 *The foul and the fragrant; Odour and the French social imagination.* Oxford: Berg. [Originally published as *Le miasme et la jonquille; L'odorat en l'imaginaire social, XVIIIe-XIXe siècles.* Paris: Aubier Montaigne, 1982.]

Curtin, Philip D.
1989 *Death by migration; Europe's encounter with the tropical world in the nineteenth century.* Cambridge: Cambridge University Press.

Djojohadikusomo, Margono
1973 *Reminiscences from three historical periods.* Jakarta: Indira.

Douglas, Mary
2002 *Purity and danger; An analysis of concepts of pollution and taboo.* London: Routledge. [Originally published in 1966.]

Elias, Norbert
1994 *The civilizing process; The history of manners and state formation and civilization.* Oxford: Blackwell. [Originally published as *Über den Prozess der Zivilisation; Soziogenetische und psychogenetische Untersuchungen.* Basel: Haus zum Falken, 1939.]

Haan, F. de
1923 *Oud Batavia; Platenalbum.* Batavia: Kolff.

Headrick, D.R.
1981 *The tools of empire; Technology and European imperialism in the nineteenth century.* New York: Oxford University Press.

Knaap, Gerrit
1999 *Cephas, Yogyakarta; Photography in the service of the sultan.* Leiden: KITLV Press.

Locher-Scholten, Elsbeth
1997 'Summer dresses and canned food; European women and Western lifestyles in the Indies, 1900-1942', in: Henk Schulte Nordholt (ed.), *Outward appearances; Dressing state and society in Indonesia*, pp. 151-80. Leiden: KITLV Press. [Proceedings 4.]
2000 *Women and the colonial state; Essays on gender and modernity in the Netherlands Indies, 1900-1942.* Amsterdam: Amsterdam University Press.

McLaughlin, Terence
1971 *Dirt; A social history as seen through the uses and abuses of dirt.* New York: Dorset Press.

Manderson, Lenore
1996 *Sickness and the state; Health and illness in colonial Malaya, 1870-1940.* Cambridge: Cambridge University Press.

Nieuwenhuys, Rob
1961 *Tempo doeloe; Fotografische documenten uit het oude Indië, 1870-1914.* Amsterdam: Querido.
1982 *Komen en blijven; Tempo doeloe – een verzonken wereld: Fotografische documenten uit het oude Indië, 1870-1920.* Amsterdam: Querido.

Owen, Norman G. (ed.)
1987 *Death and disease in Southeast Asia; Explorations in social, medical and demographic history.* Singapore: Oxford University Press. [Asian Studies Association of Australia, Southeast Asia Publications Series 14.]

Reid, Anthony
1989 'Elephants and water in the feasting of 17th century Aceh', *Journal of the Malaysian Branch of the Royal Asiatic Society* 62: 25-44.

Said, Edward W.
1979 *Orientalism.* New York: Vintage.

Schama, Simon
1987 *The embarrassment of riches; An interpretation of Dutch culture in the Golden Age.* New York: Knopf.

Smith, Virginia
2007 *Clean; A history of personal hygiene and purity.* Oxford: Oxford University Press.

Taylor, Lou
2002 *The study of dress history.* Manchester: Manchester University Press.
Vigarello, Georges
1985 *Le propre et le sale; L'hygiène du corps depuis le Moyen Age.* Paris: Seuil.
Wright, Lawrence
1960 *Clean and decent; The fascinating history of the bathroom and the water closet and the sundry habits, fashions and accessories of the toilet principally in Great Britain, France and America.* London: Routledge and Kegan Paul.

3

The epidemic that wasn't
Beriberi in Bangka and the Netherlands Indies

Mary Somers Heidhues

Perhaps all Dutch schoolchildren learn about Dr Eijkman's chickens. By feeding the fowl either paddy, brown rice, or white rice,[1] he was able to indicate that a diet of white rice caused a paralysis of the legs that resembled the nerve damage experienced by victims of the puzzling human disease called beriberi. The material in the bran or pericarp (*zilvervlies*) of the rice, which was removed by industrial milling, protected the chickens from what he called *polyneuritis gallinarum*, chicken polyneuritis, and, by a later extension, human beriberi. His insights, his good luck, and not least, his meticulous record-keeping earned him a Nobel Prize (shared with the Englishman F.G. Hopkins) in 1929 (Boomgaard 2006:205).

Christiaan Eijkman's results, published in the medical journal *Geneeskundig Tijdschrift voor Nederlandsch-Indië* in 1896, appeared to go against prevailing medical wisdom about the causes of disease. Diseases were contagious, arose from uncleanliness, or from 'miasmas', obnoxious if invisible vapours that escaped from the soil and made unsuspecting victims feverish, weak, bloated, or whatever the symptoms might be. Other creative explanations included bad air, enriched by a 'fermentation', or, where sleeping quarters were already well ventilated, the blame went to nocturnal drafts

---

1 The sources speak of '*afgewerkte*' versus '*half afgewerkte*' rice (or rice in '*zilvervlies*') that is, white versus brown, and finally, unhusked rice. (Paddy is an English term; the Indonesian word for unhusked rice kernels that are separated from the stalk is *gabah;* sometimes *gabah* means the – inedible – husks themselves.) To avoid confusion of the processes and the terms of husking, pearling, and so on, this text retains the terms paddy-brown-white distinction as far as possible. White rice may in addition be polished to remove the residue of the other processes and make the grains more shiny, sometimes it is also coated. For an exhaustive treatment of traditional methods of preparing rice, see Abé 2007, on terminology, pp. 32-37 and 50-89, while a summary of industrial methods is on pp. 74-5. Abé (2007:89) believes the common English appellation 'husk' is not technically correct but that the outer skin should be called 'hull'. Carpenter (2000:17-23) also details traditional and industrial treatment of rice.

under tropical conditions. By Eijkman's time, however, progressive scientists believed that diseases were spread by microscopic germs, passed from person to person or through other channels.

In fact, Eijkman himself took years to recognize that the mysterious ingredient in brown rice was not a protection against some kind of poisonous toxin or infectious agent, but an essential dietary component, the lack of which could cause severe nerve damage and even death. Today, this substance has the name of vitamin B1 or thiamin, while beriberi is one of the well-known if relatively rare vitamin deficiencies. A whole field of nutritional science has since arisen.

Eijkman's discoveries took a long time to gain widespread acceptance in the medical world, at times he himself doubted the consequences of his research. Convinced that a disease must be of infectious origin, he himself even criticized others who adhered to the 'food deficiency' theory of the disease.[2]

Only after further research, much of it in the Netherlands Indies, did most scientists – Eijkman included – accept that beriberi was a nutritional deficiency. Prevailing ideas about hygiene, contagion, and the spread and prevention of disease had stubbornly stood in the way of comprehending what was happening to the victims and why. Finally, some scientists closed the discussion by

Figure 1. C. Eijkman, circa 1900

[2] Carpenter 2000:55. See also Eijkman's Nobel Prize acceptance statement, reprinted in Jansen 1957:168-78.

isolating crystalline thiamin, which is easily destroyed by the usual methods of searching for it, making it available for treatment. In the 1920s and 1930s, others determined its chemical composition, unlocked the mechanism of the disease itself, and found the prophylactic dosage necessary for humans (Carpenter 2000:108-15). For years, however, ideas of cleanliness or contagion turned out to be enemies of appropriate treatment for the victims.

Not a new or unknown disease, beriberi appeared to be reaching epidemic proportions in certain parts of the world in the late nineteenth century. This chapter sketches the experience of beriberi between the 1850s and 1914 in the Netherlands Indies and especially on the tin-mining island of Bangka (then spelled Banka), where the disease among the Chinese mine coolies was a serious, even deadly, and stubborn problem. Here and elsewhere, officials and medical specialists were pressed to take measures against the disease – measures that for decades were exercises in futility.

BERIBERI IN HISTORY: A GLOBAL DISEASE

Known from observation for centuries and in a number of different lands, beriberi acquired a variety of names, but descriptions of the symptoms show the disease was the same. In many lands, it appeared seasonally, as for example in Japan, where it tended to show up in the wetter, hot months of July and August, only to disappear again toward October, and where it was called *kakke*, a name derived from the Chinese.

For the most part (Japan is an exception), it was a disease of the tropics. It affected mostly, although not exclusively, rice-eaters. Some authors think it showed up among Roman armies on their expeditions to the Near East, and the Chinese described it centuries ago. A German employee of the Verenigde Oost-Indische Compagnie (VOC, East India Company), Albrecht Herport, on his way to the East Indies in the mid-seventeenth century, reports how, when bad weather buffeted the ship, they had 'many sick men [...] many suffered from barbieri (this is a paralysis of the extremities)'.[3] Once ashore, these victims usually recovered – or fell prey to another disease.

Bontius was among the first to describe the symptoms of beriberi in the Netherlands Indies. Early Portuguese missionaries in

---

3 'viel kranck Volck..., etliche lagen an der Barbieri, (ist ein Erlamung an den Gliederen)' (Herport 1930:34-5).

Ambon in the sixteenth century also suffered from it.[4] No one was really sure what the cause might be, but if the illness was not too severe, the symptoms would disappear by themselves, especially if the victim got rest and better food.[5] The Japanese often dealt with seasonal beriberi by adding small red adzuki beans to their diet – legumes are an excellent source of the vitamin, as later came to light. On the other hand, sometimes victims continued to have problems long after the disease retreated, and it might leave them susceptible to other illnesses.[6] Only if the paralysis had become so severe that it affected vital organs like the lungs and heart was death the inevitable outcome.

NEW PROBLEMS IN THE NINETEENTH CENTURY

In the late nineteenth century, beriberi was becoming both more common and much more deadly. Suddenly, the disease would appear in a group of people, often young men, often immigrants, and, for some reason, often the most strapping individuals, who would seem to be the picture of health, good nutrition, and immunity to disease. The 'epidemic' appeared selectively: natives of a place were seldom affected. Common along the seacoast, it was rare in the interior. At first, Europeans were seldom victims and observers speculated that this was a disease of Asians. The sickness also appeared to be an urban phenomenon, hovering around ships or certain buildings, such as prisons, barracks, hospitals, asylums, sometimes only in certain stories of a building. Wetness or dampness, overwork, and poor hygiene seemed to contribute, while exposure to other diseases might complicate the symptoms and make diagnosis difficult. Above all, beriberi had something to do with rice.[7]

In the Netherlands Indies in the second half of the nineteenth century, beriberi suddenly appeared among certain definable groups:

---

4 Carpenter 2000:24. For Valentijn's and Bontius's descriptions of beriberi, see Editor 1854. Interestingly, Bontius insists that 'it is not mortal of itself' unless muscles of the heart or thorax were affected (excerpted in Editor 1854:516).

5 Even earlier, at the dawn of the seventeenth century, Van Neck described beriberi: 'Deese siecte, na onx vermoeden, ontstont ons van de rijs, die wij doen wel 16 maenden lanck gegeten hadden, deur faute van broot' (This disease, in our opinion, appears from the rice we have been eating for sixteen months, for lack of bread) (*Vierde schipvaart* 1980:231-2). The antidote was, if possible, to land and get fresh fruits and meat.

6 For example Scheube (1896:163), 'Der häufigste Ausgang der Beriberi ist die Genesung' (The most frequent outcome of beriberi is recovery).

7 Scheube (1896:140-1) gives a contemporary medical view of the etiology and spread of the disease.

prisoners, coolies in the tin mines or in plantations, those on board ships (especially the native personnel), inhabitants of certain institutions like hospitals or orphanages, and finally, the army. Clearly, it was on the increase, both in frequency and severity. But why?

The connection with institutions meant that persons for whose well-being the government was ultimately responsible – not just criminals – were suffering. The search for explanations became more urgent after 1870 when large numbers of soldiers fighting in the Aceh wars succumbed. There, first natives, then Europeans sickened, refuting the theory that Europeans might be 'immune' to the disease. By 1884, at the latest, the search for the cause and appropriate treatment had become urgent.

Meanwhile, in 1883, beriberi in the newly-formed Japanese Imperial Navy was sending sailors to the hospitals in droves. Neither the weather nor unsanitary, crowded conditions aboard ship seemed to be the problem. Naval doctor Kanehiro Takaki noticed that the food given the sailors was wanting in protein (which he measured as 'nitrogen'). After a particularly disastrous outbreak of sickness aboard a training vessel in 1883, he convinced authorities to change the food supply in the following year, adding meat, condensed milk, bread, and vegetables to the diet, while correspondingly reducing the rice intake. In contrast to the previous year's voyage, on that of 1884 there were no deaths and only fourteen sick, all of them men who had refused to eat their allotments of meat and milk (a hint that dietary habits would complicate treatment). The successful experiment led to a general change in the sailors' diet. By 1886 there were no more deaths and only three cases of the disease in the entire Imperial Navy. Takaki's case rested, he received baronial honours, but his colleagues did not believe his conclusions (Carpenter 2000:10-3).

Even earlier, in 1873, a Dutch naval surgeon named Van Leent had equally good results with Javanese naval personnel serving on the run to Aceh. When up to 60 per cent of them came down with beriberi while at sea, he determined that they should get the same diet as the Dutch sailors (few of whom caught the disease). Sickness rates dropped steeply.[8] However correct this treatment might have been, how could he convince Javanese to eat pea soup, sausages, and cheese?[9]

---

8 Van Leent, cited in Carpenter 2000:12-3. See Leent 1880.
9 Eijkman, cited in Jansen 1959:170-1. Some did resist the change in food; Takaki's subjects were also averse to meat, milk, and bread. Cultural resistance to dietary change remained a problem and probably torpedoed some well-intentioned efforts. As is known today, many Asians also do not tolerate milk.

Both these doctors published their results, Takaki in English-language journals, Van Leent in the flagship of the Netherlands Indies' health services, the *Geneeskundig Tijdschrift voor Nederlandsch-Indië*. Nevertheless, many colleagues pooh-poohed their results - or failed to read them for reason of language.[10]

If the altered diet was unattractive to Asians, a worse alternative was for the victim to fall into the hands of Western and Western-trained doctors. Medications and treatments a state-of-the-art medical text of 1896 proposed to 'help' the unfortunate sufferer included: various laxatives or purgatives, calomel, digitalis, bloodletting, morphine, arsenic, iron, belladonna, quinine, a syrup combining 'strychnine, phosphoric acid, sodium sulfate, sulfate of iron oxide and quinine sulfate', and electric shocks for damaged nerves (Scheube 1894:202-3, 1896:170). External applications were rubdowns with eucalyptus or capsicum and cold showers. As late as the mid-nineteenth century, one doctor recommended drawing blood, using leeches, or moxibustion,[11] which later fell from favour. Luckily, the victim might get extra fruits, meat, and port or red wine, for prevalent opinions still agreed that rest and good food were helpful. Unfortunately, most caregivers often failed to apply this wisdom, continuing to deny the importance of diet as a preventive.

On a lighter note, when beriberi appeared at a Protestant seminary for native missionaries in Depok in the 1880s, investigators claimed that lodgings and food were excellent and the young men had plenty of fresh air. Therefore, they prescribed each student a large glass of milk laced with brandy and sugar a few times daily, a treatment that promised to be popular but that was unfortunately not tried elsewhere.[12] Often, better food and rest did help but usually only slowly, and the sickest died in spite of the interventions (Scheube 1894:204).

Why some treatments succeeded was still a mystery. Apart from solutions like those of Takaki and Van Leent, nineteenth-century medical men's wisdom failed stubbornly. Demographic epidemiology seemed to lead nowhere. Each time a population was identi-

---

10   Carpenter (2000:10-3) points out that the Japanese Navy employed English-trained medical men, but the Imperial Army relied on Germans and German-trained doctors, and Army specialists dismissed the experience of the sister service. The Japanese Army nearly had to withdraw during the Russo-Japanese War (1904-1905) because over 90,000 men fell seriously ill with beriberi (Carpenter 2000:88-9). The navy had no problems.
11   Lindman 1854:156-7. Moxibustion, from Chinese traditional medicine and related to acupuncture, has been known in the West since the seventeenth century. It consists of burning small amounts of medicinal herbs above or on certain points of the body.
12   Berg 1886:65-6. Cow's milk is a good source of vitamin B1.

fied as especially susceptible to beriberi, other groups in different environments fell prey to the disease. On the other hand, if it was a miasma from the earthen floors of the sleeping quarters, why were dwellings with proper wooden floors affected? Rain and cold weather seemed to promote the disease, but in some places it was most severe in the hot, dry season.

CLEANLINESS VERSUS DIET

Not for nothing has the nineteenth century (in fact the second half of it) been called the 'Century of Hygiene'. Spurred by discoveries in bacteriology and contagiousness of diseases, many scientific minds focused solely on identifying the agent responsible for the spread of what they still presumed was an infectious disease.

Yet during these same decades, signs multiplied that beriberi was not a contagious disease and not caused by some kind of germ, mould, toxin, parasite, or bacillus (Scheube 1894:205). Scurvy was, of course, long known as a disease of sailors; since the eighteenth century adding certain foods to ships' provisions had met the challenge, even before the relevant vitamin (C) was discovered. As mentioned, fresh meat, fruit, and vegetables were also an early treatment for beriberi. Because of their preference for 'scientific' explanations, however, too many researchers refused to believe that changes in diet might be the answer.

What had worsened the nutritional situation and stood behind the 'epidemic,' was the introduction of the industrial milling, pearling, and polishing of rice in major centres in the late nineteenth century, such as Bangkok, Saigon, or Rangoon, and also in Java. However, it was not a one-to-one situation, as will be seen.

Unhusked rice (paddy) can keep well if it is dry and protected from vermin, as villagers all over Asia knew. Shortly before cooking it, they pounded and winnowed the grain by hand. Occasionally, they harnessed water or animal power to the task. This method, although removing both the husk and the bran (in a single process), did so imperfectly, thus retaining much of the food value in the germ and the layers surrounding the rice kernel.[13] Spoilage was not a problem because peasants did not store this rice but prepared it just before consumption.

13 According to Abé (2007:53-8), traditional methods of handling rice remove only a fraction of the bran, even as little as 20 per cent.

Exporting unhusked paddy was, because of its higher weight, not commercially desirable. Some exporters did export 'cargo rice', that is rice with the husk but not the bran removed, which is called here 'brown rice'. Rangoon, the major supplier of the East Sumatra tobacco plantations and a supplier for Bangka in the twentieth century, shipped most of its export rice as 'cargo rice'.[14] Husked rice, however, unless completely dried and otherwise protected, spoils easily if the bran is not thoroughly removed. Thus large grain exporters would usually remove as much of the bran as possible; in addition, white rice was simply more attractive to consumers. Apart from its unfamiliar taste and consistency, brown rice requires longer cooking time.

Before the industrial age, lots of human power, sometimes supplemented by simple machines, could produce very white rice with little or no bran. This was done in Japan as early as the eighteenth century, but the labour involved meant it was available only to the rich.[15] Then, in the course of the nineteenth century, new machines came into play. In the southern United States (where rice was a commercial commodity, not a staple),[16] steam-driven rice mills replaced hand mills, becoming common by the 1830s.[17] Siam imported machinery for a steam-driven rice mill, probably its first, from the United States in 1858 (Terwiel 1983:184). By the end of the century major rice exporters, whether in Rangoon, Bangkok, or Saigon, were thoroughly mechanized.

Not the steam engine itself is to blame, it merely provided the power. After the paddy was husked, special cones removed the bran and outer layers of the grain in a process sometimes called 'pearling'. The rice might pass through as many as four cones (Latham 1998:22-5; Grist 1955:227-9, 248-9). As a result consumers eating machine-prepared white rice, which was typically polished after removal of the bran, were getting more or less pure starch. When cooks washed it thoroughly before cooking, a common practice among both Javanese and Chinese, especially when cooking for a group, then cooked it in plenty of water, pouring off the excess, they removed any residual vitamins.

Such de-vitaminized rice was the typical food of armies, ships' crews, inmates of various institutions, and coolie labourers – and later of urban populations. Not surprisingly, beriberi turned up

14 Private communication, Yoshio Abé.
15 This contributed to the pre-industrial prevalence of beriberi in Japan.
16 Private communication, Yoshio Abé.
17 www.er.nps.gov/nr/TwHP/wwwlps/lessons/3rice/visual4.htm (accessed 26-4-2007) (picture and description of a steam-driven mill in Georgetown County, South Carolina).

among such diverse groups as the Philippine militia, orphans, prisoners, students at a Christian seminary near Batavia, coolies in Malaya and the Netherlands Indies, and even members of the Siamese police force who received rice allotments from the government. Furthermore, 'institutional' diets were usually deficient in other foods such as fresh vegetables, legumes, or meats that might make up for what the cooked rice now lacked.

Rural natives were largely 'immune', to beriberi, not because of some special genetic resistance, but because, in addition to some vegetables and side dishes, they were still consuming hand-milled rice, or rice milled by simple mechanical devices, which retained the beneficial parts of the grains that the modern mills removed. The 'epidemic' of beriberi had been set loose by modern technology.[18]

INTERNATIONAL FOCUS ON RICE

Beriberi had become an international problem in the late nineteenth century, but national thinking limited the search for a solution. One attempt to 'globalize' the search for an answer came from the Americans in the twentieth century. Determined to be a model colonialist in the Philippines (against all odds), they soon faced 'outbreaks' of beriberi, in particular among the native militia, the Philippine Scouts. They took two steps: they changed the diet, after reading of similar steps taken by Dutch and British colonial officials, adding potatoes and bread in place of some of the rice (whether the Scouts were happy about this is not recorded), and they invited neighbouring countries to a conference in 1910.

Thumbing his nose at his countryman Takaki's work, the Japanese delegate still blamed a microorganism, while some other participants held out for parasites or toxicity. In the end though, the majority of those present supported a resolution that blamed beriberi on 'continuous consumption of white (polished) rice as the staple article of diet...'.[19] This result should have been authoritative, but what was to be done in the Netherlands Indies?

18 In Japan, the white rice preferred by urban populations could be achieved by aggressive hand-milling. In addition, particularly during the hot summer, many people favoured a 'cooling' diet of little more than rice and tea. Apparently, Japan's rural people often sold their rice, a higher-priced commodity, and themselves consumed more barley and wheat (both of which are well provided with the appropriate vitamin). See Carpenter 2000:8-9. Alternatively, they did not pound rice so thoroughly for their own consumption.
19 Carpenter 2000:80-3. Americans often call white rice 'polished' rice to distinguish it from the 'brown' variety. Polishing was an additional process, following removal of the bran by pearling.

BERIBERI IN THE NETHERLANDS INDIES

The Netherlands Indies government bought much of its rice, often through local ethnic Chinese dealers, from mainland Southeast Asian exporters (sometimes via Singapore) or from centres in Java. This rice fed the Netherlands Indies army, navy, the tin miners (except those who purchased rice for themselves or were in non-government operations), prison inmates, and other institutional groups. Just such groups had become a 'laboratory' for ideas about hygiene, cleanliness, ventilation, and disinfection.[20]

In Batavia, the *Geneeskundig Tijdschrift voor Nederlandsch-Indië*, founded under a slightly different title in 1851, devoted more articles to the question of beriberi than to any other topic during its first three decades of publishing. Eijkman's contribution of 1896, about polished rice was just one of many submissions that purported to explain this mysterious, explosively appearing 'epidemic'. Other authors, often armchair 'experts', continued to challenge the experiences of a Van Leent, Takaki, or Eijkman.

A review of the index to the *Geneeskundig Tijdschrift voor Nederlandsch-Indië* gives some idea of the geographic and demographic distribution of the sickness and offers an insight into how prevailing ideas about contagion and hygiene stood in the way of confronting the evidence. Observers who had experience with a single group of sufferers only or other authors who were grinding their own axes sent most of the contributions. One problem was that they may even have been dealing with health problems that were not, or not exclusively, beriberi, for correct diagnosis was often difficult. The major proponents were those supporting the idea of either infection, poisoning, or deficient food.[21] The idea of infection was probably the most persistent, although beriberi repeatedly proved to be non-contagious. This in turn gave rise to multiple suggestions for prevention.

The second group favoured some kind of poisoning from the grain itself, analogous to the example of ergotism, which was caused by a fungus that grows on rye. The toxins cause severe nerve damage (especially in the limbs) and hallucinations. At the time, pellagra, too, was thought to be from a poison in maize, although it was later shown to be a deficiency disease.[22] Some suggested the

---

20 Corbin 1982:123. I thank Kees van Dijk for this reference to miasmas and the battle against them.
21 As emphasized in Langen 1927:5-7.
22 Ergotism has been known since at least the sixteenth century; a fungus on rye produces oversized 'kernels' of rye called mothercorn, which contain the toxin ergotamine (Dieren 1887:7-9). Modern mills remove these. Pellagra, a deficiency disease, spread with the introduction of maize as a staple grain in the eighteenth century; it comes from a deficiency of vitamin B3 (niacin) in, for example, a one-sided diet of (untreated) maize or other grain. For a time, it was also attributed to a toxin in maize (as in Dieren 1897).

agent was in spoiled fish, since salted fish was a regular item in coolie and other diets. The idea of a nebulous but poisonous 'miasma', rising from the soil, also died hard. After all, in beriberi, the feet were affected first (Scheube 1896:142).

When deficiency returned again and again as a probable cause, some contributors countered that many victims were not only physically sound, but ate hearty, apparently nutritious meals. Furthermore, among any given population eating the same diet, some sickened and others did not.

The outbreak among soldiers in the Aceh War after 1870 made it a military necessity to explain and eliminate the disease. Beriberi cases among Europeans in the Netherlands Indies army climbed from 2411 in 1878 to 5338 in 1884, while at the same time, the number of those sick with malaria, although higher, was retreating (44,552 in 1878, 19,501 in 1884). The statistics for 1885-1908 show that beriberi rates then declined from about 40 per cent of all native troops and 24 per cent of Europeans to less than 10 per cent from 1898 onward (Wijckerheld Bisdom 1911). Since the deficiency theory was not accepted at this time, what produced the good results? The men were ordered to disinfect their quarters and clothing after 1886 (see below for this treatment), and, more usefully, the diet was improved to include more protein and fat.[23] The end of the 'concentrated line' of defence in Aceh probably helped. Greater mobility after the lifting of the line may have given soldiers access to native rice and a better variety of fresh foods. Another possibility is a change in the rice supplier.[24] Whatever the reason, the apparent benefits to Aceh's military did not yet help other groups – a health problem in the army, and that in wartime, was far more serious than one among coolies or prisoners.

NEW RESEARCH

By the 1880s the idea of improving nutrition had again receded into the background (Donath and Veen 1945:75-6) as was evident in 1884 when the government appointed a commission which included Eijkman and two scientists from Utrecht, C.A. Pekelharing (a pathologist) and C. Winkler (a neurologist), to investigate the situation. Having no time for experiments, the prestigious doctors

---

23 Dieren 1897:94. These foods incidentally contained more vitamin B1.
24 From the end of 1888, rice provisions came from the Pamanukan-Ciasem area of West Java (Gelpke 1890:147). The 'concentrated line' was a kind of 'clear and hold' defence line behind which the Dutch forces were actually confined.

resorted to a theory of infection well-suited to the superficial experience of beriberi as an 'epidemic'. In his preliminary report of 1888, Pekelharing insisted that he had isolated an infectious agent from the blood of patients and from the air (or rather the walls) of the quarters where they lived. Agreeing that the disease was not contagious, he identified the real culprit as '*vuil*' – filth. The earthen floors of living quarters should be well-drained and after becoming wet, they should be cleaned and disinfected, and kept dry (although he also noted that the supposed infectious agents he had collected were resistant to dryness). Clothing and quarters should also be disinfected. This disease spread not through contaminated food but through *inhalation* (Pekelharing 1888). His recommendations – disinfect the living quarters – dominated the following attempts to rein in the disease (including those in Aceh).[25]

Actually, Pekelharing was at the cutting edge of medical science with his 'micrococci'. The germ theory of disease was in its infancy, finally displacing the pre- Pasteurian ideas of 'miasma' and bad air (although some writers clung to the miasma hypothesis as late as

Figure 2. Commission on beriberi (*De Amsterdammer*, 23-9-1888)

---

25 Nationaal Archief (NA), The Hague, Ministerie van Koloniën (Koloniën), 1850-1900, nummer toegang 2.10.02, inventarisnummer (inv. nr) 6480, Mailrapport (MR) 1890, 433+.

1890).²⁶ In the 1850s, the riddle of the cholera epidemic in London had been solved without looking for microbes.²⁷ In the 1880s, however, men like Louis Pasteur, Robert Koch, and others were developing the theory of infectious diseases and isolating the bacterial agents that caused these infections. But Pekelharing, however up-to-date, was mistaken.

Fortunately, Eijkman, who had been sent to Bangka in 1888,²⁸ remained in the Netherlands Indies and continued investigations by experimenting with animals. In 1896, he correctly pointed to highly-milled white rice as a cause of (or in his initial opinion a *contributor* to) beriberi, depending on how thoroughly it was milled, and how carefully it was cooked. Although Eijkman had put his finger on the crucial factor, he first thought that white rice either contained a toxin (like ergotamine) or somehow lacked the antidote to whatever external infectious or toxic agent was causing beriberi. By 1898, however, he recommended that prisoners be fed brown rice. Subsequent research had convinced him.

Following Eijkman, his successor G. Grijns ruled out decisively the idea of a toxin in rice and brought the research much farther, also suggesting the value of legumes in preventing beriberi. In 1897, A. Vorderman had demonstrated the value of brown rice when he undertook a statistical analysis of prisoners in Java, with data gathered from visiting all of Java's 101 prisons, consulting medical data from some 250,000 inmates. His results showed that beriberi was 300 times more common where prisoners consumed white rice than where brown rice was the rule. Such results would seem conclusive, but his study attracted little positive resonance.²⁹ Finally, D.J. Hulshoff Pol experimented with feeding mung beans to inmates of a mental hospital in Bogor. He published his results, which showed both the preventive and curative power of the beans, in 1902 and 1904.³⁰ Legumes would later prove to be an important part of anti-beriberi diets.

---

26 A recent article about Siam distinguishes between 'pre-Pasteurian' and 'Pasteurian' medicine, the former involving 'miasmas,' the latter, 'germs' and contagion (Davisakd Puaksom 2007).
27 In London, demographic epidemiology – isolating the source by seeing where victims lived and then, in this case, finding most victims used a single well for drinking water – did the trick (Johnson 2006). Only later did researchers identify the microbes, long after closing the well ended the epidemic.
28 NA, Koloniën, 1850-1900, 2.10.02, inv. nr 6469, MR 1888, 519+.
29 The Vordermann study is discussed in Carpenter 2002:46-51. Most of the rice was neither completely 'brown' nor completely 'white' and Vordermann distinguished, by analysing samples, between 'mostly brown', 'mixed', and 'mostly white'. Many prisoners were only incarcerated for a few days and had no time to get sick. In 'mostly white' prisons, however, up to one-fourth of long-term inmates developed the disease.
30 Carpenter 2000:52-63; Donath and Van Veen 1945:76-7. Hulshoff Pol himself also clung to the infection theory for a time.

Modern observers might easily challenge the many misguided theories of the disease, but beriberi researchers were treading new territory. The presence of very severe, even deadly forms of the disease made the traditional solutions of 'better food' or 'strong food' (as ancient Chinese texts proposed) insufficient. Differences in susceptibility to beriberi among individuals complicated the search. Certain factors like the need to perform hard physical labour or the presence of fevers, for example from malaria, raised the body's nutritional requirements and thus contributed to deficiencies. This also partly explains why outbreaks did not affect all persons in a group, and also why often the most physically 'healthy' young men seemed to be the earliest affected.

This brief account simplifies the arguments and counterarguments, as well as the achievements, greatly profiting from the wisdom of hindsight. Nonetheless, the failure to implement promptly what knowledge was available to change the fate of the seriously, often mortally, ill deserves criticism.

BERIBERI ON BANGKA

From the first reports about the disease in the 1850s to the radical improvement in the 1910s, decades of helplessness and futility nagged officials on this little island, but the disease itself plagued the workers. Most of the tin workers, the so-called coolies, were Chinese, usually immigrants. If the story of the scientists' search seems in retrospect like a success story – albeit with a fair amount of infighting – the situation on the ground was a decades-long tragedy.

Bangka was an ideal place to give support to either the 'miasma' or the 'infection' theory of beriberi. A visitor to the mines in the 1880s saw things this way:

> The mine buildings look alike everywhere [...] four buildings at right angles to one another, which form, in the middle, a wide inner court. The front building, made of planks [...] contains a row of benches and tables; here the labourers [...] take their meals [...]. The two side buildings serve partly as kitchen, partly as sleeping quarters for the unmarried workers [...]. These living quarters make a poor impression. In most cases, they are old, neglected buildings, scarcely ever repaired, and where cleanliness would be sought in vain. The sleeping areas in particular are quite dirty. (Posewitz 1886:99.)

The miners lived in neglected housing, surrounded by *vuil*. Their work required them to stand in water for long periods, the upper body exposed to the sun, hardly health-promoting.[31] New arrivals (*sinkeh*) frequently joined the mines – usually once a year – and they were more susceptible to the disease than local-born Chinese, called *peranakan*, which made officials suspect that *sinkeh* might be introducing the disease from China or Singapore. Other diseases, malaria, syphilis, influenza, and so on, produced symptoms that both contributed to the outbreak and confused the diagnosis (Langen 1927:76-85).

Not surprisingly, the first report in the *Geneeskundig Tijdschrift voor Nederlandsch-Indië* on beriberi, observed in 1853, was from Bangka. A medical officer reported the presence of some twenty patients in the hospital of Mentok, most of them Europeans or natives, not Chinese coolies. He ascribed the sickness to mysterious 'cosmic-telluric influences, unknown up to now'.[32] Previous accounts had blamed cold weather, rain, bad food, bad water, a polluted atmosphere – but none of this seemed to fit the cases in Bangka. Perhaps it was really a miasma.[33] In February of the following year, official reports noted several cases among workers in the district of Toboali, sixteen sickened and three died. General malnutrition may have been to blame, for by August, when the government supplied extra rice, salt and oil to meet the crisis, cases vanished.[34] Thus, the disease began as a sporadic occurrence, not confined to the mines, but within a few decades, it was a major problem on that island and concentrated among the coolie labourers.

ORGANIZATION OF TIN MINING AND COOLIE WELFARE

The appearance of the sickness on Bangka may have been partly the result of changes in the structure of the mining operations themselves. True, Bangka had been dependent on imported rice ever since outside labourers came from China to work the mines in

---

31 Kappen 1860:515. Interestingly, this author already insisted that 'well-fed individuals are not affected by beri-beri' (Kappen 1860:511), while others insisted that nutrition of all the men was adequate. Standing in water gave rise to arthritic complaints, but not beriberi.
32 Since 'cosmic' means extra-terrestrial, and 'telluric' means terrestrial, from earth, this would certainly cover a wide array of possible causes.
33 Lindman 1854:132, 150. Lindman noted that he also experienced an 'epidemic' of beriberi in Probolinggo in 1849 and thought the lack of information in the medical literature was because the disease had been relatively unknown before then. As noted, descriptions of the disease existed from the seventeenth century or earlier.
34 Arsip Nasional Republik Indonesia (ANRI), Jakarta, Bangka 3B/7, General Report 1854.

the mid-eighteenth century, if not earlier. The island's yearly rice production, mostly from dry-field *ladang*, barely sufficed for the native rural population, and occasionally even they had to import rice to make up a shortfall after a bad harvest.

When tin-mining by groups of Chinese labourers began in the eighteenth century, the ruler of Bangka, the Sultan of Palembang, exchanged rice and other necessities for the tin produced. When first the British, then the Dutch, took over the island directly in the early nineteenth century, the system of food advances and tin purchases remained largely the same, only the administrators changed.

Under the British and Dutch, initially, work gangs of miners organized in cooperative kongsis (benevolent associations of overseas Chinese) mined and smelted the tin. The workers chose a headman from among them, following their own bosses, while each had a share in the work and the profit. The kongsis purchased rice and cooking oil on credit from representatives of the government power. They were themselves responsible for other food, and most early kongsis had a garden and pigsty of their own, perhaps purchasing salted fish from local fishermen.

From about the middle of the nineteenth century, the situation of coolies appears to have deteriorated. The mine-working kongsis became mere sub-contractors as the government extended control over the operation of the mines. At the same time, the old system of shareholding was retreating. More and more, workers in the mines were not shareholders, and shareholders were not workers but tradesmen and townsmen who invested by purchasing arriving coolies and selling them as labourers to the mines.[35] Little incentive remained for the kongsi headmen to consider the interests of workers who were no longer his co-owners (Diest 1865:21). The kongsis still existed, but they were no longer autonomous, being under the ultimate direction of government-employed mine engineers, whose instructions, after 1880, they had to follow (*Jaarverslag Bankatinwinning* 1912:xlii).

The (Chinese) mine headmen did not need to fear the workers, for the government was on the side of the headmen in any dispute. Probably, care for the food of the workers receded proportionately. By 1880, non-shareholders – coolies – outnumbered shareholders in the mines and the relationship continued to change in favour of non-shareholders (*Koloniaal verslag* 1880:200). These, however, were facilitating conditions, not the cause of beriberi outbreaks.

Another change occurred in 1884, when the government stopped delivering rice and instead offered the mines a cash

---

35 This change was noted – and lamented – as early as 1853 (*Koloniaal verslag* 1853:168).

advance equivalent to the purchasing price of the rice (*Jaarverslag Bankatinwinning* 1912:xlv). The coolies themselves only saw cash at the end of the mine year, when the tin was smelted and sold. During the year they depended on the mine headman for food and other supplies. Only in 1902 did they begin to get small monthly cash advances to buy supplementary food or other items (*Jaarverslag Bankatinwinning* 1912:liii). For much of this time, the coolies received inadequate diets for men performing hard labour, and complaints mounted as sometimes the rice itself was hardly edible because of improper storage.

SYMPTOMS AND SUGGESTIONS

Statistics on morbidity and mortality of tin miners on Bangka attributed to beriberi - although incomplete and defective – illustrate the seriousness of the challenge in the mines. European overseers were not constantly present in the mines and many cases may have gone unnoticed. Diagnosis, as noted, was often difficult.

Table 1. Reported cases of beriberi and deaths, Bangka

Year[36]	Number of sick	Deaths attributed to beriberi	Total number of workers[37]
1854	16	37	184
1860	110 (Sungaiselan)	37	7,296
1863	some (Merawang)	–	7,402
1865	large number (Merawang, Pangkal Pinang, Sungaiselan)	–	7,288
1869	reported among military	–	7,506
1871	'many' (several districts)	–	7,391
1872	'less'	–	7,964
1881	'many cases' (Mentok)	–	7,588
1882	'a few', Chinese and native (Mentok)	–	7,525
1883	some (Marawang, Sungaiselan); 30 % of miners in Sungailiat	–	7,195

36 As an indication, the table gives available statistics on numbers of sick. Note that not all years are included.
37 Number of miners varied during the year. Later numbers represent an average.

1884	various cases (four districts)	—	7,195
1886	'sporadic'	—	n/a
1887	'a few'	—	n/a
1888	539	105	n/a
1889	previous victims recovered, but some new cases	—	n/a
1890	'many' (Mentok)	—	8,818
1893	'rare'	500[38]	8,860
1894	800 (circa)	342	12,345
1895	169 evacuated[39]	600 (circa)	n/a
1896	591 evacuated[40]	—	10,349
1897	709 evacuated[41]	123	11,310
1898	319 evacuated	107	13,083
1899	158 evacuated	—	n/a
1900	186 evacuated	—	n/a
1901	329 evacuated	—	n/a
1902	346 evacuated	almost 100	13,205
1903	525 evacuated[42]	210	14,229
1910	1260	—	19,823
1911	823	—	21,292
1912	800 (circa)	—	22,296
1913	639	12	21,436
1914	26	—	21,406
1915	0	—	19,050

[Numbers include shareholders, paid laborers, charcoal-burners for the smelters, and workers in privately-operating mines. Source: *Koloniaal verslag*, various years; *Jaarverslag Bankatinwinning* 1912, 1913, 1914; General Reports, Political Reports, various years]

38 This figure obviously contradicts the idea that beriberi was 'rare'.
39 To China. Others who were sicker were sent to Bogor for treatment and rest and then to China.
40 Probably to Bogor. Previously, the sick had been sent to Singapore or China and discharged there.
41 According to NA, Koloniën, Openbaar Verbaal, 1901-1952, 2.10.36.04, inv. nr 214, V 1-12-1903, no. 38, the number was 449. This is the source of the following numbers of evacuees.
42 These were evacuated between 1 January and 28 March. *Koloniaal verslag* 1903 says only 388 were evacuated.

3 *The epidemic that wasn't*

Until the 1890s, the number of workers was about 7,000-8,000 and rose slowly in that decade to 10,000-13,000. After 1903 (14,000), the number climbed to reach 20,000 during the 1910s. In bad years, the number of sick was 5-6 per cent of the force, but the number in an individual mine or mine district could be much higher.

Apart from collecting numbers, how did the colonial authorities treat the disease and what preventive measures did they take? The Chinese were expected to care for the sick in the mines, but they had little incentive to do so, especially if they thought the disease was contagious, as they apparently feared was the case with beriberi. Reportedly, they isolated the victims, perhaps in a small hut away from the mine, gave them a bit of rice and water, and left them to die. After a few days, if the provisions had disappeared, they added more, but did not, for fear of contagion, remain to see how patients were faring.[43] In any case, the number of coolies with beriberi soon overwhelmed any residual ability of the mine kongsis to care for them. In some mines, one-third or even more of the labourers were sick, so that the mine authorities finally had to take general measures.

Figure 3. Chinese tin miners on Banka, circa 1920 (KITLV 34679)

43 *Jaarverslag Bankatinwinning* 1912:liv; Kappen 1869:513. This may be a legend, for it was repeated from account to account.

Still officials mostly wrung their hands. The tiny Chinese hospital on the island cared for only 29 sick and infirm persons in 1852; it became totally inadequate for the dozens, even hundreds of sick.[44] As numbers increased, leaving the mines to look after the sick became problematic.

The first cases, relatively few, appeared to be seasonal. As late as 1883, the sickness was said to have retreated toward the end of the year, but in 1884 it returned in Mentok, Jebus, and Sungaiselan. Five cases also appeared in Pangkal Pinang between March and September.[45] Five cases also appeared in Pangkal Pinang between March and September. Mines with high proportions of *sinkehs*, that is, recent arrivals (who were never shareholders) also had the largest number of victims. On the other hand, in Jebus, where as a rule the miners were local-born Chinese *peranakan*, who often did not live on the mine premises, beriberi appeared to be comparatively rare.

BELITUNG

While in Bangka the question occupied engineers and bureaucrats, in Belitung, then called Billiton, the second tin island of the Netherlands Indies and a home of private enterprise, the disease was running a dramatic course. Because Belitung's production there was in the hands of a largely privately-owned company, official sources have less information about conditions there. Tin mining only opened officially in 1852. The disease seems to have picked up rapidly after that, especially in the 1880s, and it ended earlier than on Bangka. Seven hundred miners died of beriberi as early as February-March 1863.[46] A mine specialist working in the interior in the following year reported that 63 per cent of the Chinese in his mine died, of unknown diseases, within a single month, while health conditions for the Europeans in the early years were equally disastrous (Heerklotz 1868:87-8). In 1888-1889 there were 550 cases of beriberi. In the following year, among 8,334 workers, there were 588 cases, of whom 41 died. Some 441 victims of beriberi were 'evacuated' to China.[47] In 1908, of 12,500 workers, 700 were

---

44 *Koloniaal verslag* 1852/53:54; ironically, the government stopped supporting the hospital, which had been financed by a tax on remittances to China, in 1854. ANRI, Bangka 3B/7, General Report 1854.
45 ANRI, Bangka 5/9, 5/10, General Reports 1883, 1884.
46 As noted, the diagnosis may have been wrong in some cases (Swaving 1871:4).
47 *Koloniaal verslag* 1890:14, 232. 'Evacuation' here was a euphemism for getting them out of sight, probably many died because the ships´ food was as bad or worse than that in the mines and there was no help available when they reached Chinese ports. Official publications of the Billiton Company usually depict the miners as satisfied and healthy.

sick. This was the turning point, for in the following year, 1909, of 13,600 miners, only four were sick (Van der Heijden 1918:57-8).

As in Bangka, immigration and beriberi seem to have been positively correlated, and recruitment of new workers rose dramatically after the 1880s. Typically, several hundred arrived yearly, and if there were shortfalls of rice production in southern China, many arrivals already showed early symptoms of the disease when they landed.[48] Coolies certainly received inadequate food during their journey, by junk, to the South.[49] The presence of beriberi in the Straits Settlements, which was a recruiting area for miners, also drew blame. Was the disease being imported? (Jennissen 1911:503, 507).

Like Bangka, Belitung went through stages of explanations and treatments. In the 1870s (1874-1876 was an especially bad time), company employees fought beriberi with ventilation. In the 1880s, they still blamed miasmas and contagion and burned down old buildings, abandoning others. Because cleanliness seemed essential, chlorine and caustic soda disinfected remaining quarters. More positively, the authorities encouraged maintaining gardens and raising animals to improve the diet. By 1888, the mining company began to send less serious cases to Bogor in hopes of returning those recovered to the mines, but this answer proved to be too expensive and they soon dropped the policy.[50]

After dwindling between 1893 and 1903, the disease suddenly peaked in 1903-1904. Again, nearly 300 were evacuated, most of them *sinkeh*. Once more, bad conditions in southern China seemed to be invading Belitung. New coolies underwent health inspections in Hong Kong and Singapore so that the sick could no longer be hired or enter the island. Java rice, which had been blamed for the outbreak in 1903, was now supplanted by imported (mostly white) rice from Siam or Rangoon, but this was not the answer. Finally, in 1908, the officials decided to take the work of Eijkman and others seriously. All imports of white rice stopped. The mining company provided the mines with brown rice (*beras merah*) only. After that year, all cases of beriberi came from persons living outside the mines who still subsisted on 'wholly' whitened rice.[51]

---

48 The time spent aboard ship may have added to the problem.
49 Heerklotz (1868:49) visited a junk in the bay of Tanjung Pandan, Belitung, in 1864. He claims the coolies received rice and Spanish pepper twice daily but no other food, and many died en route. About half of those who made it could expect to die in the mines.
50 Jennissen 1911:504. Gelpke (1890:146), comments on the irony that the military stationed in Bogor often suffered from beriberi 'epidemics', while chain-gang prisoners (and later tin miners) were evacuated to the same place to recover from beriberi.
51 Jennissen 1911:507. Jennissen (1911:510-1) interestingly points out that in the Straits Settlements, Indians were largely free of beriberi, for they traditionally ate *beras masak*, parboiled rice, which was unacceptable to other Asians because of its taste. The success story of brown rice is also told in *Gedenkboek* 1927:166.

BANGKA (FINALLY) COMES AROUND

Bangka underwent similar stages, but moving the authorities to act took years longer. In the end, the health situation began to affect the colonial pocketbook, where it hurt most. Tin production on Bangka had peaked in 1856 at over 100,000 piculs (a picul is about 62 kilograms) and then fell to about 80,000 for the next ten years, falling further to 69,000 in 1869. In the 1870s, it hovered around 65-70,000 piculs (*Jaarverslag Bankatinwinning* 1912:xxxviii, xli; *Koloniaal verslag* 1870:155). Other factors also depressed production, of course, but an official report in 1871 does ascribe the decline in tin production to beriberi in several districts, as well as to bad weather. In 1884, a combination of drought and beriberi seriously hindered production, some mines even closed down.[52] Bad results recurred in the following year.[53] With international demand for tin and local demand for labourers growing, such losses were unacceptable. The late-nineteenth-century transition to mechanization in the form of steam-driven water pumps, to keep the diggings free of flooding more efficiently, and of various other machines, actually increased the need for workers. In addition, thanks to better methods of exploration, more workers were needed to open new, promising sites or to exert the extra effort needed to exploit nearly played-out ones.[54] In the late 1890s and into the first years of the twentieth century, beriberi was a major contributor to the annual death rates of 2-3 per cent among the miners. The export of the sick to China, Singapore, and later Bogor, where many nevertheless died of the disease, probably made the death rate appear lower than it really was.[55]

'Evacuation' of sick miners continued partly because of the persistent belief – contradicting virtually all of the medical literature – that beriberi was somehow contagious. In late 1895, Bangka's highest official, its Resident, summed up the measures taken to combat or treat beriberi: in the district towns were houses for the sick, except in Merawang (which is close to Pangkal Pinang). Many of the sick, however, were being shipped out with six (Straits) dollars in pocket money to Singapore, where they could look for work and were – according to the rationale – better off than in China. (How they could seek work when they were weak, paralyzed, or con-

---

52 ANRI, Bangka 1/17 Political Report 1871; NA, Koloniën, 1850-1900, 2.10.02, inv. nr 6354, MR 1872 and inv. nr 6442, MR 1884.
53 NA, Koloniën, 1850-1900, 2.10.02, inv. nr 6450, MR 1885, 675.
54 On mechanization and labour demand, see Heidhues 1992:60-1.
55 Of those sent to Bogor, 5-6 per cent were said to have died.

fused is not clear.) New regulations said they should be returned to China, but many did not wish to go there, at least not at once, because they hoped to find work in the Straits. There could be no question of keeping them in Bangka, where they would be a burden and besides they were – once more – 'contagious'.[56]

Meanwhile, the beriberi sanatorium in Bogor was now open to Bangka coolies. By 1894, as previously in Belitung, the sick who were well enough to travel were sent to Bogor to recover and then back to China. In 1903, however, trouble arose in Batavia, when coolies on their way to Bogor passed through busy areas of the city. The sight of the men, shuffling or being carried on ox-carts in various stages of helplessness from the harbour to the train station, caused a near-riot and a new solution was necessary.[57]

China was not a satisfactory destination either. The men hoped to return to China eventually, but not without cash. Furthermore, the East Sumatran tobacco plantations, which also hired coolies in China, feared that the image of the sick returnees dumped at the harbours was giving the Netherlands East Indies a bad name, impeding their own recruitment there.[58] In view of the problems connected with evacuation, including resistance from the coolies, in 1911, the authorities determined to transfer all care for the sick to Mentok. Once recovered, the men could return to the mines or to China.[59]

Was the problem homemade or coming from abroad, sneaking in with the newly arriving *sinkehs*? In 1898, mine officials on Bangka stopped all recruitment in Singapore, partly from fear that they might 'import' beriberi from there.[60] On the other hand, a few years later, Bangka's bad reputation led the Hong Kong authorities to close down coolie recruitment there, reopening it only in 1907 (*Jaarverslag Bankatinwinning* 1912:li), and the island continued to enjoy a terrible reputation among potential recruits in China.

Since evacuation was no answer, preventive measures were necessary, but as long as the cause of the disease was a mystery, what measures were appropriate? The results of the Pekelharing mission soon reached the island. In 1884, a governing official took

56   Letter of Resident of Bangka, 25-11-1895, in: NA, Koloniën, 1850-1900, 2.10.02, inv. nr 6516, MR 1896, 8.
57   NA, Koloniën, Openbaar Verbaal, 1901-1952, 2.10.36.04, inv. nr 214, V 1-12-1903, no. 38.
58   NA, Koloniën, 1850-1900, 2.10.02, inv. nr 6510, MR 1894, 1157+ and inv. nr 6512, MR 1895, 240+.
59   *Jaarverslag Bangkatinwinning* 1912: liv-lviii, 19. Probably this was also the cheapest solution.
60   Letter from Mentok, 30-3-1898, in: NA, Koloniën, 1850-1900, 2.10.02, inv. nr 6520, MR 1898, 3+; see also inv. nr 6518, MR 1896, 19+, 21+. As noted, Bangka continued to 'export' beriberi victims to Singapore, discharging them with a bit of pocket money.

every opportunity to urge the mining kongsis to follow the rules he pointed to for preventing beriberi (however futile they might have been), and this official even mobilized the Lieutenant of the Chinese, not to mention two Catholic missionaries, to propagandize disinfection when they visited the mines.[61] In any case, Pekelharing's idea of disinfecting all quarters and all clothing might have worked for the military, ships, or prisons, but not in the kongsis of Bangka, especially where buildings had dirt floors and coolies were lucky to have a single set of clothes.

In that same year, the leading mine engineer and a military pharmacist examined the tin ore and found 'microscopic worms (*wurmpjes*)'. Since the pharmacist insisted that these little worms were also found in the intestines of beriberi victims who were autopsied, the sick must be infecting themselves with parasites, transferring them to the water they used to wash ore, where they multiplied. Tell the miners, he proclaimed, to boil their drinking water.[62] How could the miners take him seriously, when they themselves probably never drank water without boiling it. As early as 1852, it was well-known that, in the absence of tea, they drank an infusion made from leaves of *jambu biji* (guava).[63] The admonition to boil water merely showed how ignorant the pharmacist and engineer were of the miners' life.

In 1888, care for the sick improved. Over six hundred patients (both miners and prisoners) were cared for in a provisional sick bay in Pangkal Pinang, most of them from Blinyu, where in one mine as many as 60 per cent of the labourers had been sick, presumably in spite of the wave of decontaminations. The authorities also recruited native medical personnel as caretakers. The government also built sick houses (*ziekenloodsen*) close to the mine sites but isolated from the other quarters (to prevent contagion). There the sick were to get 'improved food.' Prisons, another centre of the disease, were disinfected – as recommended.[64]

Still, how could it be that no one was looking at the diet of the coolies? The statistics show that beriberi continued and even grew after all the disinfecting activities. Furthermore, if the sick were getting better food, why wasn't better food available for all?

As Eijkman and his colleagues realized, rice needed examination. What kind of rice did the coolies eat and where did it come from?

---

61 NA, Koloniën, 1850-1900, 2.10.02, inv. nr 6441, MR 1884, 62.
62 NA, Koloniën, 1850-1900, 2.10.02, inv. nr 6443, MR 1884, 215. The idea of a parasite also appears in Erni (1884). Nasty parasites abounded, but they were not causing beriberi.
63 For example, ANRI, Bangka 3B/5, General Report 1852.
64 ANRI, Bangka 5/14, General Report 1888. 'Improved food' might have helped but many were too sick to eat.

3 The epidemic that wasn't

Figure 4. Tin mining in Blinyu, Bangka, circa 1920 (KITLV 34570)

RICE IMPORTS

Industrially milled rice dominated the imports to the islands. Some data is available for the 1880s, when this rice came primarily from Java. In 1883, a shortfall in the local harvest necessitated imports of 765,000 kg from Singapore – in this year there is no record of imports from Java.[65] In 1884 400,000 kg milled rice was imported from Singapore and a small amount from Surabaya.[66] In the following year new rules on provisioning mines put the job in the hands of local (mostly) Chinese traders, who imported from Batavia, Singapore and Palembang, apparently diversifying the suppliers. The other important part of the coolie diet, salt fish, was caught,

---

65 In addition to importing rice for non-miners in times of shortages, sailing ships to Riau-Lingga or even Singapore sometimes exported small amounts from local growers.
66 ANRI, Bangka 5/9, 5/10, General Reports 1883, 1884.

bought, and salted on the island.[67] In 1885, rice arrived from Java, Palembang, Singapore and Saigon, a new supplier, but apparently only about 50,000 kg from the latter.[68] In 1887, 100,000 kg white rice arrived from Singapore, 370,000 from Batavia, 700,000 from Indramayu, 240,000 from Ceribon, 150,000 from Tanjungpandan, and 500,000 from Palembang (these statistics refer to the ports, not the producing areas, so the rice may have originated elsewhere). Smaller amounts came from Banten and Joana, while almost 140,000 kg brown rice came from Palembang and a small amount from Ceribon.[69] Why the amounts jumped so high after the previous year is unknown. Perhaps it had to do with shortfalls or with the opening of more storage capacity. Import figures for 1888 list over 3 million kg from Banten (a decimal error?), 300,000 from Batavia, 100,000 from Indramayu, 450,000 from Palembang, and smaller amounts from Ceribon, Joana, Tegal and Panarukan. Brown rice arrived from Palembang (140,000) and a smaller amount from Batavia. Of more than 2 million kilograms of white rice imported in 1889, nearly half came from Indramayu and one third from Banten. In addition, 130,000 kg of brown rice came from Palembang and Banten. In 1890, Banten, Palembang and Indramayu, and also Ceribon were the major suppliers, and the ratio of white to brown rice was 10:1 or even higher for these years. However, in 1890 an additional 400,000 kg entered from Singapore – where it originated is unknown.[70] By the beginning of the twentieth century, much – if not all – rice for the island was coming from Saigon's modern rice mills.[71]

Not just rice but food in general had become a problem. Repeated complaints about the quality of the coolies' diet reached the authorities, who were inclined to believe them.[72] Batavia sent more examiners to assess the situation on Bangka. Following a rebellion of miners, accounts of bad treatment, and the increase of

---

67 ANRI, Bangka 5/11, General Report 1885. From 1885 to 1890, rice shipments from Saigon to the Netherlands Indies were interrupted, to be resumed in 1891, probably as a result of an official visit to Saigon. See Salmon 1994.
68 This figure may have a decimal error.
69 ANRI, Bangka 5/13, General Report 1887.
70 ANRI, Bangka 5/15 and 5/21, General Reports 1889 and 1890.
71 NA, Koloniën, Openbaar Verbaal, 1901-1952, 2.10.36.04, inv. nr 214, V 1-12-1903, no. 38. Interestingly, in 1897, the contract for delivering 120,000 piculs (almost 7,500,000 kg) of rice to the island was awarded to Khouw Kim An, later *Majoor* of the Chinese in Batavia (Letter of 1-6-1897, in: NA, Koloniën, 2.10.02, inv. nr 6519, MR 1897, 338+). According to Salmon 1994, the first steam-driven rice mill in Saigon was founded in 1869, and by the 1890s there were five or six of these modern mills. Straits Chinese dominated the export of rice from Saigon, except that to China, which was mostly in Cantonese hands.
72 NA, Koloniën, Openbaar Verbaal, 1901-1952, 2.10.36.04, inv. nr 214, V 1-12-1903, no. 36.

beriberi, as well as complaints about treatment of the sick sent to Bogor, B. Hoetink, an Officer for Chinese Affairs, visited the island in 1902 and produced a scathing criticism of the situation of workers for which he blamed the government as the responsible party.[73]

Bad food was a part of Bangka's bad reputation. De Jongh, a mine engineer sent to investigate in 1903, nevertheless claimed that all kongsis still maintained gardens and pigsties, feeding the animals with leftover rice or the remains of arak-brewing. For the coolies, some meat must have been available (although pork was a holiday food), and each day, fresh or salt vegetables complemented the rice and salt fish.[74] De Jongh thought the food was adequate, but the small amounts of side-dishes in reality did not compensate for the lack of nutrients in the rice.

More years passed before Bangka's authorities implemented a first effective countermeasure. Grijns had shown that adding legumes to the diet could combat beriberi, and also D.J. Hulshoff Pol had underlined his results with a controlled experiment (above). At first it would appear that the tin mines fairly promptly implemented these insights (published in 1902 and 1904) in their prescribed diets. In November 1907, a visiting missionary noted that the miners in Blinyu received, in addition to rice, various vegetables, dried fish, and a portion of mung beans, 'the latter as a preventive against beriberi' (Kortenhorst 1908:228). The statistics show that this must have been either not adequate or not universal, for the beriberi problem continued. Numbers of sick continued to climb, defying the work of Eijkman, Grijns, Vorderman, and Hulshoff Pol. What the scientists had learned, the administrators continued to ignore, for whatever reason.

As of 1914, Bangka's authorities finally moved, six years after this step was taken on Belitung.[75] Only brown rice, *zilvervliesrijst*, was to be provisioned to the mines.[76] Brown ('red') rice, imported from Java or Rangoon, would be the only form of rice distributed. The sick would continue to be treated in Mentok, which also improved the statistics. The general death rate among the miners dropped from over two per cent in 1906-1908 to one per cent in 1912-1913. The occasional later case of beriberi was of little significance.

73 NA, Koloniën, Openbaar Verbaal, 1901-1952, 2.10.36.04, inv. nr 214, V 1-12-1903, no. 38.
74 NA, Koloniën, Openbaar Verbaal, 1901-1952, 2.10.36.04, inv. nr 214, V 1-12-1903, no. 36.
75 In 1913, shortly before this move, the mining administration was separated from the general government administration and became a wholly government-owned company, Banka Tinwinning.
76 *Jaarverslag Bankatinwinning* 1913:19. Vorderman's statistical results were, as will be recalled, published in 1897. See also the directive *Voorwaarden* 1914.

Although beriberi retreated and working conditions improved incrementally, other diseases would rise to take their place. When the death rate again climbed above two per cent in 1914, the major contributor was malaria, which caused more losses – above all lost work days – than beriberi ever had (*Jaarverslag Bankatinwinning* 1913:19-23). At least that could be fought, experts and administrators agreed, with mosquito nets.

CONCLUSION: FALSE STEPS, FALSE CONCEPTIONS

The history of knowledge conventionally focuses on breakthrough ideas and conceptual leaps. But the blind spots on the map, the dark continents of error and prejudice, carry their own mystery as well. How could so many intelligent people be so grievously wrong for such an extended period of time? How could they ignore so much overwhelming evidence that contradicted their most basic theories? These questions, too, deserve their own discipline – the sociology of error.[77]

One lesson from this account could be the need to move away from accepted ways of thinking. The medical breakthrough in ascribing diseases to 'germs' or 'filth' prevented many people from looking at the relationship of beriberi with diet, even though the role of food in treating or preventing beriberi had been part of common wisdom from very old times. Of course, changing and improving the coolies' diet would also have cost money (and probably effort). For a long time, this was not an alternative.

Another insight is the extent to which administrators and researchers were also often preoccupied with one disease at a time. Diseases have their day, it seems. When smallpox receded in the 1850s, beriberi gained prominence in the minds of officials and contributors to the *Geneeskundig Tijdschrift voor Nederlandsch-Indië*. Once the beriberi problem appeared solved, malaria became a focus.

Surely, however, another factor leading these men astray was the ease of ascribing something to poor hygiene – enabling, in a certain way, a 'blame the victim' diagnosis of the problem. 'Chinese are by nature dirty', officials noted,[78] as if this excused the situation.

---

77 Johnson 2006:15. Johnson was referring to the dismal failures in London's 1854 cholera epidemic.
78 NA, Koloniën, Openbaar Verbaal, 1901-1952, 2.10.36.04, inv. nr 214, V 1-12-1903, no. 38. Even Hoetink underlined that conditions in Southern China were in any case not better than on Bangka.

Susan Sontag (1990) once warned about the metaphorization of diseases, first tuberculosis, then cancer, finally AIDS. In the eyes of Western administrators and scientists, beriberi had become a metaphor for squalor. Coolies were assumed to be the 'dregs' of southern Chinese society. Indeed the miners lived in terrible poverty. Quarters were crowded and airless, the area around the barracks often filthy. Coolies were miserably clad, if they had not brought a blanket from China, the men covered themselves with used rice sacks when sleeping. A ready excuse appeared with the new arrivals from China, where, as everyone claimed to know, conditions were very poor, probably far worse (so the common perception) than in the mines.

A twentieth-century truism points out that if humans are treated in inhuman fashion, they become something less than human in the eye of the beholder. The concentration on filth and infection, or on importing the disease from China, in the end, offered an easier explanation for administrators than would a complete revision of the miners' diet – for which they themselves, who were responsible for supplying the rice, were to blame. Perhaps this 'epidemic' was also a metaphor for their callousness.

REFERENCES

Unpublished sources

Arsip Nasional Republik Indonesia, Jakarta
Bangka, General Reports

Nationaal Archief, The Hague
Ministerie van Koloniën, 1850-1900, nummer toegang 2.10.02
Ministerie van Koloniën, Openbaar Verbaal, 1901-1952, nummer toegang 2.10.36.04

Published sources

Abé, Yoshio
2007 Le 'décorticage' du riz; Typologie, réparition géographique et histoire des instruments à monder le riz. Paris: Éditions de la Maison des Sciences de l'Homme.
Berg, C.L. van den
1886 'Een bezoek aan het seminarie voor inlandsche zendelingen te Depok, naar aanleiding van daar voorgekomen gevallen van beri beri', *Geneeskundig Tijdschrift voor Nederlandsch-Indië* 25:57-66.

Beri-beri
1854 'Beri-beri', *Geneeskundig Tijdschrift voor Nederlandsch-Indië* 3:514-9.

Boomgaard, Peter
2006 'The making and unmaking of tropical science; Dutch research on Indonesia, 1600-2000', *Bijdragen tot de Taal-, Land- en Volkenkunde* 162:191-217.

Carpenter, Kenneth J.
2000 *Beriberi, white rice, and vitamin B; A disease, a cause, and a cure.* Berkeley, CA: University of California Press.

Corbin, Alain
1982 *Le miasme et la jonquille; L'odorat et l'imaginaire social, XVIIIe-XIXe siècles.* Paris: Aubier Montaigne.

Davisakd Puaksom
2007 'Of germs, public hygiene, and the healthy body; The making of the medicalizing state in Thailand', *The Journal of Asian Studies* 66-2:311-44.

Dieren, E. van
1887 *Critiek op de beweringen van Prof. Pekelharing omtrent de beri-beri.* Arnhem: Van der Zande.
1897 *Beri-beri: eene rijstvergiftiging; Critisch-historische bijdrage tot de kennis der meelvergiften.* Amsterdam: Scheltema and Holkema.

Diest, P. van
1865 *Bangka, beschreven in reistogten.* Amsterdam: Stemler.

Donath, W.F. and A.G. van Veen
1945 'A short history of beri-beri investigations in the Netherlands Indies', in: Pieter Honig and Frans Verdoorn (eds), *Science and scientists in the Netherlands Indies*, pp. 75-8. New York: Board for the Netherlands Indies, Surinam and Curaçao.

Erni, H.
1884 'Eene beri-beri epidemie op Sumatra', *Geneeskundig Tijdschrift voor Nederlandsch-Indië* 23:95-109.

Gedenkboek
1972 *Gedenkboek Billiton, 1852-1927.* Vol 2. 's-Gravenhage: Nijhoff.

Gelpke, C.O.
1890 'Ein Beitrag zur Bestreitung der Beriberi', *Geneeskundig Tijdschrift voor Nederlandsch-Indië* 30:144-53.

Grist, D.H.
1955 *Rice.* London: Longmans, Green.

Heerklotz, Dedo
1868	Reise und Aufenthalt in Niederländisch-Ostindien. Oederan: Schlesinger.

Heidhues, Mary F. Somers
1992	Bangka tin and Mentok pepper; Chinese settlement on an Indonesian island. Singapore: Institute of Southeast Asian Studies. [Social Issues in Southeast Asia.]

Herport, Albrecht
1930	Reise nach Java, Formosa, Vorder-Indien und Ceylon, 1659-1668. Haag: Nijhoff. [Reisebeschreibungen von Deutschen Beamten und Kriegsleuten im Dienst der Niederländischen West- und Ost-Indischen Kompagnien 1602-1797]

Heijden, H.N. van der
1918	'De hygiënische verzorging der arbeiders-immigranten in de Buitenbezittingen', Koloniale Studiën 2:45-84.

Jansen, B.C.P.
1959	Het levenswerk van Christiaan Eijkman, 1858-1930. Haarlem: Bohn. [Published in honour of the centenary of the Association for the Nederlandsch Tijdschrift voor Geneeskunde, 1857-1957.]

Johnson, Steven
2006	The ghost map; The story of London's most terrifying epidemic, and how it changed science, cities, and the modern world. New York: Riverhead Books.

Kappen, E.F.J. van
1860	'Beri-beri onder de mijnwerkers in het distrikt Soengeislan (Eiland Banka)', Geneeskundig Tijdschrift voor Nederlandsch-Indië 10:510-7.

Kortenhorst, A.S.J.
1908	'Vormreis van Monseigneur E.S. Luypen naar het eiland Banka', Berichten uit Nederlandsch-Oost-Indië voor de leden van den Sint Claverbond 20:211-29.
1909	'Vormreis van Monseigneur E.S. Luypen naar het eiland Banka', Berichten uit Nederlandsch-Oost-Indië voor de leden van den Sint Claverbond 21:3-30.

Langen, C.D. de
1927	Beri-beri; Een klinische studie van voeding en ziekte in Nederlandsch-Indië. 's-Gravenhage: Naeff.

Latham, A.J.H.
1998	Rice; The primary commodity. London: Routledge.

Leent, F.J. van
1880   'Mededeelingen over beri-beri', *Geneeskundig Tijdschrift voor Nederlandsch-Indië* 20:272-310.

Lindman, L.
1854   'Beschrijving der op het eiland Banka waargenomene beri-beri gedurende het jaar 1853', *Tijdschrift der Vereeniging tot Bevordering der Geneeskundige Wetenschappen in Nederlandsch-Indië* 3:131-59.

Pekelharing, C.A.
1888   'Mededeelingen omtrent de stand van het onderzoek naar de oorzaak en het wezen der beri-beri', *Geneeskundig Tijdschrift voor Nederlandsch-Indië* 27:121-50.

Posewitz, T.
1886   'Die Zinninseln im Indischen Ozean: Part II: Das Zinnvorkommen und die Zinngewinnung in Bangka', *Földtani Intézet* (Jahrbuch der Ungarischen Geologischen Reichsanstalt) 8:57.

Salmon, Claudine
1994   'De Batavia à Saïgon; Notes de voyage d'un marchand chinois (1890)', *Archipel* 47:155-191.

Scheube, B.
1894   *Die Beriberi-Krankheit; Eine geographisch-medicinische Studie.* Jena: Fischer.
1896   *Die Krankheiten der warmen Länder; Ein Handbuch für Ärzte.* Jena: Fischer.

Sontag, Susan
1990   *Illness as metaphor and AIDS and its metaphors.* New York: Anchor Doubleday.

Swaving, C.
1871   'Een woord over een kongsiehuis en de sterfte onder de mijnwerkers op Billiton', *Geneeskundig Tijdschrift voor Nederlandsch-Indië* 14:1-16.

Terwiel, B.J.
1983   *A history of modern Thailand, 1767-1942.* St Lucia/London/New York: University of Queensland Press.

Vierde schipvaart
1980   *De vierde schipvaart der Nederlanders naar Oost-Indië onder Jacob Wilkens en Jacob van Neck, (1599-1604).* Uitgegeven door H.A. van Foreest en A. de Booy. Vol. 1. 's-Gravenhage: Nijhoff. [Werken uitgegeven door de Linschoten-Vereeniging 82.]

Voorwaarden
1914   *Voorwaarden van aanbesteding voor de levering van rijst in zilver-*
               vlies ten behoeve van de mijnwerkers op het eiland Banka. Batavia:
               Landsdrukkerij.
Wijckerheld Bisdom, R.F.J.
1911   'Overzicht van het totaal aantal overledenen en van de met
               malariaziekten en beri-beri behandelde, afgekeurde en
               aan die ziekten overleden militairen van het Nederlandsch-
               Indische Leger gedurende de jaren 1885 tot en met 1909',
               in: *Feestbundel ter herinnering uitgegeven bij het verschijnen van*
               het 50ste deel Geneeskundig Tijdschrift voor Nederlandsch-Indie,
               pp. 395-403. Batavia: Javasche Boekhandel en Drukkerij.
               [Uitgegeven door de Vereeniging tot Bevordering der
               Geneeskundige Wetenschappen in Nederlandsch-Indie.]'

4

Hygiene, housing and health in colonial Sulawesi

David Henley

This chapter uses European sources to sketch a picture of health and hygiene conditions in precolonial and colonial Sulawesi. Colonial observers gave exaggerated attention to Indonesian shortcomings in the field of hygiene, particularly personal hygiene, and their public health implications. Nevertheless it does appear that standards of both personal and public hygiene have improved significantly over the past century, and that this has been one cause of the concurrent improvement in health conditions. The processes involved have included changes in medical awareness, social norms, house design, and settlement location.

Northern Sulawesi – the colonial Residency of Manado, comprising the modern provinces of North Sulawesi, Central Sulawesi, and Gorontalo – offers a good scope for research on questions of population and health in precolonial Indonesia due to a history of late but intensive colonization and a valuable combination of administrative and anthropological records (Henley 1997a, 1997b, 2001, 2002, 2005a, 2005b, 2006). Minahasa, in North Sulawesi, was a stateless, tribal area at the beginning of the nineteenth century, but following pacification in 1809 it became the scene of compulsory cash crop cultivation and almost complete conversion to Christianity. Central Sulawesi was not occupied by the Dutch until after 1900, but missionary-anthropologists described its peoples in rare detail during the years immediately preceding and following its conquest. This chapter uses European sources from the nineteenth and early twentieth centuries to sketch a picture of hygiene conditions in the region on the eve of Dutch rule. An attempt is then made to assess how those conditions changed, and with what consequences for public health, in the colonial and postcolonial periods.

Predictably, no European of the colonial period was impressed by standards of either personal or public cleanliness in northern Sulawesi. Many of the recorded comments on the subject clearly reflect the prejudices of the time, attributing infectious diseases largely to the unhygienic habits of the 'natives' or 'Alfurs' themselves. Nicolaas Graafland (1867-69, I:256), a famous nineteenth-century missionary of Minahasa, expressed the general view when he declared simply that 'the pagan Alfur is dirty to a grave degree'. On the nearby Sangir islands, his colleague Steller (1866:29, 31) accused local people of 'carelessness regarding their persons, clothing, and food' and noted that the open space beneath their stilt houses served as 'a living area for goats, pigs and chickens, which, rooting in the mud for food, exacerbate the lack of cleanliness and make life in the house above neither healthier, nor more pleasant for the olfactory organs'. As late as the 1920s, a Dutch medical doctor wrote of Minahasans that 'as far as cleanliness and concepts of hygiene are concerned, even the most cultivated among them stand miles below what in Western culture was already regarded a century ago as the minimum civilized level' (Bouvy 1924:382).

Today such self-important rhetoric makes an almost satirical impression, evoking amusement rather than shock. Among Indonesianists, moreover, the view has taken hold in recent years that health and hygiene conditions were in fact substantially better in precolonial Indonesia than in early modern Europe, notably because Indonesians customarily made more use of water for washing and bathing (Reid 1987:37-8; 1988-93, I:50). Under these circumstances it is tempting to dismiss colonial complaints about the unhygienic character of traditional Indonesian lifestyles as nothing more than prejudice and propaganda. A look at the descriptive details of the accounts in question, however, suggests that their strident quality was often more a matter of naive observation than of blinkered misrepresentation, and that the situations described did differ substantially from those prevailing in the same locations at later dates.

MORBIDITY AND MORTALITY

Statistical and qualitative sources alike paint a grim picture of health conditions in Sulawesi prior to the twentieth century (Henley 2005a:249-87). Roughly a quarter of all children born died in infancy – mostly of respiratory diseases, tetanus, dysentery, and malaria – and at least a third before reaching adulthood. Most of those who did reach adulthood died in their 50s. Once in every generation a smallpox epidemic killed about one person in every six, and sometimes more. In those places where malaria was endemic, it pushed the child mortality rate up beyond 40 per cent; where it occurred in the form of occasional epidemics, it weakened the adult population and increased the frequency of miscarriages and stillbirths. Gastroenteritic diseases, tuberculosis, goitre, and beri-beri were all common, while almost everyone was affected at some point in life by yaws. In some places most of the population was also permanently affected by chronic skin disease. Conditions were particularly bad in malarial localities with little good drinking water, such as the Banggai islands off the east coast of Central Sulawesi.

> On Banggai, which consists almost entirely of swamp, malevolent fevers reign almost the whole year round, killing many of the inhabitants and giving others a sickly and weak appearance. The inhabitants of Peling, where there is an almost complete lack of good drinking water – what there is is brackish and turbid – are much afflicted by stomach illness and plagued by skin diseases, which give both men and women a repulsive appearance. (Bosscher and Matthijssen 1854:96-7.)

Cholera, transmitted via water polluted with the faeces of sufferers, afflicted the whole region in seven great epidemics between 1828 and 1915, killing at least 10,000 people each time. Dysentery was another major epidemic threat. Intestinal parasite infections were also extremely common: in Tondano (Minahasa) in 1931, 63 per cent of the population was found to be infected with hookworm and 27 per cent with roundworm; in Sangir the proportions were 33 per cent and 54 per cent respectively.[1]

The reported prevalence of skin disease is particularly significant in relation to the hygiene question. On Banggai even kings were affected (Figure 1), while a slave without skin disease commanded double the price of a *kalanding*, as those with scaly skin were called (Kruyt 1932:251). The populations of other parts of the region, too, all suffered to a greater or lesser degree.

> Skin diseases like scabies, *Dajakse schurft* [*Tinea imbricata*] and other fungal skin infections are part of the normal equipment of the population here. Fairly harmless in themselves, they contribute via the effects of constant scratching to the danger of secondary infection with all its consequences (sores, abscesses, blood poisoning). Yaws, too, finds ready access to the body through the damaged skin.[2]

---

[1] A.Ph. van Aken (resident), 'Memorie van Overgave van de residentie Menado', 1932, pp. 218, in: Nationaal Archief (NA), The Hague, Ministerie van Koloniën (Koloniën), Memories van Overgave, 1852-1962, nummer toegang 2.10.39, inventarisnummer (inv. nr) 306.
[2] K.F. Avink (gezaghebber), 'Aanvullende Bestuursmemorie onderafdeling Kolondale', 1935, pp. 7, in: NA, Koloniën, Memories van Overgave, 2.10.39, inv. nr 1214.

| *David Henley*

Figure 1. Raja (king) of Banggai, blind and with skin disease, as sketched by a Dutch visitor in 1678. (Nationaal Archief (The Hague), VOC 1345, f. 193).

In the Poso area of Central Sulawesi in the 1890s, according to missionaries Adriani and Kruyt (1950-51, II:198), 'perhaps half of the population was afflicted by a scaly skin disease'. In the Palu Valley, 'practically everybody' was said to suffer from scabies (Tillema 1926:222). Most notorious in this respect, however, were the Sangir and Talaud islands, where the spectacular and disfiguring fungal infection *Tinea imbricata* (Figures 2 and 3) was particularly common. 'I truly believe', wrote one Dutch visitor in 1825, 'that there is no other place where this disease is found so frequently as on the Sangir islands' (Van Delden 1844:376). A century later some even claimed that 'almost every native' of Sangir and Talaud was afflicted by *Tinea imbricata* (Käyser 1918:41) and while this may have been somewhat exaggerated a government doctor confirmed in 1914 that on Talaud 'more than 90 per cent of the population' was 'suffering from various kinds of skin disease' (Roep 1917:426). The connection proposed by many colonial observers between poor hygiene and skin disease is confirmed by the fact that the areas where skin problems were particularly prevalent, including Talaud, parts of Sangir, and Banggai, were also areas where, for geological

4 Hygiene, housing and health in colonial Sulawesi

Figure 2. Tinea imbricata (forearm). (Käyser 1911:202).

and topographic rather than climatic reasons, there was a seasonal shortage of fresh water.

Today, by contrast, visible skin disease is the exception rather than the rule even in those areas where it was formerly almost universal, while cholera and dysentery, although not unknown, have likewise become incidental dangers rather than unavoidable facts of life and death. Mortality statistics confirm that great changes for the better occurred during and after the colonial period. In Minahasa, where death rate figures are available for the years 1849-1870, a combined epidemic of dysentery, cholera, measles and malaria in 1853-1854, when about 10 per cent of the population died, was the last great mortality crisis of its kind; later epidemics, although numerous, were much less lethal. While epidemic crises were damped, background mortality in relatively normal years also showed a clear downward trend (Figure 4). When the crisis year of 1854 is excluded from the calculation, the average recorded crude death rate over the period 1860-70, at 25.9 per thousand, is still 2.3 per thousand lower than in the years 1849-59. A little over a century later in 1971, the death rate in North Sulawesi had fallen to under 15 per thousand, and the infant mortality rate to under 15 per cent (Jones 1977:116). Not, of course, that improved hygiene was the only factor here; also crucial were medical and nutritional improvements, to which I will return briefly in my conclusion.

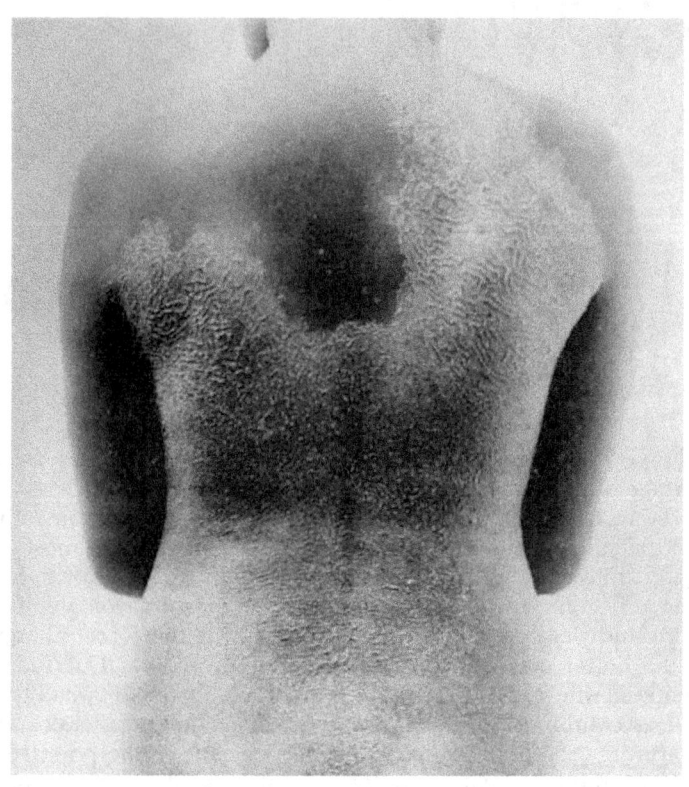

Figure 3. Tinea imbricata (back). (Käyser 1911:204).

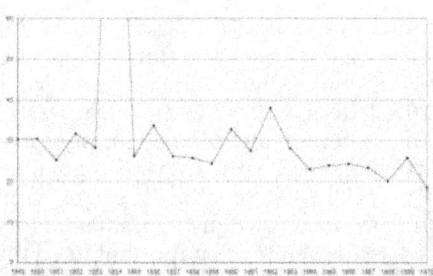

Figure 4. Recorded annual death rate (per 1,000 inhabitants), Minahasa, 1849-1870. Note: death rate in 1854 = 133 per 1,000 (point off scale). (adapted from Henley 2005a:365).

| David Henley

LIFESTYLES AND LIVING CONDITIONS

In those localities where water happened to be plentiful and accessible, bathing was always a popular activity. The American sea captain Woodard (1969:102) observed at the end of the eighteenth century that the people of the Palu Valley bathed 'twice a day in fresh water', and even the missionary Steller (1866:31) conceded that adults on Sangir made 'quite some use' of water for bathing. But in many places the availability of water for washing, and even drinking, was inherently limited. Northern Sulawesi is mountainous and dissected, with few large water catchment areas. Drinking water came mostly from small streams and shallow wells, the level of which was liable to run low in times of dry weather, leading to intensified water pollution and outbreaks of stomach disease. On the low-lying Talaud islands, with their coralline rocks and thin soils, droughts were regularly followed by drinking water shortages and epidemics (Ebbinge Wübben 1889:207; Jellesma 1911:1242). In the early twentieth century, poor drinking water was also blamed for poor health conditions in Donggala (Grubauer 1913:579), Togian,[3] Tagulandang (Frieswijck 1902:472), and especially Gorontalo.[4] 'It seems to me', wrote one Dutch official in Gorontalo town in 1923, 'that a piped water supply must be regarded as an even more important need than a hospital'.[5]

Under precolonial conditions, access to water was further impeded by the geography of settlement. In most areas rotational swidden farming was the backbone of the economy, and low-level warfare a constant fact of life. The typical settlement therefore had two components: a permanent, central nuclear village, built on a hilltop and fortified for defense, and a surrounding patchwork of bush fallow and cultivated fields, the latter studded with temporary dwellings and huts (Figures 5 and 6). Since most fields were made on hill slopes to facilitate bush clearance and ensure good drainage, the scattered swidden houses where people spent much of their lives were not always close to streams. In the nuclear settlements, meanwhile, problems of hygiene were likewise 'exacerbated by lack of water, since the villages, because they were built in high places, were everywhere distant from rivers and streams' (*Fragment* 1856:27).

> Here there was little space and the houses stood crowded together; the ground was almost completely covered with refuse, and the clos-

---

3 E.L. van Son (gezaghebber), 'Aanvullende memorie inzake de onderafdeling Poso', 1935, pp. 12, in: NA, Koloniën, Memories van Overgave, 2.10.39, inv. nr 1212.
4 A.Ph. van Aken (resident), 'Memorie van Overgave van de residentie Menado', 1932, pp. 219, in: NA, Koloniën, Memories van Overgave, 2.10.39, inv. nr 306.
5 J.E. Edie (assistent-resident), 'Memorie van Overgave van de afdeling Gorontalo', 1923, pp. 27, in: NA, Koloniën, Memories van Overgave, 2.10.39, inv. nr 1188.

est water source was usually at the foot of the hill. On these hilltops, moreover, people were very much exposed to wind and rain, against which the poorly-built houses offered little protection. These conditions, direct consequences of warfare, were more harmful to the population than war itself. (Adriani and Kruyt 1950-51, I:77.)

The houses in the core village were typically large, built on tall piles and accommodating a number of related nuclear families, each with its own hearth. European observers invariably described them as insanitary: British naturalist Sydney Hickson, visiting the village of Karaton in Nanusa (Talaud) in 1886, provides a memorable example.

> Each house accommodated several families, and I was told that in some cases as many as five hundred individuals were crowded into one of these dwellings. They were built upon wooden piles, many of them seven feet above the level of the ground, and the refuse of the kitchen and all manner of filth had accumulated for years beneath each house so as to diffuse a stench which is beyond my powers of description. Had the village been visited by a sanitary inspector with the necessary powers instead of by a Resident without, there can be no doubt of the first step he would have taken to restore the village to a fairly sanitary condition. (Hickson 1889:160.)

Figure 5. Nuclear village in defensive hilltop site, Poso area, Central Sulawesi, circa 1905. (Adriani and Kruyt 1912-14, Plate 43).

Figure 6. Swidden houses, To Wana area, Central Sulawesi, circa 1975. (Atkinson 1989, Photograph 2).

This may in fact have been an extreme case, not only because the houses on Talaud were large even by Sulawesi standards, but also because Hickson arrived there in the wake of a cholera and malaria epidemic. Healthy adults, according to many sources, normally defaecated 'in the woods', in streams, or, in coastal villages, on the beach, where the results were washed away by the tide; only the sick, along with children and old people, habitually did so at home through holes in the floor platform (Tillema 1922:179, 197-8, 217, 236-7). Evidently there was much variation here, however, for other observers reported having 'reason to suspect that on occasion, the inhabitants of a village are obliged by the accumulated dirt to set up their houses in a new location' (Sarasin and Sarasin 1897:278). Among some groups, including the Sea-Sea of Peling in Banggai, human faeces were systematically deposited underneath the house as food for pigs penned up there.

> These people live in rather large [...] houses on piles; the space underneath the house is used as a pigsty, to which end it is entirely fenced in. All domestic waste without exception, including faeces, is cast down through the floor as pig fodder. A thick layer of manure is found underneath such a house, and the resulting stench is already unbearable even at a considerable distance. (Tillema 1922:236.)

In Minahasa too it was an 'old custom' to defaecate at night into 'the pigsty, which is constructed partly under the house' (Tillema 1922:188). In the Palu Valley people did so into the space where sheep and goats were penned overnight, an arrangement prohibited after the imposition of Dutch rule on the grounds that 'these spaces under the houses formed veritable breeding-places for vermin and dirt, and were the origin of many diseases' (Hissink 1912:82-3). Even where defaecation mainly occurred outside the village, sanitary conditions still left much to be desired, human waste typically creating a 'stinking mess' in the undergrowth (Tillema 1922:217) while pollution of streams affected downriver settlements (Roep 1917:414; Tillema 1922:208).

Colonial observers believed that the crowded conditions in the big village houses facilitated the transmission of disease, and later research in New Guinea confirmed that the prevalence of respiratory and skin disease is significantly correlated with the average number of people sharing a house (Feachem 1977:173-4). Lack of windows and constantly smouldering hearth fires made for a permanently smoky interior, which led to conjunctivitis and other eye problems (Adriani and Kruyt 1950-51, II:201), together no doubt with respiratory disease (Feachem 1977:139, 173-7). Individual behaviour patterns, finally, cannot be discounted as factors affecting the sanitary situation, even if colonial observers were inclined to exaggerate their significance. The link between personal hygiene and

| David Henley

the prevention of infectious disease, after all, was not understood by precolonial Indonesians any more than it was by Europeans prior to the eighteenth century. 'Cleaning of the body after defaecation', noted the hygiene propagandist Tillema (1922:198) on the basis of correspondence with missionaries and colonial officials living in pagan areas, 'generally does not occur'. Bathing, however frequent, was done more for refreshment than for cleanliness as such (Bouvy 1924:382). Infants (Figure 7 and 8) were reportedly seldom bathed at all and appeared, according to one early twentieth-century missionary, 'unspeakably dirty' (Woensdregt 1930:327).

Figure 7. Infant in cradle with older child, Poso area, Central Sulawesi, circa 1920. (Adriani and Kruyt 1950-51, Plate 75).

4 *Hygiene, housing and health in colonial Sulawesi*

Figure 8. Children and infants in temporary field shelter, Poso area, Central Sulawesi, circa 1920. (Adriani and Kruyt 1950-51, Plate 86).

COLONIAL AND POSTCOLONIAL CHANGES

Some of the most significant changes in health conditions under colonial rule resulted from the geographical regrouping of the population, and from modifications to traditional domestic architecture. Both of these developments were partly direct results of colonial policy, and partly spontaneous responses by the indigenous population to the new political situation. In the interests of taxation, political control and schooling as well as hygiene, wherever colonial power became established the Dutch authorities promptly ordered the relocation of nuclear settlements from defensible hilltops to more accessible sites close to roads and streams. Since pacification removed the rationale for defensive settlement, and roadbuilding together with the expansion of trade made accessibility increasingly attractive from an economic point of view, this policy was seldom strongly resisted. Although the relocation sometimes increased the malaria risk, it was usually a sanitary advance in so far as it improved access to water (Adriani 1915:469; Tillema 1922:208).

A parallel change was the replacement of big multiple-hearth houses by smaller dwellings (Figure 9). Everywhere in northern Sulawesi, whether in the few towns (of which the largest, Manado, had a population of under 30,000) or in the villages, by the 1920s the typical house contained between one and three nuclear families (Tillema 1922:194, 219, 231; 1926:203). Again this was partly a matter of Dutch hostility to the unhygienic and 'uncivilized' traditional structures, partly a matter of individual preferences now that the large semi-corporate kin groups which had occupied the big houses were losing their political and economic importance to the state and the market respectively (Henley 2005b). As noted, the trend toward individual household dwellings almost certainly helped in some degree to control infectious disease (Alexander and Alexander 1993:258). In many cases the new houses were more European in design as well as smaller than their predecessors, featuring shorter supporting piles, larger windows, and a separate kitchen area instead of central hearths in the living quarters. This, however, was more of a mixed blessing in health terms, since the elevation and smokiness of the old houses had both served, albeit not by conscious design, to repel mosquitoes and thereby combat malaria (Knapen 1998:89-90; Snellen 1990:120-7).

Figure 9. Small family houses, Tentena (on Lake Poso), Central Sulawesi, circa 1930. (Adriani and Kruyt 1950-51, Plate 59).

4 Hygiene, housing and health in colonial Sulawesi

Certain supervisory measures taken by the Dutch authorities to keep the new houses and settlements clean may have been more significant. In terms of external appearances, their results were certainly impressive. Hickson (1889:213) described the Minahasan town of Tondano in 1886 as consisting of 'rows of pretty little houses, each one – almost a model of neatness and cleanliness – surrounded by a garden of flowers and shrubs'. The 'perfection of tidiness' displayed in the new model villages of Minahasa, complained another British observer of the same period, 'would be almost irritating were it not for the beauty of the flowers and the tropical vegetation' (Guillemard 1886:171). By the early twentieth century, strict sanitary regulations, not all of them cosmetic, were being enforced even in remote places like the islands of Talaud.

> The external order and neatness of the villages is thus generally very adequate, and certainly not inferior to that of many Dutch country villages. If a *kampung* head allows his village to become neglected he is punished, in an extreme case dismissed, and if the compound of a house is not properly maintained the owner is fined, or, if he repeats the offence, imprisoned. As already noted, the level of order and cleanliness inside the houses, so important for health, does leave much to be desired. In times of emergency, however, intervention extends into the interior of the house. Last year, for instance, when dysentery was prevalent, the authorities took various countermeasures and issued an order (among others) that nobody should drink other than boiled water. Those caught breaking this regulation were summarily punished by the native judge. (Roep 1917:419.)

Quarantine measures taken by the colonial authorities against epidemic diseases certainly had some success. During a cholera epidemic in 1914, for instance, an infected woman who arrived by sea in Buol was immediately isolated, together with everyone who had been in contact with her, in a specially built barrack, and the local population escaped unaffected.[6] In 1915, and again in the following year, it was reported that 'tough measures' taken by the government had limited the spread of cholera in Central Sulawesi (*Koloniaal verslag* 1916:34, 1917:35). The incidence of this disease declined throughout Indonesia toward the end of the colonial period: between 1921 and 1927, in fact, there was apparently not a single case in the whole archipelago (Netherlands Indies Medical and Sanitary Service 1929:56). Another area in which colonial intervention was significant was that of child-

---

6 W.J.D. van Andel (gezaghebber), 'Memorie van Overgave van de onderafdeling Bwool', 1921, pp. 6, in: NA, Koloniën, Memories van Overgave, 2.10.39, inv. nr 1186.

birth - originally a highly dangerous event for both mother and child, not least because it was customary to cut the umbilical cord with a non-sterile bamboo knife. In 1856 the first two women from North Sulawesi were sent to Java for training as midwives, and in 1936 ten qualified midwives were working in Minahasa alone, where their services were said to be in popular demand.[7]

There is some evidence, too, that standards of personal hygiene improved during the colonial period. In mission schools in nineteenth-century Minahasa, according to Graafland (1867-69, I:257), children learned 'to clean themselves properly on the order of the schoolmaster', while cleanliness in clothing and cooking also improved in spontaneous imitation of European norms. By the early twentieth century, skin disease had become much less common in Minahasa,[8] and in Central Sulawesi too it was reported that 'people are gradually becoming ashamed' of skin disease, 'as a result of which the population diligently helps to cure it by using soap, so that the number of people affected has fallen significantly' (Adriani and Kruyt 1950-51, II:199). Another improvement was the increased use of footwear, which reduced the chances of hookworm infection (Bouvy 1924:394; Tillema 1922:196). It is not certain that religious conversion itself automatically gave rise to more positive assessments of indigenous hygiene on the part of missionaries and other European observers, some of whom tended if anything to be more critical of the behaviour of Christianized Indonesians than of that of unconverted pagans.

Whereas the draconian sanitary and quarantine regulations of the colonial era did not on the whole survive Indonesian independence, changes in public habits such as the use of soap – and certainly of footwear – have been more permanent. And in some other aspects of public hygiene, the postcolonial era has seen greater advances than the colonial one. An example is the provision of clean fresh water, an area in which the colonial authorities were strong on rhetoric, but never actually accomplished more than a few improved wells and a modest municipal piped water system in the regional capital of Manado. Public water supplies and sewerage have not been strengths of post-independence governments either, but small electric water pumps have compensated for this on a decentralized basis by making underground water more widely and reliably available than in the past for drinking, bathing and washing.

---

7   A. Stuurman (assistent-resident), 'Memorie van Overgave van de afdeling Manado', 1936, pp. 113, in: NA, Koloniën, Memories van Overgave, 2.10.39, inv. nr 1177. See also Bouvy 1924:373.
8   A. Stuurman (assistent-resident), 'Memorie van Overgave van de afdeling Manado', 1936, pp. 105, in: NA, Koloniën, Memories van Overgave, 2.10.39, inv. nr 1177.

CONCLUSION

Individually, most of the arguments just presented are to some extent open to question or counterargument. While the reduction in the numbers of people sharing houses, for instance, made for less infectious disease, the colonial concentration of larger numbers of people in single settlements, and the concurrent growth of commerce, probably had the opposite effect (Tillema 1922:208). Even in relation to the most obvious and dramatic hygiene improvement of the colonial period, the striking reduction in skin disease, it is still possible to be sceptical: medication was undoubtedly another factor here alongside improving personal hygiene (Adriani and Kruyt 1950-51, II:199), and the assertion by some commentators that the use of soap was a revolutionary innovation in indigenous culture is contradicted by the acknowledgement in other sources that before soap and shampoo became available, coconut oil was widely used for the same purposes (Riedel 1886:79; Van Spreeuwenberg 1845-46:34).

Even if it is accepted that important hygiene improvements took place during and after the colonial period, just how closely these were associated with the concurrent fall in mortality is ultimately impossible to say. This uncertainty is hardly surprising considering that even in the case of the best documented and most historically important mortality decline of all, that of Great Britain during the industrial revolution, there is still an open debate over what factors were primarily responsible: improving nutrition, as classically argued by Thomas McKeown (1976), or public health and municipal sanitation, as first comprehensively proposed in a counterthesis by Simon Szreter (1988). In my own published research on Indonesia, at the end of the day I lean more to the 'nutritional' than to the 'sanitary' position (Henley 2005b). Although actual famine was historically rarer in Southeast Asia than in some other parts of the world, and although disease was usually the immediate cause of death, mortality rates – particularly among the very young and the very old – were always sensitive to levels of food availability, and the incidence of malnutrition was reduced when the commercialization of rural economies led to intensified production and exchange of food crops and products (Henley 2005a:317-62). Nevertheless it is apparent from what has been said above that a strong case can also be made that a lack of cleanliness – in the sense of clean bodies, clean water, and avoidance of contact with disease-carrying people and materials – considerably contributed to the high death rates in precolonial times, and that the colonial and postcolonial periods have seen significant improvements in this respect.

REFERENCES

Unpublished sources

Nationaal Archief, The Hague
Ministerie van Koloniën, Memories van Overgave, 1852-1962, nummer toegang 2.10.39

Published sources

Adriani, N.
1915 'Maatschappelijke, speciaal economische verandering der bevolking van Midden-Celebes, sedert de invoering van het Nederlandsch gezag aldaar', *Tijdschrift van het Koninklijk Nederlandsch Aardrijkskundig Genootschap* (2nd series) 32:457-75.

Adriani, N. and Alb.C. Kruyt
1912-14 *De Bare'e-sprekende Toradja's van Midden-Celebes*. Batavia: Landsdrukkerij, 's-Gravenhage: Nijhoff. Three vols.
1950-51 *De Bare'e sprekende Toradjas van Midden-Celebes (de Oost-Toradjas)*. Amsterdam: Noord-Hollandsche Uitgevers Maatschappij. Three vols. [Verhandelingen der Koninklijke Nederlandse Academie van Wetenschappen, Afdeling Letterkunde, Nieuwe Reeks 54, 55, 56.]

Alexander, Jennifer and Paul Alexander
1993 'Economic change and public health in a remote Sarawak community', *Sojourn* 8:250-74.

Bosscher, C. and P.A. Matthijssen
1854 'Schetsen van de rijken van Tomboekoe en Banggai, op den oostkust van Celebes', *Tijdschrift voor de Taal-, Land- en Volkenkunde van Nederlandsch-Indië* (*TBG*) 2:63-107.

Bouvy, A.C.N.
1924 'Uit en over de Minahasa I. De Minahassa en de geneeskunst', *Bijdragen tot de Taal-, Land- en Volkenkunde* 80:365-96.

[Delden, A.J. van]
1844 'De Sangir-eilanden in 1825', *Indisch Magazijn* 1(4-6):356-83; 1(7-9):1-32.

Ebbinge Wübben, F.A.
1889 'Naar de Talaut-eilanden', *Tijdschrift van het Koninklijk Nederlandsch Aardrijkskundig Genootschap* (2nd series) 6:201-12.

Feachem, Richard G.A.
1977 'Environmental health engineering as human ecology: An example from New Guinea', in: Bayliss-Smith and Richard G. Feachem (eds), *Subsistence and survival; Rural ecology in the Pacific*, pp. 129-82. London: Academic Press.

Fragment
1856 'Fragment uit een reisverhaal', *Tijdschrift voor Nederlandsch Indië* 18-1:391-432; 18-2:1-38, 69-100, 141-60.

Frieswijck, E.
1902 'Aanteekeningen betreffende den geografischen en ethnografischen toestand van het eiland Tagoelandang (afdeeling Sangi- en Talaut-eilanden)', *Tijdschrift van het Binnenlandsch Bestuur* 22:426-38, 469-89.

Graafland, N.
1867-69 *De Minahassa. Haar verleden en haar tegenwoordige toestand.* Rotterdam: Wijt. Two vols.

Grubauer, Albert
1913 *Unter Kopfjägern in Central-Celebes; Ethnologische Streifzüge in Südost- und Central-Celebes.* Leipzig: Voigtländers Verlag.

Guillemard, F.H.H.
1886 The *cruise of the Marchesa to Kamschatka & New Guinea, with notices of Formosa, Liu-Kiu, and various islands of the Malay Archipelago.* Vol. 2. London: John Murray.

Henley, David
1997a 'Carrying capacity, climatic variation, and the problem of low population growth among Indonesian swidden farmers: evidence from North Sulawesi', in: Peter Boomgaard, Freek Colombijn and David Henley (eds), *Paper landscapes; Explorations in the environmental history of Indonesia*, pp. 89-118. Leiden: KITLV Press. [Verhandelingen 178.]
1997b 'Goudkoorts: mijnbouw, gezondheid en milieu op Sulawesi (1670-1995)', *Spiegel Historiael* 32:424-30.
2001 'Malaria past and present: The case of North Sulawesi, Indonesia', *Southeast Asian Journal of Tropical Medicine and Public Health* 32:595-607.
2002 'Population, economy and environment in island Southeast Asia: An historical view with special reference to northern Sulawesi', *Singapore Journal of Tropical Geography* 23:167-206.
2005a *Fertility, food and fever; Population, economy and environment in North and Central Sulawesi, 1600-1930.* Leiden: KITLV Press. [Verhandelingen 201.]

2005b   'Population and the means of subsistence; Explaining the historical demography of island Southeast Asia, with particular reference to Sulawesi', *Journal of Southeast Asian Studies* 36-3:337-72.
2006   'From low to high fertility in Sulawesi (Indonesia) during the colonial period; Explaining the "first fertility transition"', *Population Studies* 60-3:309-27.

Hickson, Sydney J.
1889   *A naturalist in North Celebes; A narrative of travels in Minahassa, the Sangir and Talaut islands, with notices of the fauna, flora and ethnology of the districts visited.* London: John Murray.

Hissink, [C.]
1912   'Nota van toelichting, betreffende de zelfbesturende landschappen Paloe, Dolo, Sigi en Beromaroe', *Tijdschrift voor Indische Taal-, Land- en Volkenkunde* 54:58-128.

Jellesma, E.J.
1911   'De Talauer-eilanden (Residentie Menado)', *De Indische Gids* 33-2:1236-43.

Jones, Gavin W.
1977   *The population of North Sulawesi.* Yogyakarta: Gadjah Mada University Press. [Department of Demography, Australian National University, Indonesian Population Monograph Series, 1.]

Käyser, J.D.
1911   *Voordrachten over tropische huidziekten.* Batavia: Javasche Boekhandel en Drukkerij.
1918   *Verpleging van huidziekten in de tropen.* Amsterdam: De Bussy.

Knapen, Han
1997   'Koortsachtig koppen tellen in de binnenlanden van Zuidoost-Borneo (1700-1900)', *Spiegel Historiael* 32:444-9.
1998   'Lethal diseases in the history of Borneo; Mortality and the interplay between disease environment and human geography', in: Victor T. King (ed.), *Environmental challenges in South-East Asia*, pp. 69-94. Richmond, Surrey: Curzon Press. [Nordic Institute of Asian Studies, Man and Nature in Asia Series 2.]

Koloniaal verslag
1848-1941   *Koloniaal verslag* [title varies]. 's-Gravenhage.

Kruyt, Alb.C.
1932   'De bewoners van den Banggai-archipel', *Tijdschrift van het Koninklijk Nederlandsch Aardrijkskundig Genootschap* (2nd series) 49:66-88, 249-71.

McKeown, Thomas
1976 *The modern rise of population.* London: Edward Arnold.
Netherlands Indies Medical and Sanitary Service
1929 *Control of endemic diseases in the Netherlands Indies.* Weltevreden: Landsdrukkerij.
Reid, Anthony
1987 'Low population growth and its causes in pre-colonial Southeast Asia', in: Norman G. Owen (ed.), *Death and disease in Southeast Asia,* pp. 33-47. St. Lucia: University of Queensland Press.
1988-93 *Southeast Asia in the age of commerce, 1450-1680.* New Haven, CT: Yale University Press. Two vols.
Riedel, J.G.F.
1886 'De Topantunuasu of oorspronkelijke volksstammen van Centraal Selebes', *Bijdragen tot de Taal-, Land- en Volkenkunde* 35:77-95.
Roep, B.
1917 'Hygiëne op de Talaudeilanden', *Tijdschrift voor het Binnenlandsch Bestuur* 53:414-33.
Sarasin, Paul and Fritz
1897 'Über den Zweck der Pfahlbauten', *Globus; Illustrierte Zeitschrift für Länder- und Völkerkunde* 72:277-8.
Snellen, W.B.
1990 'Success and failure of malaria control through species sanitation – some practical examples', in: W. Takken et al., *Environmental measures for malaria control in Indonesia; an historical review on species sanitation,* pp. 81-127. Wageningen: Agricultural University. [Wageningen Agricultural University Paper 90-7.]
Spreeuwenberg, A.F. van
1845-46 'Een blik op de Minahassa', *Tijdschrift voor Nederlandsch Indië* 7-4:161-214, 301-33; 8-1:23-49.
Steller, E.
1866 *De Sangi-archipel.* Amsterdam: De Hoogh.
Szreter, Simon
1988 'The importance of social intervention in Britain's mortality decline c.1850-1914; A re-interpretation of the role of public health'. *Social History of Medicine* 1:1-37.
Tillema, H.F.
1922 *'Kromoblanda'; Over 't vraagstuk van 'het wonen' in Kromo's groote land.* Vol. 5-1. 's-Gravenhage: Uden Masman.

1926   *Zonder tropen geen Europa!* Bloemendaal: [Privately published.]

Woensdregt, Jac.
1930   'Het kind bij de To Bada in Midden Selebes', *Koloniaal Tijdschrift* 19:321-35.

Woodard, David
1969   *The narrative of Captain David Woodard and four seamen who lost their ship while in a boat at sea, and surrendered themselves up to the Malays in the island of Celebes; Containing an interesting account of their sufferings [...], and their escape from the Malays, [...] also an account of the manners and customs of the country.* London: Dawsons of Pall Mall. [Facsimile of the second edition, 1805.] [First edition 1804.]

5

Being clean is being strong
Policing cleanliness and gay vices in the Netherlands Indies in the 1930s

Marieke Bloembergen

Cleanliness and colonial policing are connected in an important way. This seems to be the message of some advertisements in the Netherlands Indies colonial police journals around 1940, and they clearly addressed the colonial police. One promoting Purol (Figure 1), for example, pointed to the importance of clean feet and clean socks for policing; Lifebuoy soap advertisements stressed the importance of fresh body odour in order to stay firm (Figure 2), and one even promised protection against German measles (*rode hond*, literally 'red dog') (Figure 3). This last one also seemed to celebrate the sheer bodily pleasure of showing masculine beauty. These ads caught my attention during my research on the dirty work of empire – or colonial policing in the Netherlands Indies.[1] They all seem to transmit the important message that being clean is being strong. Looking at these pictures from a present-day point of view and with hindsight, they also provide an awkward comment on the peculiar episode of vice policing that will be discussed in this chapter: the pursuit of homosexuals in the Netherlands Indies colonial society during 1938 and 1939. For, might the last advertisement possibly be an appeal to gay eroticism in the masculine organization of the colonial police?

The so-called 'vice scandal' – as the mass arrests of homosexuals in the Netherlands Indies in 1938-1939 came to be known – has been investigated from the perspective of the victims and (European centred) homosexual subcultures.[2] Here I focus especially on the role of the police in this remarkable project of moral cleaning, to come to a further understanding of the problem of colonial policing in the late colonial state.

---

1   Bloembergen 2007, 2009. The present article is a slight revision of a case study in Bloembergen 2009:299-332.
2   It is strange that this well-known vice scandal has not yet been used as an entrance for the still to be written study of masculinity and homosexuality in the Netherlands Indies. On the case itself, see Kerkhof 1982, 1992. See also Koenders 1996; Aldrich 2003.

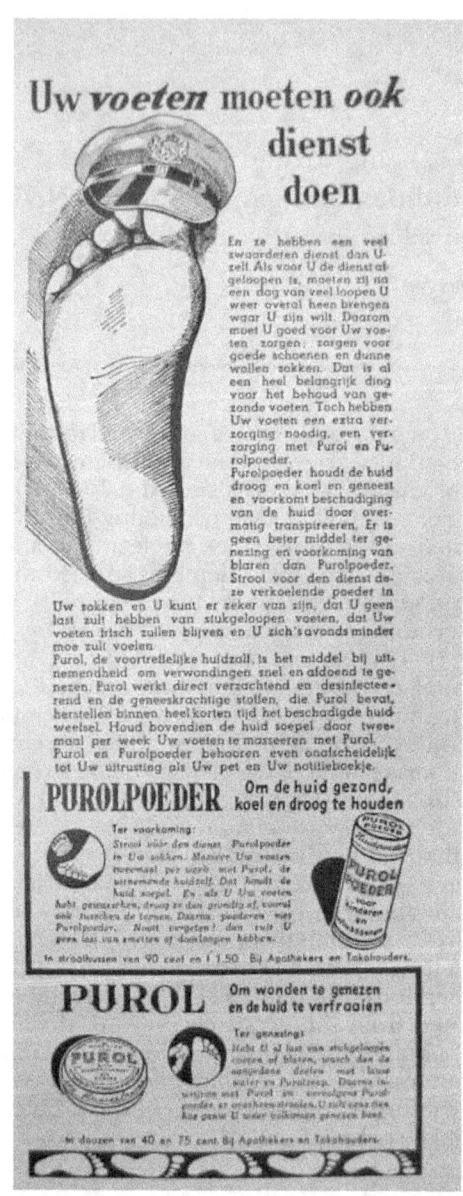

Figure 1. Your feet have to serve as well [...] Purol powder. To keep the skin clean, cool and dry.' Purol advertisement, published in *De Politie*, 1941.

Figure 2. 'Who said that he had never heard of LIFEBUOY? Especially in the service, when so much is asked of your body, it is important to remain fresh and fit.' Lifebuoy advertisement, published in *De Politie*, 1941.

Figure 3. 'LIFEBUOY not only refreshes you, but it also prevents you from B.O. (Body Odour).' Lifebuoy advertisement, published in *De Politie*, 1937.

THE VICE SCANDAL

Between December 1938 and May 1939, the colonial police arrested around 225 men throughout the Netherlands Indies, mostly Europeans, many of whom had good social standing. A number of them were even high officials of the Netherlands Indies colonial administration. These men were suspected of having had sexual relationships with persons of the same sex under the age of 21, which was against the law in the Netherlands Indies (as it was in the Netherlands) in accordance with Article 292 of the Indies Criminal Law. 171 of them were found guilty. The Netherlands Indies newspapers followed this remarkable mass arrest of homosexuals – which had never happened before on such a scale in the Netherlands Indies – with great interest and referred to it as '*de grote schoonmaak*' (the great spring-cleaning), '*zedenschoonmaak*' (moral cleaning) or '*het reinigingsproces*' (the cleansing process). At the same time they introduced the suspects of homosexual sex – at first by full name, later on by initials, town, and occupation – as representatives of a '*poel der verwording*' (cesspool of vice) and '*vies gedoe*' (dirty stuff).[3] This, in a nutshell, was the 'vice scandal'.

What can this explosion of 'moral cleansing' tell us about the functioning of the colonial police and the late colonial state? Apparently, this hunt was motivated by standardized conceptions of 'clean' and 'cleaning'. In the process of hunting down suspects, the police may have enhanced these notions, and contributed to the stigmatization of homosexuality in the colony in general, and the individual victims in particular. At first sight, these police raids on homosexuals were part and parcel of the colonial state's multidimensional politics of hygiene and civilization.[4] But, when we consider the colonial state's previous policy towards sexual offences or towards homosexuality, and the regular occupations of vice squads in the Netherlands Indies, the aim of this moral cleansing is not so obvious. The stated aim of the police raids in 1938-1939 was to only track down those homosexuals who had committed paedophilia (the minority age being until 21), which was a violation of article 292 of the Indies' penal code. It was, however, obvious that police investigation methods were directed against homosexuals in

---

3 In the period 27 December 1938 until 16 May 1939, the *Bataviaasch Nieuwsblad* used 26 times '*Het reinigingsproces*' (the cleansing process) as the heading for news-articles on tracing and prosecuting homosexuals, once, on 10 March, '*schoonmaak*' (cleaning), and within that same article 'spring cleaning'. For '*poel der verwording*', *Nieuws van den Dag voor Nederlandsch-Indië*, 27-12-1938 and '*vies gedoe*', *Indische Courant*, 9-1-1939, both quoted in Kerkhof 1982:61, 69.
4 See, among others, Abalahin 2003.

general. The mass arrests of homosexuals were therefore the more remarkable since, until then, the existence of homosexuality in the Netherlands Indies was well known, and generally tolerated. More importantly, homosexuality in itself was not against the law in the Netherlands Indies (nor in the Netherlands) (Kerkhof 1982:25-8).

The history of homosexuality and European and indigenous perceptions of homosexuality in the Netherlands Indies still need to be investigated and written. But it may be inferred that, along the lines of imported Christian notions, the majority of the European community in colonial society regarded homosexuals as unnatural, abnormal, or unclean. Moreover, a few critical Indonesian reactions to the 'vice scandal' indicate that at least in the eyes of some Indonesian spokesmen – representatives of the modern educated Indonesian elite – homosexuality was a disease, even a danger.[5] But these comments, like the upheaval in the European newspapers in 1938 and 1939, were made in hindsight. One of the Indonesian sources I am referring to, *Bahaja homo-sexualiteit dan bagaimana membasminja* (The danger of homosexuality and the ways to overcome it), by the Minangkabau author Maisir Thaib – a warning guide for parents of boarding school students in West Sumatra – implies indirectly that until then, also within indigenous societies the practice of intimate boy friendships was at least tolerated. In short, it seems that until the vice scandal of 1938, homosexuality was not an official public problem.

The moral cleansing forces of the colonial state, police and private organizations (European and indigenous associations) were directed against prostitution and traffic in women and children. It was only during the 'vice scandal' that these forces also turned against homosexuality as representing a general offence against public decency and a crime. How can this sudden apparent need for moral cleansing – within the white European colonialist group – be explained? And how did it fit within the program of the colonial police, and their modern colonial vice squads?

POLICING COLONIAL CLEANLINESS AND THE PROBLEM OF CIVILIZATION

The modern colonial police force, set up in the first two decades of the twentieth century, was the face of the colonial state. It was in the interest of this state, if it wanted to be civilized and mod-

---

[5] Thaib 1939. On the context and the message of this book, see Hadler 2008. See also the reaction to the vice scandal of the Indonesian nationalist Thamrin in the Volksraad (Advisory Council) below.

ern, to have an effective and professional police force that could ensure public safety and enforce (political) order, while at the same time performing in an emphatically civilized way. By organizing a civilized police force that would guarantee society's need for safety, the colonial government ideally could acquire the cooperation and consent of its subjects. Moreover, through modern policing, civilization, cleanliness, decency, and hygiene could be assured – all, of course, according to an ideal of modern European standards. This could help prevent infectious diseases and maintain vigilance, and also mark a civilized state.

Fear and concern, control and the urge to 'civilize', were leading motives behind three important police reforms that the colonial government implemented in the first two decades of the twentieth century. This resulted in a more or less professional police force that consisted of the old *bestuurspolitie* (Administrative Police, dating from the nineteenth century), the modern city police (created in 1911-1914), the *veldpolitie* (Field Police: a mobile, well-armed and barracked police for security surveillance in rural areas, created in 1918-1920), and, mainly for political control, the *gewestelijke recherche* (Regional Investigation Department). At the central level, the Attorney General controlled this force; the Director of Interior Administration was in charge of management. At the local level the highest European administrators of the Binnenlands Bestuur (Interior Administration), or the Residents, headed the police force in their own provinces. This colonial police force was almost entirely staffed by Indonesian recruits. In the 1930s, 96 per cent of the police, out of a force of 34,000, was Indonesian. Typical for the colonial hierarchy – in which not only race, but also class mattered – only a few of them, members of the Indonesian elite, got access to the higher ranks, especially in the 1930s.

This modern colonial police force was organized both as a tool for political control and as a civil security tool – at least as a more civilized tool than the army. Where the army ensured colonial authority by the sheer presence of its force and the supremacy of its violence, the 'modern' colonial police were instructed and trained to act professionally – in a strong, constrained, sedate way, and to postpone violence as long as possible while dealing with any public security problem.[6] Also, they were meant as a tool of 'civilization' to

---

6 For a first code for violence restriction for the police in the Netherlands Indies, see 'Voorloopig reglement van tucht voor het personeel der algemeene politie in Nederlands-Indië', in *De Nederlandsch-Indische Politiegids*, January 1917, Article 2.13. Like its following revisions, this article was open for interpretation. See also the handbook used at the police academy in Sukabumi by Dekker and Tacoma (1938).

bring order, safety, cleanliness, and decency – into colonial society. This idea became part of the self-image of the policemen who were trained at the police academy in Sukabumi, which was set up in 1914, and opened for almost all ranks at the beginning of the 1920s.[7] A police handbook of the 1930s opened with the government policy, formulated as a defence against criticism and police violence, that it aimed for a force of 'men of high principles of life, strong moral and character traits' – in short, to be strong (Dekker en Tacoma 1938).

How the modern colonial police imagined their task is well illustrated by the frontispiece of *De Politie*, the journal of the Association for Inspectors and Head-Inspectors of Police in the Netherlands Indies (Figure 4). This was one of four police associations, all set up at the end of the 1910s, beginning of the 1920s, which reflected the striving for police professionalization and civilization from within the police force. The frontispiece of *De Politie* showed a fit Roman soldier, armed with the sword of order and the torch of enlightenment, who guarantees law and order, neatness and civilization. Although the soldier became more muscular over the years – appealing to strong masculine fascist art in the 1930s – the content of this image never changed (Figure 5). This desired image of 'civilized police' had two sides: police that in a firm, upright and effective way provide the social need for safety, and police as a tool of the colonial forces of civilization: *oom agent* (Uncle) in the *desa* (village), who reports infectious diseases, and who ensures that everyone keeps their yards neat and tidy, and behaves well.

The image of civilized police and the idea of civilization and neatness through policing seemed to become more important in the 1930s. With further development of Indonesian nationalism and fiercer political policing, it became harder for the colonial authorities to ignore opposition to colonial rule. After the violent repression of the communist revolt of 1926-1927 (in which a large number of Muslims participated), mass arrests and the internment of around 1300 alleged communists without trial, the colonial government subsequently refined and extended the organization of political policing and enlarged the police force in general (Bloembergen 2006, 2009:247-97; Poeze 1994). The international economic crisis, which forced the government to cut down policing expenses, did not hamper the artificial image of *rust en orde* (law and order) or

---

7   The programme at the police academy was twofold: on the one hand recruits were trained in semi-military discipline, the use of arms (rifles, sabres and pistols) and physical exercises, and on how to recognize a 'communist conspiracy'. This programme reflected the needs of a police state-in-progress; on the other hand, recruits were educated in the principles of a constitutional state, criminal law and justice, and methods and rules of *civilized* modern policing – including restrictions on police power, and instructions on the use of force (Bloembergen 2009:203-46).

Figure 4. Frontispiece of *De Politie*, 1937

Figure 5. Frontispiece of *De Politie*, 1942

5 Being clean is being strong

zaman normal (normal times) as the 1930s have been characterized. The threat of war in Europe and Asia, however, cast a dark shadow over this false image of peacefulness and security. Meanwhile, the police, more visible because of the extension of political policing, and being watched while watching, had become the standard for the quality of colonial government (Idenburg 1961:143).

Against this background, moral policing could become an important assignment of the modern colonial police, even more important than formerly. Modern police vice squads could prove the 'civilized' intentions of this repressive colonial state. This was also how some members of the new generation of modern educated police trainees from the police academy in Sukabumi, working for the city police forces in Java's main cities, Surabaya, Semarang and Batavia, saw their task.

POLICING CLEANLINESS AND VICES

Surveillance of cleanliness and public decency became a formal task of policing in colonial administrative towns in the Netherlands Indies from the last quarter of the nineteenth century, and remained so for the modern colonial police force operating in the 1920s and the 1930s. This task was a means to colonial civilization, public hygiene, order and – ideally, from the perspective of colonial government – control.

With regard to the policing of cleanliness and *zedelijkheid* (public decency), and as a proof of their modernity, the new city police force in the main cities developed special vice squads, part of the city police's criminal investigation departments.[8] The initiators, for example in Surabaya, were intermediate ranking European police officers who considered public decency an important and modern good, and who thereby identified with the icon of their association's journal, the Roman soldier – not only because of his sword, but also because of his torch of enlightenment. Not only the intermediate ranks, but also the highest rank in the modern police force identified and associated with the colonial forces of civilization – at least in the main cities (*Zedenpolitie Amsterdam* 1925; *Zedenpolitie Batavia* 1925, 1926). The chief superintendents of the city police forces in Batavia, Semarang and Surabaya all had seats on the directory boards of a number of private 'civilizing' institutions, such as

---

8 On the characteristics and early practice of the modern city police forces, see Bloembergen 2007.

Pro Juventute (For the Youth), the Association for Hygienic Education, or the Society for the Protection of Animals.

In the 1920s and 1930s the fight against prostitution and the trade in women and children became the aim of an international purity crusade. Different institutions in the Netherlands Indies got involved in this fight as well. In that regard, the police and/or their special vice squads had to deal with the Regeeringsbureau voor de Bestrijding van den Handel in Vrouwen en Meisjes en dien van Ontuchtige Uitgaven (Governmental Office for the Fight against Trade in Women and Girls and Indecent Publications), which the Government had set up in 1913. There were also all sorts of private associations, European and indigenous engaging in this fight, such as the already mentioned Pro Juventute and the Perkoempoelan Pembasmian Perdagangan Perempoean dan Anak-Anak (Association for the Suppression of Trade in Women and Children).[9] These 'purifying forces' concentrated primarily on prostitution and traffic in women and girls. Street prostitution of boys, apparently, was not their concern, as long as they were not European, as we shall see later.[10]

Homosexual sexual offences in general did not get special attention, as can be deduced indirectly from the available criminal statistics – however unreliable these might be.[11] This also appears from the content of the journals of the four police associations. These showed no interest in homosexual vices, with one exception in 1936, which became meaningful, as we shall see below. This lack of interest is not surprising, since homosexuality in itself was not an offence, only some acts were. Apparently it was male sexual abuse of women and girls, rather than of boys, that had priority.[12] It was only after the vice scandal, that several medical specialists, who

---

9 For more examples, see Abalahin 2003. On Pro Juventute, and attitudes of the colonial state and colonial society towards youth delinquency, and youth re-education, see Dirks 2011.

10 Street boys and young male vagabonds who, via the police, ended up in private and state sponsored juvenile re-education facilities mainly did so because of petty crime and vagrancy. These juvenile re-education facilities were primarily male oriented. Personal communication Annelieke Dirks, 9-6-2008, PhD thesis 'Juvenile delinquency, colonial civil society and the late colonial state in the Netherlands Indies, circa 1880-1942'. (Leiden University, 2011). The vice scandal of 1939 apparently made a difference to this policy, as we shall see below.

11 From the Criminal Statistics based on material provided by the European Law Courts before 1935, it is hard to determine if those men, who were prosecuted for 'general' sexual vices, committed the crime as defined by Article 292. Kerkhof counted an average of 10 men yearly. Only since 1935 the criminal statistics distinguished the category of 'sexual offences'. On the basis of these, Kerkhof (1982:27) counted in 1935:3, 1936:6, 1937:5, 1939:171, and in 1940:20 European men prosecuted for the offence of Article 292.

12 *Handel in meisjes* 1929; *Onthullingen vrouwenhandel* 1928; *Politie en prostitutie* 1917; *Scherpere bestrijding prostitutie* 1929; Stern 1927; *Technische zaken* 1926; *Zedenpolitie Amsterdam* 1925. The journal for the Association of Indonesian Policemen, *Medan Polisi Boemipoetra*, showed no special interest in this topic in the 1920s.

during the vice scandal played a role as experts, wrote on related topics, for example on how to determine the age of a young men – which implied Indonesian men – or on how to interrogate youngsters (Adriaanse 1940; Müller 1941).

How, in the period before the 'vice scandal', police authorities in the Netherlands Indies dealt with possible homosexual relationships in the colonial police force is hard to find out and deserves further research. The weakness with which homosexuality was associated did not match the representation of the police as a tool of violence that was also the face of the colonial state. From the suggestive Lifebuoy advertisement mentioned above, the bodily training and gymnastics at the Police School, and the very fact that policing was male work, it may be inferred that it existed, or the possibility should not be discounted. A police recruit's diary from 1928 reveals that 'homosexuality' was a topic during a first-aid course for superintendents at the Police School in Sukabumi as a disease and thus probably as a warning too. The owner of the diary, a colonial soon-to-be superintendent of police as well as a Catholic butcher's son fresh from the Netherlands, was upset. He had never heard of such a thing, he wrote. His classmates appeared to have been full of this topic on the day, and he wondered 'how the world could be so wrong'.[13]

The policy towards homosexual police officers became clear enough during the vice scandal in 1938, in which at least four European police officers were arrested and interrogated as suspects. Three were found guilty. These weak spots, as they were regarded then, were inconspicuous within the massive number of other European homosexuals who were arrested, and in terms of the attention the press paid to the highest and most famous of them. For the police, the vice scandal would, on the contrary, turn out to be an event that not so much showed the weakness, but rather the strength and healthy morals of the police, and thereby of the state.

PURITY CRUSADE

The Netherlands Indies' vice scandal started in the heart of colonial civilization, the capital city, Batavia. It was there, in early 1937, that the Chief Superintendent of the Batavian city police, P. Dekker, for the first time had to give account to his superiors,

---

13 Diary of P. van der Poel, in: Nederlands Instituut voor Militaire Historie (Netherlands Institute for Military History), The Hague.

the Resident of Batavia, and the new Governor-General A.W.L. Tjarda van Starkenborgh Stachouwer, for the police's policy towards homosexual vices in Batavia. The immediate occasion was a petition of the board of the Christelijke Staatspartij (CSP, Christian State Party) to the Governor-General in December 1936 in which it complained about the 'rampant sin of homosexuality [...] among very well-known persons, men of good position in society'. The CSP-board admonished the Governor-General to make the police investigate the matter thoroughly – especially among the civil service – and report to the government so that it could take measures against this 'evil'. The police should not only act against those who committed the offence of having sexual relations with young men under age, but also against 'the evil' among grown-up men in general.[14]

The CSP-board justified its request on three grounds. One was the free local paper, *De Ochtendpost* (Morning News), that in its gossip column 'Batavian Nouvelles' informed its readers extensively about the way Batavian men (and women) of very good position spent their nightlife. Another one was an article in the police journal *Het Politieblad* (The Police Journal), entitled 'Ontucht en diefstal' (Vice and theft), from which the CSP-board concluded that there must be a connection between 'crime and the deviant sin'.[15] A third factor was the rumour that the PPAA, the indigenous Association for the Suppression of Trade in Women and Children, was bracing itself to expose vice scandals. The CSP board concluded that 'European society could not stay behind'.[16] Thus, worried about European sexual deviant vices, and facing initiatives of a purity crusade from indigenous society, the board of the CSP thought it was urgent to show that European society was not weakening, but strong.

In Batavia, the police authorities showed no worries at all when the Governor-General, via the Attorney General (in charge of central police), asked them for a reaction to the CSP's petition. Chief

14 Petition, Board of CSP, 8-12-1936, in: Nationaal Archief (NA), The Hague, Ministerie van Koloniën (Koloniën), Geheime Mailrapporten, serie AA, 1914-1952, nummer toegang 2.10.36.06, inventarisnummer (inv.nr) 144, Mailrapport (MR) 1937, 989+. See also Kerkhof 1982:32-6.
15 Ibidem. Unfortunately, I have not found either of the two articles mentioned in this letter (yet). *Het Politieblad* was the journal of the association for policemen of the lower intermediate ranks, the Algemeene Politiebond van Politiepersoneel in Nederlandsch-Indië (The General Police Association). Until 1931 it was known as the Association for Head Constables and Chief Inspectors in the Netherlands Indies.
16 Petition, Board of CSP, 8-12-1936, in: NA, Koloniën, Geheime Mailrapporten, 2.10.36.06, inv. nr 144, MR 1937, 989+.

5 Being clean is being strong

Superintendent of Police P. Dekker conceded that the police kept a list of names, but a very unreliable one, not to be used, and secret. Although he referred to homosexuality as 'evil' he also, in a laconic way, pointed to the fact that the police could not act against homosexuals: not 'as long as an homosexual didn't interfere with men under age, violate public virtue, or commit crimes'. The Resident confirmed that there was no need to worry: so far there were no vice scandals in Batavia, and the police were watching. In his letter to the Governor-General, Attorney General G. Vonk also insisted that 'the police in general should refrain from investigating an official, of whom it is only a surmise that he goes around with adults from the same sex, which is not a crime'. Neither rumours, nor conjectures, nor the unreliable name-list could serve an investigation against acts that were not liable to punishment.[17]

Thus, the CSP came away empty handed. It could not convince the police authorities in the Netherlands Indies of the relationship between homosexuality, crime and the weakening of public morals. The topic remained in the air, however, throughout 1937 and 1938. This was partly due to a more successful Christian lobby from the Netherlands where the government happened to sharpen legislation towards sexual vices;[18] and there was a minor homosexual vice scandal in Surabaya early in 1938, which became a favourite topic for further gossip and moral indignation in the Netherlands Indies newspapers. Continuing Christian lobbying in the Dutch Parliament resulted in the request of the Minister of Colonies, H. Colijn, to Governor-General Van Starkenborgh Stachouwer, to explain rumours about the increase of homosexuality in the Netherlands Indies, and the weakening of public morals in the colony. The Governor-General, again, denied there was a problem. Another reason for more attention for the topic – or more gossip – in the Netherlands Indies newspapers, enlivened by the minor vice scandal in Surabaya, was because of the obsessive indignation of one particular conservative newspaper-editor, H.C. Zentgraaff from the *Javabode*, with the free lifestyle of the group of Western artists, scientists and tourists that flocked to Bali in this period. In his eyes, they were vicious, exemplified by the eccentric German artist, Walter Spies, who also happened to be and act publicly homosexual.[19]

---

17 Resident of Batavia to Attorney General, 22-1-1937; Attorney General to Governor-General, 27-1-1937, in: NA, Koloniën, Geheime Mailrapporten, 2.10.36.06, inv. nr 144, MR 1937, 989+.
18 On this episode, see Koenders 1996:249-63.
19 See Zentgraaff looking back in the *Javabode*, 5-1-1939, quoted in Kerkhof 1982:59.

131

| Marieke Bloembergen

A MORAL WINDFALL ON THE SUSPICIOUSNESS OF SWIMMING
AND CYCLING IN SUKABUMI

In November 1938, the Batavian police were tipped off that a well-known homosexual, staying at a hotel in Batavia, received under-aged men in his hotel room. At that moment, in the climate of public moral indignation about homosexuality as a weakening vice, the police must have realised they had a good chance to perform as a successful civilizing force and ensure colonial decency – in short, to show that they were strong, and to show off colonial moral strength. Two weeks of observation were enough to confirm this tip and arrest the man, a certain W.G. van Eyndthoven, who had never made a secret of his being homosexual.[20] The police only realized what a good prey they had, when they found in Van Eyndthoven's hotel room a huge collection of letters between Van Eyndthoven and homosexuals in the Netherlands and the Netherlands Indies. These letters seemed a windfall for successful moral policing. They were the basis of a secret police investigation, taking place in Batavia in the first two weeks of December 1938, into the nature and reach of a possible network of homosexuals in the Netherlands Indies. They therefore can help us to get an idea of police investigation methods into the vice scandal.

In two senses Van Eyndthoven's private correspondence formed a clue for the police investigation: first, the letters alerted police to their senders and to their male friends, who all became suspects because of their connection to Van Eyndthoven; and second, they provided insight into the jargon and vocabulary, the pet names and coded words that some authors used, and that, according to police suspicions, might reflect secret, deviant and even forbidden behaviour. Thus the police found out that Van Eyndthoven and some of his connections used the word '*onbetaalbaar*' (priceless) to refer to '*bijzonder genotvolle belevenissen*' (very pleasant experiences).[21] This coded language was indeed part of the sub- or counter-culture, which homosexuals developed as a reaction to their exclusion, or to the fact that public opinion regarded their sexual preference as deviant (Kerkhof 1982:32-6). However, since the relationship between language and 'reality' is hard to coin in general, the police here went along a very slippery road of interpretation and proof

---

20 Attorney General Marcella to Governor-General Van Starkenborgh Stachouwer, 6-3-1939, in: NA, Koloniën, Geheim Archief, 1901-1940, nummer toegang 2.10.36.51, inv. nr 546, Verbaal 25-4-1939, E16; see also Koenders 1996:309.
21 Police interrogation G., procès-verbal, 1-12-1938, in: Arsip Nasional Republik Indonesia (ANRI), Jakarta, Archive of Binnenlands Bestuur (BB), 3409.

finding. In this context anything could be meaningful and suspicious – such as an invitation to come for 'a fresh nose', a swim, and a bicycle ride in Sukabumi, which the police found among Van Eyndthoven's letters. Ironically, the unlucky sender was a young pupil of the police academy in Sukabumi.[22]

On 1 December 1938 the Superintendent of Batavia's police criminal investigation department, William Edward Böck, cross-examined recruit police officer H.A.I. Geraerts, the sender of the suspicious invitation. The two policemen met at the breeding place of the modern colonial police, the police academy in Sukabumi. Böck's first aim was to establish the nature of the connection between Geraerts and Van Eyndthoven (whom he had interrogated two days before) in order to get a further picture of the presumed homosexual network in the Netherlands Indies, and to figure out if Geraerts was gay. Therefore, Geraerts had to clarify all the names and pet names of homosexuals that the police had derived from Van Eyndthoven's letters. Geraerts cooperated as far as he could, admitted to having friendly relations with Van Eyndthoven, but denied being attracted to men or to have experienced gay sex. He maintained that his proposal to Van Eyndthoven to pass by for a swim and a bicycle ride was as innocent as possible.[23] On the surface, his invitation fitted the clean and fresh hilly air of Sukabumi. Under the circumstances, appearances were against him. Geraerts seemed not only to have known Van Eyndthoven well; it was precisely the place where he had met Van Eyndthoven that made him even more suspicious: a certain private house in the colonial entrepreneurial town Medan (Sumatra).

Young, fresh and green, Geraerts arrived in the Netherlands Indies in November 1937 – most impressively by bicycle – together with a male companion, W.H.H. Peltzer, both in search of their fortune. The house in Medan was one of the first places they stayed in the Netherlands Indies. It was well known in Medan as a meeting place for homosexuals. Geraerts and Peltzer might have not been aware of that, but must have realized sooner or later. The European owner himself was gay; he lived with a young Indonesian man. They shared a bedroom. Now and then there were parties in the house, with men dancing together and kissing in public. Directed by Van Eyndthoven's private letters and with the help of their colleagues in Medan, the Batavian police knew the place by now. According to his letters, Van Eyndthoven had found this address via the Medan housing agency 'Homo-sex'. Van Eyndthoven was one of the ten-

---

22 Police interrogation G., procès-verbal, 1-12-1938, in: ANRI, BB, 3409.
23 Police interrogation G., procès-verbal, 1-12-1938, in: ANRI, BB, 3409.

ants of the house during the time that Geraerts stayed there. It was then that they first met. Van Eyndthoven rented the pavilion in the garden. Peltzer and Geraerts, for reasons of economy, shared a room in the house, and thus slept in one space – like the European owner and his Indonesian friend did. For Böck, this was very suspicious. Geraerts had to draw for him how this male household in Medan, and especially the sleeping quarters, was organized. Wisely, Geraerts showed the two beds far apart in the room (Figure 6).[24]

Böck also paid special attention to the picture postcard Van Eyndthoven sent to Geraerts from Batavia the moment he heard that Geraerts had moved to Sukabumi and enrolled at the police academy. If he were ever in Batavia, so Eyndthoven typed on his typewriter, Geraerts should come over to dredge up memories of the good old days. 'Do you remember after that meeting? Priceless!' It was especially this last word, notably handwritten, as the police report remarked, that Böck wanted Geraerts to clarify. Geraerts recognized 'priceless' to be in Van Eyndthoven's hand, but pretended not to know its special meaning. For the moment Böck left it there, either giving Geraerts the benefit of the doubt, wishing to keep up the appearance of the police, or merely postponing the fate of this useful informant.[25]

In the meantime, the police collected new incriminating information against Geraerts through interrogations with the other, now publicly gay, inhabitants of the Medan house. On request, Oesman, the Indonesian partner of the house owner, denied that Geraerts was 'like the other men'. However, he also stated that Geraerts had kissed him once or twice during a party. During that interrogation Oesman also had to account for his desire for men. He felt like

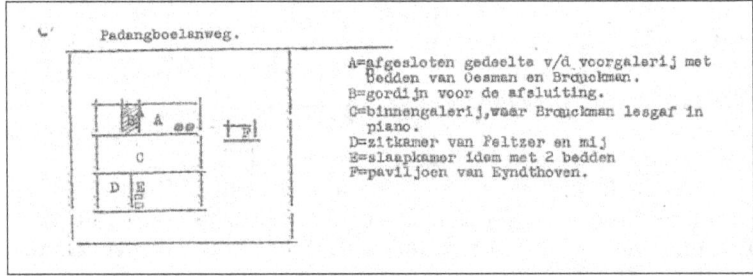

Figure 6. Drawing of how the male household in Medan was organized. Geraerts had to make this drawing during his interrogation in December 1938.

24 Police interrogation G., procès-verbal, 1-12-1938, in: ANRI, BB, 3409.
25 Police interrogation G., procès-verbal, 1-12-1938, in: ANRI, BB, 3409.

a woman, Oesman explained to his interrogator, he longed to be a woman, and to be with a man. He never felt anything for girls. 'I only care to dance with men'. Geraerts often joined the parties at the house, Oesman continued, but he never danced; once Geraerts had tried to dance with Oesman, but Geraerts couldn't dance, according to Oesman.[26] Two weeks later, the Batavian police subjected Geraerts to a second cross-examination, now at the Office of the Public Prosecutor in Batavia. Superintendent of Police J.C. Julianus, much more direct then Böck, asked Geraerts if he ever had been intimate with one or more persons in the circle of men frequenting the Medan house. Geraerts again maintained his innocence. He conceded that Oesman once kissed him on the cheek, and that he let that pass by.[27]

Presumably because most witnesses in Medan, like Oesman, stressed that Geraerts was not homosexual, the police let him go after this second interrogation. However, Geraerts remained stigmatized like the other victims of the police raids against homosexuals. He deserved the benefit of the doubt, as the interim Chief Superintendent of Batavia's police force admitted to the Head of the Police Department. The homosexual witnesses from Medan regarded Geraerts as 'somewhat naïve', he explained, and they teased him, because he did not understand their hints and ambiguous wordplays. But they also stated that Geraerts kept aloof. There were, in short, no proofs that he was gay.[28] Thus, Attorney General Marcella informed the Director of Interior Administration. But he added that the evidence of Geraerts's past in Medan, and his attitude during the interrogations, made him seem 'not particularly firm nor vigorous' in character.[29] It was up to the Director of Interior Administration to decide if Geraerts was still fit for the colonial police force. Apparently he was, for Geraerts was allowed to stay. He finished the exams for the rank of head constable, graded number 10 out of 75 candidates, and left for a post in East Java. The Governor of East Java, however, received Geraerts's files. These included the verdict of the Head of the police academy, that Geraerts had 'certain qualities, which made him less fit for the police service'.[30] Geraerts was clean, but was he strong?

26 Fragment of the interrogation of O., by the Public Prosecutor in Batavia, 30-12-1938, in: ANRI, BB, 3409.
27 Police interrogation G., procès-verbal, 7-1-1939, in: ANRI, BB, 3409.
28 Interim Chief Superintendent of the Batavia police force, to the Head of the Department of Police, 5-1-1939, in: ANRI, BB, 3409.
29 Attorney General to Director of Interior Administration, 7-1-1939, in: ANRI, BB, 3409.
30 Head of the police academy to Head of the Department of Police, 5-5-1939; Director of Interior Administration, 5-6-1939, in: ANRI, BB, 3409.

The police interrogation of Geraerts suggests that the methods in this 'secret' police investigation hardly differed from those of the Netherlands Indies' political police and their hunt for communists since the repression of the communist revolts in 1926-1927.[31] Like the political police, the Batavian special vice squad looked for keywords (in this case not pointing to communist ideology, but to homosexual jargon or coded homosexual language), connections (being befriended by Van Eyndthoven or known by him was enough reason to be suspected of deviancy), and organization. (All these clues together might indicate a criminal gang, which, in this case, traded young men under age, and which spread the weakening danger of homosexuality like a contagious disease).

BLAME AND SHAME

The secret investigation of course was not a secret anymore by mid-December, with names of the first victims published in the Netherlands Indies' newspapers – among them two well-known high officials.[32] On the basis of the findings of the Batavian police, the new Attorney General H. Marcella concluded that 'the criminal homosexuality' was of such a large scale in the Netherlands Indies, that it needed 'serious attention and stout resistance'. Thus, right after Christmas, on 27 December 1938, Marcella ordered the colonial police, the colonial administration, and all the public prosecutors throughout the Netherlands Indies as a follow up to the Batavian police investigations against gay sexual offences, to act against all persons committing 'this evil', without discrimination (with emphasis). And thus begun the systematic police campaign against homosexuals, led by the indefatigable Public Prosecutor T.M. de la Parra: from Sabang to Merauke, and from school heads to the highest officials.[33]

Within the general state of moral indignation and public wondering that went along with the police raids, it was the arrest of the Resident of Batavia, H. Fievez de Malines van Ginkel – who happened to be head of the Batavian police – that came as the greatest shock to the public. It is very likely that many people knew

---

31 On the methods of political policing in the Netherlands Indies after the communist revolts, see Bloembergen 2009:247-97; Shiraishi 1997.
32 For a broad evaluation of the Netherlands Indies' and Dutch press on the vice scandal, see Kerkhof 1982:58-77.
33 Report Attorney General, 6-3-1939, in: NA, Koloniën, Geheim Archief, 2.10.36.51, inv. nr 546, Verbaal 25-4-1939, E16; see also Koenders 1996:329.

5 Being clean is being strong

the Resident was a frequent visitor of '*de baan*' ('the lane'), or the area in Batavia where it was possible to pick up boys. Chief Superintendent Dekker himself most surely must have known.[34] The Resident's confession, in January 1939, therefore implied corruption of the Batavian city police. Both the Resident and Dekker had to justify – again – police policy towards homosexual vices. How honest had they been, when they reacted to the CSP's petition of November 1936? The Resident, who turned completely grey within three months after his arrest, had to admit in a rather predictable hearing that he had endorsed a passive policy.[35]

Dekker, who at the time had only been chief superintendent in Batavia for half a year, claimed that he was afraid he would lose his job if he reported the Resident's personal conduct. He also explained the police's policy of tolerance towards homosexual vices by lack of personnel, and changes in personnel at the Batavian vice squad. Finally, the attitude of the former public prosecutor in Batavia, now temporarily replaced by De la Parra, had been, in his view, remarkably uncooperative in cases of occasional arrests of homosexuals. As a consequence, police subordinates concluded that they could refrain from arresting homosexual suspects, as long as they were not going around with under age *European* men. Attorney General Marcella confirmed Dekker's last remark: according to him it had been an unclear policy towards homosexuality that had blinded the police to the actual 'evil'. Dekker came away with a reprimand for keeping silent about the Resident.[36]

The police operations against homosexuals remind us of the mass arrests of alleged communists – which, however, only took place after the revolts of 1926-1927 – and were in methods very comparable to political police repression. Also, they provide us with one of the few examples of preventive policing – in this case against the phantom of weakening gay vices – that were successfully directed at central level. If it were up to De la Parra, this massive investigation also would have been proceeded in a uniform way:

---

34 It turned out that Dekker actually had seen a compromising police report on the Resident dating from July 1938. In this report two young homosexuals who were involved in the Surabayan vice scandal mentioned above had pointed to the house of the Resident of Batavia, as one of the addresses they used to visit. Dekker put the report aside. This was in line with the police policy, which he had defended at the end of 1937. Report Attorney General, 6-3-1939, in: NA, Koloniën, Geheim Archief, 2.10.36.51, inv. nr 546, Verbaal 25-4-1939, E16.
35 Fragment of the cross-examination of the Resident, by Public Prosecutor A. Mieremet, 19-1-1939, in: NA, Koloniën, Geheim Archief, 2.10.36.51, inv. nr 546, Verbaal 25-4-1939, E16. 'Suspect has turned completely gray' as the *Bataviaasch Nieuwsblad*, 24-4-1939 wrote in its report on the trial of the Resident in April 1939.
36 Attorney General to Resident of Batavia, 16-2-1939; report Attorney General, 6-3-1939, in: NA, Koloniën, Geheim Archief, 2.10.36.51, inv. nr 546, Verbaal 25-4-1939, E16.

he himself travelled throughout Java to attend the hearings of suspects personally. However, at the local level not every head of police was as enthusiastic as De la Parra. The Resident of Banjumas, for example, when the public prosecutor of Semarang urged him to act against homosexuals, was not willing to cooperate since he had no wish to compromise persons of good reputation 'just like that' (Van Baal 1986). The Resident of Bali, on the other hand, apparently more willing to join this homophobic campaign than the Resident of Banjumas, reported that the police during their investigation lacked cooperation of the local population, who, in his view, were manipulated by the artistic Western troop in Bali.[37] Elsewhere, in the main cities of Java, the police successfully enforced cooperation by one-day raids against street boys, who they arrested to act as witnesses.[38] These uniform operations were not typical of the daily practice of civil or political policing. Apparently homosexuality was an easier adversary to imagine and coin, and thus bind the ethnically diverse colonial police, than 'nationalism' was.

The result was telling, as we already know. At least 223 men were taken in preventive detention (quite often for several months). By far most of them were European (among whom three policemen), but the list of detainees also counted nine Indonesians, and six representatives of other Asian population groups (one Armenian, four Chinese and one Arab). Most of these men were tried and sentenced to imprisonment, varying from periods of two months to two years.[39] The indigenous street boys, acknowledged by the colonial authorities to be prostitutes and not homosexuals, were judged differently. Those who were above the minority age were sentenced to jail because of violating the ban on streetwalking. Those below the minority age were sent to the juvenile re-education facilities managed by Pro Juventute.[40] Measures against high colonial officials, working at governmental departments in Batavia, seemed to have been decided at a faster speed. By March 1939 at least 50 gov-

---

37 Report Resident of Bali and Lombok, 2-3-1939, in: NA, Koloniën, Geheim Archief, 2.10.36.51, inv. nr 562, Verbaal 13-9-1939, Y36. On the ultimately rather successful hunt of homosexuals on Bali, see Kerkhof 1982:47-53.
38 In Batavia on 28 December; in Malang on 7 January 1938; in Bandung on 10 January; in Ceribon on 12 January. In Batavia the police again arrested, in one day, on 13 January, 36 persons among whom however only a few witnesses. *Bataviaasch Nieuwsblad*, 13-1-1939.
39 These figures are based on the list compiled by Kerkhof (1982:87-8, 108-14). Since this list merely shows initials of names, it is unclear how many Eurasian men were on it. It seems fair to conclude, however, that the raids were in the first instance directed against European men.
40 Kerkhof 1982:87. Koenders (1996:314) quotes W.J. de Haas, the Head of the Prison System in the Netherlands Indies, who asserted in May 1939, to a Dutch official, that these street boys were mainly motivated by money, and quite often supported by their families to engage in this business. A psychiatrist examined 34 of these boys and declared none to be homosexual.

ernmental officials had been arrested and interrogated; 38 of them heard that they had to go, either because they were fired, dismissed or allowed to go 'on leave'.[41] Attorney General Marcella, on request of Governor-General Van Starkenborgh Stachouwer, arranged a special measure for the dismissal of homosexual officials. Those who had only been arrested as homosexual suspects were either honourably discharged or transferred. Those who had committed paedophilia were dismissed from the service. In the future, new officials arriving from the Netherlands would need an official confirmation, stating they were not communist or 'like that' (Kerkhof 1982:43; Koenders 1996). Apart from the mass arrests and the many convictions, there were, possibly, three suicides.

A sour example of the harm this episode did to many individuals in the Netherlands Indies is the story of a well-qualified high governmental official, W.Ph. Coolhaas, who the police interrogated because of his homosexual inclinations. The government allowed Coolhaas to go on leave, but refused to take him back when his period of leave ended. After the war, Coolhaas re-applied – any job in the colonial administration would do – assuring the authorities that he had had himself cured by a Swiss psychiatrist in Zürich, pupil of the famous psychoanalyst Ernst Jung. Recently happily married, he thanked God that he was 'healed' by now and that he had found the right way in the field of sex.[42] He was strong again.

TRANSNATIONAL SCANDALS?

The Netherlands Indies' purification campaign did not stand on its own. Other, comparable homosexual scandals, resulting in similar police hunts of homosexuals took place in the 1930s in British Malaya, in the Netherlands, and in Nazi Germany. Interestingly, these scandals, although not all of the same size and scale, more or less developed in the same pattern. They all took place in a period of political and economic insecurity, and in societies marked by sharp political divisions. All the campaigns were initially directed against highly placed governmental or party officials. They started off with rumours about the homosexual behaviour of certain individuals, which were often (not always) supported by tangible evi-

---

41 Report Attorney General, 6-3-1939, in: NA, Koloniën, Geheim Archief, 2.10.36.51, inv. nr 546, Verbaal 25-4-1939, E16.
42 Coolhaas to General-Major Bongers, 23-5-1945, in: NA, Ministerie van Koloniën te Londen, 1940-1948, nummer toegang 2.10.45, inv. nr 1085.

dence, such as a diary (in the case of British Malaya) or a collection of letters (in the case of the Netherlands Indies). This 'evidence' provided the police with generous source material, and a starting point to investigate a presumed larger 'network' of homosexual officials. Most of these cases caused a huge public scandal, which was widely and intensely covered by the local and national press.[43]

This common pattern in timing, context, focus and actions against homosexuals suggests that these anti-homosexual campaigns reflected a struggle over competence and power, more than filling a need to get rid of deviant sexual behaviour. This remains a matter of speculation, however. But this was a time in which certain groups in society felt the need for strong and clear leadership. Since public morals considered homosexuals to be weak in character, they could therefore, at this particular time, be thought unfit for the kind of authority that society and insecure times needed.

Especially remarkable seems to be the parallel in timing between the campaign in the Netherlands Indies with the Nazi campaign against homosexuals in Germany – here as enemies of the state – which started to be implemented systematically from 1936 onwards. There are, however, no direct connections, nor are there indications that members of the Nationaal-Socialistische Beweging (NSB, Dutch national socialist party) in the Netherlands Indies had anything to do with the campaign in the colony. On the contrary, some members of the NSB in the Netherlands Indies were homosexuals, as was also the case in the Netherlands. And to complicate matters: as a consequence of the fierce Nazi campaign against homosexuals in Germany, both communists and members of the NSB in the Netherlands, for propaganda reasons or for self-confirmation, accused each other of incorporating homosexuals, therefore weakening their party (Koenders 1996:366-74).

But there was a Dutch connection to the Netherlands Indies anti-homosexual campaign. In its request of December 1936 the CSP, which was closely connected to the Dutch Anti-Revolutionaire Partij (ARP, Anti Revolutionary Party), may have been inspired by a huge homosexual vice scandal, the so-called 'Ries-affaire', which attracted public attention in the Netherlands from the second half of 1936 until early 1937. This Dutch scandal carried the same characteristics as the one in the Netherlands Indies: it began with the

---

43 On the scandal in British Malaya, and the circulating idea of the existence of a homosexual network in the colonial administration in the 1930s, see Aldrich 2003:194-8. On the scandal in the Netherlands (the so-called Ries Affaire in 1936-1937), and on the scandal in Germany (the Röhm Affaire in 1934) and its aftermath in the Netherlands, see Koenders 1996:295-303, 336-41. On the campaigns and scandals in Nazi Germany, see Micheler 2002.

police arresting a highly placed governmental official, the Chief Treasurer L.A. Ries, and a number of his friends who were also high officials, for having committed homosexual offences. The arrest of Ries became a public scandal which resulted in a nasty discussion on the quality of the evidence in the Dutch parliament, and which attracted the warm attention of the public and Dutch national newspapers for several months. The Dutch Minister of Finance, in the end, was happy to fire his highest official, with an argument that would now sound very familiar: 'he was of a character and mind [...] because of which he lacks, outwardly and inwardly, the kind of authority we need.'[44] He was not strong enough.

THE INDIES' SCANDAL: BEING CLEAN IS BEING STRONG

In hindsight the massive hunt for homosexuals can be understood as an attempt of the colonial authorities to appear strong and virtuous. The attempt got out of hand, but it also fitted within the conservative politics of *rust en orde*, or the *zaman normal* of the 1930s. Finally, this purifying crusade was, however, force and violence out of weakness.

At the end of the 1930s, this fake and enforced atmosphere of normalcy was extremely tense in reality, reflecting the essential weakness of the colonial state. This state was threatened by the continuous challenge of Indonesian nationalism and by a new danger, the possibility of war in Europe and Asia. Against this background, the police raids against homosexuals can be understood as an endeavour of the colonial authorities to stay firm by showing firmness. By catching the elusive, the unfathomable, and the deviant as the weak spot, they emphasized the opposite: the male heterosexual strength of the colonial state. At the same time this moral cleansing was also meant to show the civilized face of the colonial state, and thus to legitimize colonial authority to appease possible indigenous critics. In that sense, the questions of the Indonesian nationalist chairman, Mohammad Husni Thamrin, in the Volksraad (People's Council) in Batavia, on 20 January 1939, about the worrying shape 'the perverse lechery' in Batavia took, were grist to the mill of those enthusiasts who wanted to continue the campaign against homosexuals as thoroughly as possible.[45] In a double sense then, 'cleaning' society of homosexual vices meant showing that the colonial state was strong.

44 On this case, see Koenders 1996:295-306. The quotation of the Minister is on page 301.
45 Thamrin's speech was published – with approval – in the *Bataviaasch Nieuwsblad*, 21-1-1939.

This mode of thinking made its way to society through a typical way of reasoning connected to the campaign.

Those who took part in this purifying crusade – police, colonial authorities, journalists and public (letter writers) – used the same kind of vocabulary; everybody played with the idea of cleanliness and (moral) hygiene. People were talking about cleaning, cleansing, and moral strength on the one hand, and, when it came to homosexual vices, about dirtiness, viciousness and weakness in character – with crime and evil as the ultimate dirt – on the other hand. The repression of homosexual vices, in the eyes of most commentators in the Netherlands Indies newspapers, apparently meant the restoration of colonial moral strength and honour. This way of talking and writing about the scandal implied a common notion that cleaning meant showing strength, and the apparent need for that.

The trigger of the campaign in the Netherlands Indies was the publicly expressed indignation of the CSP about homosexual vices in the colony, which was specifically directed against well-known Europeans of good, official position. As has been suggested by others before, this indignation might have been fed by the increasingly conservative climate in the Netherlands Indies, and by a growing sense of insecurity, due to fear of foreign invasion and of nationalist (or communist) opposition – which the Lifebuoy soap advertisement mentioned at the beginning of this chapter also suggested. If, in that context, homosexuality moreover was related to the weakening of public morals, then the cleansing of it could become an important means to show strength and capability. Being clean, in that sense, is being strong. For the police this meant: making clean is showing strength.

Then there was, finally, the moral benefits in this particular conservative and moral hygienic climate: the discovery of the homosexual correspondence of Van Eyndthoven in Batavia, which could guarantee a successful performance of policing colonial decency, or civilization through policing. This, apparently, was especially attractive for the ambitious Public Prosecutor De la Parra, who came to Batavia only as a temporary replacement of his predecessor. The new, rather conservative Attorney General Marcella might also have been interested in an easy prey to impress his superiors (Kerkhof 1992:103). However, rumours, with the accompanying half information, suggest that not he, but Governor-General Van Starkenborgh Stachouwer – also rather conservative and relatively new – was actually the director behind the scenes for reasons of family affairs (Van Baal n.y.:329). Considering the Netherlands Indies' climate of gossip, it is hard to know the truth on this matter. However, as they were in charge of central police control, both of them were responsible.

Perhaps, in the last instance, it was not really about cleanliness, but a combination of the right climate, an easy prey, and, last but not least, ambitions that provided the basis for the suddenly overactive police operations against homosexuals in the Netherlands Indies. But this would still mean that the whole cleansing process was meant to show that being clean is being strong.

REFERENCES

Unpublished sources

Arsip Nasional Republik Indonesia, Jakarta
Archive of Binnenlands Bestuur

Nationaal Archief, The Hague
Ministerie van Koloniën, Geheime Mailrapporten, serie AA, 1914-1952, nummer toegang 2.10.36.06
Ministerie van Koloniën, Geheim Archief, 1901-1940, nummer toegang 2.10.36.51

Nederlands Instituut voor Militaire Historie, The Hague
Diary of P. van der Poel

Published sources

Abalahin, Andrew Jimenez
2003   *Prostitution and the project of modernity; A comparative study of colonial Indonesia and the Philippines, 1850-1940.* PhD thesis, Cornell University, Ithaca, NY.

Adriaanse, P.M.
1940   'Het verhoor van kinderen in zedenzaken', *De Politie* 23:280-1.

Aldrich, Robert
2003   *Colonialism and homosexuality.* Londen: Routledge.

Baal, J. van
[1986] *Ontglipt verleden; Verhaal van mijn jaren in een wereld die voorbijging. Deel 1: Tot 1947; Indisch bestuursambtenaar in vrede en oorlog.* Franeker: Wever.

Bloembergen, Marieke
2006   'Koloniale staat, politiestaat? Politieke politie en het rode fantoom in Nederlands-Indië, 1918-1927', *Leidschrift* 21-2:69-90.

2007 'The dirty work of empire; Modern policing and public order in Surabaya, 1911-1919', *Indonesia* 83:119-50.
2009 *De geschiedenis van de politie in Nederlands-Indië; Uit zorg en angst*. Amsterdam: Boom, Leiden: KITLV Uitgeverij.

Dekker, P. and S.H. Tacoma
1938 *De politie in Nederlandsch-Indië; Hare beknopte geschiedenis, haar taak, haar bevoegdheid, organisatie en optreden*. Tweede herziene druk. Soekaboemi: Insulinde. [First edition 1929.]

Dirks, Annelieke
2011 *For the youth and the future; Juvenile delinquency, colonial civil society and the late colonial state in the Netherlands Indies, 1900-1942*. PhD thesis, Leiden University.

Hadler, Jeffrey
2008 *Muslims and matriarchs; Cultural resilience in Indonesia through jihad and colonialism*. Ithaca, NY: Cornell University Press.

Handel in meisjes
1929 'Handel in meisjes', *De Nederlandsch-Indische Politiegids* 13:47-8.

Idenburg, P.J.A.
1961 'Het Nederlandsche antwoord op het Indonesische nationalisme', in: H. Baudet and I.J. Brugmans (eds), *Balans van beleid; Terugblik op de laatste halve eeuw Nederlandsch-Indië*, pp. 121-51. Assen: Van Gorcum. [Ons XXste eeuwse Verleden, in Memoires en Biografieën 3.]

Kerkhof, Gosse
1982 'Het Indische zedenschandaal: een koloniaal incident'. MA thesis, Universiteit van Amsterdam.
1992 'Het Indische zedenschandaal: een koloniaal incident', in: Raymond Feddema (ed.), *Wat beweegt de bamboe? Geschiedenissen in Zuidoost Azië*, pp. 93-118. Amsterdam: Spinhuis.

Koenders, Pieter
1996 *Tussen christelijk réveil en seksuele revolutie; Bestrijding van zedeloosheid met de nadruk op repressie van homoseksualiteit*. PhD thesis, Rijksuniversiteit Leiden.

Micheler, Stefan
2002 'Homophobic propaganda and the denunciation of same-sex-desiring men under national socialism', *Journal of the History of Sexuality* 11-1/2:95-130.

Müller, J.
1941 'Het onderzoek van misdrijven tegen de zeden verband houdende met het geslachtsleven', *De Politie* 14:477-82.

Onthullingen vrouwenhandel
1928 'Nieuwe onthullingen over vrouwenhandel', *De Nederlandsch-Indische Politiegids* 12:38-9.

Poeze, Harry A.
1994 'Political intelligence in the Netherlands Indies', in: Robert Cribb (ed.), *The late colonial state in Indonesia; Political and economic foundations of the Netherlands Indies, 1880-1942*, pp. 229-46. Leiden: KITLV Press. [Verhandelingen 163.]

Politie en prostitutie
1917 'De politie en de prostitutie', *De Nederlandsch-Indische Politiegids* 1:8.

Scherpere bestrijding prostitutie
1929 'Is scherpere bestrijding der prostitutie gewenst?', *De Nederlandsch-Indische Politiegids* 13:56-9.

Shiraishi, Takashi
1997 'Policing the phantom underground', *Indonesia* 63:1-46.

Stern, W.
1927 'Jeugdige getuigen bij misdrijven tegen de zeden', *De Nederlandsch-Indische Politiegids* 11:173.

Technische zaken
1926 'Technische zaken; De lotgevallen van meisjes, die op jeugdigen leeftijd zijn aangerand', *De Nederlandsch-Indische Politiegids* 10:136-7.

Thaib, Maisir
[1939] *Bahaja homo-sexualiteit dan bagaimana membasminja*. Fort de Kock: Djambek.

Zedenpolitie Amsterdam
1925 'Zedenpolitie te Amsterdam', *De Nederlandsch-Indische Politiegids* 8:307-9.

Zedenpolitie Batavia
1925 'Eene speciale afdeeling zedenpolitie voor Batavia', *Orgaan van den Bond voor Ondercommissarissen en Politieopzieners in Nederlandsch-Indië* 9:47-51.
1926 'Eene speciale afdeeling zedenpolitie voor Batavia', *Orgaan van den Bond voor Ondercommissarissen en Politieopzieners in Nederlandsch-Indië* 10:78-83.

6

Washing your hair in Java

George Quinn

On the evening of 7 May 1997 I joined more than 10,000 people crammed into a pilgrimage complex known as the Vanishing Place of King Joyoboyo (*Pamuksan Sri Aji Joyoboyo*) in the village of Menang about eight kilometres from Kediri in East Java. It was the eve of the first of Suro (also called the first of Muharram) which is New Year's Day in both the Islamic and Javanese calendars. On this date people flock to holy places across the island of Java to usher in the New Year with various rituals that connect the past with the future.

As night fell a thick queue of pilgrims jostled towards Joyoboyo's shrine.[1] On the steps of the shrine they sank to their haunches and approached the central sanctum in an awkward 'squat walk'. Licks of bright orange flame jumped from several incense burners as pilgrims paid homage to 'Grandfather' (*Eyang*) Joyoboyo and prayed for his blessing in the coming year.

Towards midnight the crowd around me thinned. People were drifting off somewhere. I joined a small group and went about 500 metres through the surrounding rice fields to a spectacular bathing place called Tirto Kamandanu. It consists of two concrete bathing pools, one for men and one for women, inside a walled compound. Towering above the baths is a giant stone image of the Hindu god Wisnu, and backing this an equally massive image of the elephant-headed god Ganesha. Entry to the complex was through a large, Balinese-style, split gate.

In the late night gloom scores of men were waist-deep in the water of the men's pool, or squatting at the rim of the pool, washing their hair. Some were using soap or commercial shampoos, others

---

1   The historical King Joyoboyo (more correctly but less usually spelt Jayabhaya) was a Hindu-Buddhist ruler of Kediri in the middle years of the twelfth century. Today he is popularly regarded as the ancestor of Java's kings and is accorded a veneer of Islamic identity. The pilgrims at his shrine would almost all have called themselves Muslims.

were simply dipping their hands into the water and vigorously wetting their hair. Women were doing the same in the pool next door (although I didn't personally witness this). When I asked what was going on, one young man – blinking through the lather streaming down his face – replied that he had come to Joyoboyo's vanishing place to renew his commitment to patience (*sabar*) in the face of life's trials, and to renew his trust in Allah (*tawakal*). Stoic patience and a fatalistic trust in destiny ruled by Allah are traditional virtues still much admired in Javanese society today. By ritually bathing and washing his hair on New Year's eve the young man hoped to wash away the stains of the past year in order to be clean and ready for the challenges of the new year.

There is a special term in Javanese for washing the hair, *kramas*. In the form *karamas* the word appears in Old Javanese texts where it has the meaning 'something with which to wash the hair' (Zoetmulder 1982, I:801). The Old Javanese verbal derivative *akaramas* means 'to wash one's hair, and it is this word, minus its weakly stressed prefix *a-*, that has survived into modern Javanese and has been borrowed into modern Indonesian'.[2]

Traditionally hair was thoroughly cleaned with *banyu landha*, called lye in English. In fact *banyu landha* is still widely used to wash the hair in rural society today. *Banyu landha* is made by burning dry stalks of rice (*merang*), preferably in a clean clay vessel. The charred stalks and the ashes are doused in hot water and left to soak overnight. The liquid is then strained and is ready to use as a kind of shampoo. *Banyu landha* is rich in saponin, a compound that has foaming characteristics and is highly alkaline. When used to wash the hair it dissolves the acidic oils in the hair and scalp and removes the scaly surface of hairs, leaving the scalp clean and the hair rather stiff and dry. Traditionally, after washing with *banyu landha*, the condition of hair was restored by massaging it with an extract of coconut oil called *cem-ceman*. This restored lankness, shine and oily acidity to the hair.

Traditionally, ritual washing with a special *kramas* component has been part of the major moments of transition in the human life span – marriage, giving birth, and death. According to Koentjaraningrat (1985:361) a Javanese girl goes through a ritual *kramas* ceremony after her first menstruation. In the lead-up to marriage *kramas* also has an important part to play. On the day before the formal marriage ceremony (*panggih, temu panganten*) the bride takes

---

2 It is possible that *kramas* is related to the Malay-Indonesian *-remas* (to knead / squeeze / crumple something) and the Javanese *rames* (mixed together, of food on a plate). Both terms are suggestive of the massaging and the congestion of suds and hair that accompanies *kramas*.

Figure 1. Cem-ceman

part in a bathing ritual called *siraman*. The bride and groom (in separate places) are doused with perfumed water. In more elaborate *siraman* ceremonies a make-up expert (*juru paes*) or an older relative carefully washes the bride's hair using *banyu landha* or a modern detergent-based shampoo.

In the seventh month of pregnancy a woman undergoes the *mitoni* or *tingkeban* ritual involving, among other things, ritual bathing or *siraman* with water collected from seven wells and perfumed with flower petals (Koentjaraningrat 1985:352-3). Thereafter, again according to Koentjaraningrat, between the *mitoni* ceremony and the birth the prospective mother has to observe many taboos and is required to wash her hair once a week using *banyu landha*. On the 40th day after a woman has given birth she undergoes a ritual purification assisted by a healer (*dhukun, wong pinter*) or midwife (*dhukun bayi*). The components of the ceremony are similar to those of the Islamic *ghusl* – the ritual cleansing of the whole body – with *kramas* using *banyu landha* traditionally an important component of the ceremony. Similarly, after death the body of the deceased is thoroughly washed. Traditionally this process also includes careful washing of the hair using *banyu landha* (Geertz 1960:69; Tanojo 1963:14).

Ritual washing of the hair is also part of preparations for the Islamic Fast (*pasa, siyam*). Traditionally, at least in Central Java, there were three stages of preparation for the Fast: *nyadran* (visiting the graves of ancestors, praying for their repose and tidying up the graves), *padusan* (ritual washing) and *megengan* (usually a *slametan* meal with prayers on the night before the commencement of the Fast). *Padusan* is conducted on the day before the commencement of the Fast and may involve the ritual cleaning of key household implements like mats, kitchen utensils, implements for hulling and pounding rice and so on. *Padusan* was, and for some people still is, conducted at ritual bathing places like Umbul Cokrotulung near Klaten, Umbul Pengging between Kartasura and Boyolali, Umbul Kayangan in Wonogiri district and Umbul Berjo in Karanganyar (Tok Suwarto 2005). *Padusan* invariably demands special washing of the hair. This is 'a physical and spiritual preparation to clear, clean and sanctify the mind so that when the Fast begins you are not distracted by base appetites' (Tok Suwarto 2005).

And as we have seen, ritual washing, including *kramas*, remains a significant component in preparations for the New Year. Pre-New Year bathing and *kramas* may be conducted in private at home, but very commonly it is a public affair in conjunction with visits to holy grave sites or, in a few places, with New Year's Eve immersion (*kungkum*) rituals at the confluence of rivers or in springs, as happens at the Tugu Suharto site in the western suburbs of Semarang.

6 *Washing your hair in Java*

The ritual washing of hair seems to derive its power from a convergence of four main elements. First, from ancient times hair – especially women's hair – has had a fetishized character. It is a body-part – even a bought-and-sold artifact – with special symbolic significance that seems to be both psycho-sexual in character and related to the regulation of Javanese society with its Islamic religious order.

Anthony Reid (1988:79-80) observes that in pre-modern Southeast Asia 'hair was a crucial symbol and emanation of the self' and 'enormous care was given to the care of the hair, to ensure that it was always black, lustrous, abundant, and sweet-smelling'. For both men and women the refusal to cut the hair, and conversely the shaving of the head, have been seen as acts that can confer power on an individual, or at the very least define a person's social status. In a Javanese story, the husband of Ratu Kalinyamat – the queen of sixteenth-century Jepara – was murdered on the instructions of Arya Penangsang of Jipang. In her quest for justice Ratu Kalinyamat meditated naked and vowed never to cut her hair until her husband's death had been avenged. As her hair grew, so too her sexual allure and the moral authority of her cause grew, attracting the attention of Sultan Adiwijaya who successfully engineered the murder of Arya Penangsang.

There is a popular tradition that Prince Diponegoro commanded his followers to cut off their hair to distinguish themselves from fellow Javanese who were Dutch collaborators and whose hair was normally long in the fashion of the day (Reid 1988:82; Yudhistira 2007). Nyi Ageng Serang, the elderly aristocrat who became an ally of Prince Diponegoro, is reputed to have shaved her head bald while fighting the Dutch. For a woman this was a shocking act of self-mutilation. She abandoned her femininity and became in effect a 'man' – that is, a ruthless guerilla fighter bereft of the weakness, softness and beauty that was traditionally seen as a characteristic of femininity embodied in a full head of hair.[3]

Second, the ritual washing of hair takes place at key moments of transition from one state to another – the transition from everyday living to the liminally holy fasting month of Ramadhan, from an old year to a new one, from childhood to sexually mature adulthood, from childlessness to motherhood, from unmarried to married life, and the ultimate change of state... from life to death. In the incident I observed at the Vanishing Place of King Joyoboyo, the ritual washing of hair took place around midnight - at the exact moment when the old year morphed into the new.

---

3   There are many examples of hair as fetish in more recent Javanese history. During the *Revolusi* (1945-1949) many nationalist fighters refused to cut their hair (Yudhistira 2007). Of special interest is the 'long hair' (*rambut gondrong*) controversy of the 1970s, which I see as an instance of resistance by the older generation to the adoption of long hair by young men who 'didn't deserve it'.

151

Third, in ritual contexts – including in ritual contexts today – hair is washed in *banyu landha* made from rice stalks. It seems to me possible that there is symbolic significance in the use of rice stalks. Rice stalks are used not only because they are a source of alkaline foaming saponins, but because rice has immense symbolic importance in Javanese society embodied in the myth of Sri and Sadono.[4] Indeed the very appearance of rice may be symbolically appropriate to the *kramas* ritual – it grows in paddy fields like hair growing on the head and flourishes when it is bathed in water.

Finally, the power of the *kramas* ritual must come in part from its presence in popular story. To give one example, in an almost universally known episode drawn from Java's classical cycle of shadow plays – the *wayang purwa* – Drupadi, the wife of Wrekudara (also called Bima) is insulted and humiliated by Dursasana. Drupadi vows that she will wash her hair in the blood of Dursasana. Dursasana suffers a terrible death at the hands of Wrekudara during the Bharatayudha battle. Wrekudara sucks up Dursasana's blood and deposits it in his battle helmet and it is there that Drupadi washes her hair in her tormentor's blood.

It is a commonplace of anthropology that in many societies, perhaps universally, hair is a powerful symbol of sexuality as well as a component in the symbolic regulation of the social-religious order. In religious contexts water (and its transformation, blood) is widely seen as a purifying agent that can revivify a degraded life.[5] In Javanese society hair is decidedly multi-signifying. On the one hand it is a crown (*mahkota*) growing from the sacrosanct precinct of the head. It is a symbol of human beauty, perseverance and power. On the other hand it symbolizes bestial character and problematic sexuality. It is a remnant of animality that reminds us of the depths of defilement and depravity that we are capable of descending to. In the iconography of the classical shadow theatre that underpins so much of the modern iconography of Java, the depraved, rapacious ogres are hairy, and especially have long unkempt hair on their heads (in addition to other markers of bestiality like fangs, bulging eyes, loud voices, big loping jerky strides and florid faces).

Just as Drupadi washed away the stain of her defilement through a ritual act of *kramas*, so also the present *kramas* is a ritual of purification that has religious and sexual meaning. It both extirpates

---

4 Sri (more fully, Dewi Sri) is the indigenous rice goddess of Java who lives in countless myths and folktales. Together with her consort Sadono (who, in some versions, is her brother), Sri is the focal point of rituals intended to secure good rice harvests and general agricultural fertility.
5 For key studies see, for example, Leach 1958; Douglas 1966; Hallpike 1969; Hershman 1974; Hiltebeitel and Miller 1998. None of the above, however, deal directly with Indonesian societies.

the accumulated mistakes and wounds of the past, and also prepares the subject of the ritual for a new start in a new estate. Hair emerges from beneath the skin, from the interior of the body, and it is constantly growing. It therefore lies at a kind of transition point between interior and exterior – at the boundary that distinguishes individuals from their environment. Perhaps this is why hair is also symbolically associated with boundaries and transition, with the marking of boundaries and with preparation to cross them.

A RITUAL IN DECLINE?

From ancient times bathing places (usually called *padusan* or *patirtan*) have been important centres of community life and religious ritual in Java. Probably the best-known surviving pre-Islamic bathing places are the Belahan and Jalatunda sites in East Java. Bathing pools were important in royal residences too, witness, among others, the Taman Sari pool in the Jogjakarta palace and the Tasikardi royal bathing pool in the centre of the ancient reservoir south of Old Banten. Early mosques were often surrounded by moats where worshippers would undertake their pre-prayer ritual ablutions (a survival of such a moat can be seen at the Grand Mosque in Old Banten), and bathing pools were to be found in many places of religious retreat, such as those that still survive at Jumprit near Parakan, Central Java, and Umbul Pengging between Kartasura and Boyolali, Central Java.

At the beginning of this chapter I described my experience of ritual *kramas* at Tirto Kamandanu bathing place adjacent to the Vanishing Place of King Joyoboyo. Let me now cite a somewhat different experience of *kramas*, reported in the Javanese-language magazine *Panjebar Semangat* in 1997.

> Purification rituals at bathing places are commonly held towards the end of the month of Ruwah. Unfortunately today these rituals seem to be losing their meaning. If you look at them in their outward guise you might think they are more popular than ever. But the fact is that purification rituals are turning into tourist attractions with people flocking to them in unprecedented numbers. Quite often the event is enlivened with music from a *dangdut* orchestra.
>
> When you think about it, it is not the purpose of purification rituals to give men and women the chance to splash around in a pool groping and pinching one another. The real purpose of the ritual is to give everyone a chance to purify themselves in the lead up to the fasting month of Ramadhan.

| George Quinn

> [...] So we shouldn't be surprised if Surti, a sincere and perhaps naive young woman, felt quite uncomfortable with what she found at Kahyangan, Dlepih near Tirtomoyo. She had set out from home with the intention of preparing for the Fast by purifying herself under the waterfall in the pool at Kahyangan, the same pool where Panembahan Senopati had once immersed himself in meditation. But after less than 10 minutes in the water she had clambered out. 'I had to get out of there', she said. 'People were just horsing around, splashing water over each other and making ribald jokes.'
>
> Raden Ngabei Suraksobudoyo, the custodian at Kahyangan, was likewise far from happy with the situation. 'But what can I do?' he said. 'They're just children, really. As long as they don't do anything genuinely debauched, I'm not going to stop them. The guardian spirit here is quite capable of distinguishing between pilgrims who come with serious intent, and casual visitors who only want to have a bit of fun.' (*Upacara padusan 1997*)

Many pilgrims, like Surti, find at best a degraded sanctity at hitherto holy sacred places - degraded to the point where they feel they can no longer wash their hair in public there in a ritually significant way. *Kramas* with commercial shampoos has largely contracted to the domestic sphere rather than in public places, though in the domestic sphere increasing prosperity has brought it to countless millions of Indonesians. Yet even in the privacy of the home *kramas* retains social-religious functions. Rather than purity it is cleanliness, as urged on citizens by the state, that is emphasized. But even cleanliness seems to be secondary to the expression of individual choice and the creation of a certain self-image that conforms to the interests of the state and the business community. Through the purchase of commercial shampoos consumers exercise their individuality in a way that establishes a personal connection with the manufacturer and with a brand name. Personal sensuality and the pursuit of luxury are dominating values driving the use of shampoo. Advertisements portray shampooed hair as shiny, bouncy and easy to manage – attributes that the modern state and its business allies expect of citizens and consumers. Shampooing the hair is also a tactile, very sensual act that makes hair sexually attractive – but (and this is important) *safely* sexually attractive. The act of shampooing the hair and displaying the results of shampooing the hair exude a sensuousness and sexuality that is not threatening to conservative community values, the state, or to the conduct of business.

Kramas also remains important to the public expression of religious piety. Muslim women are urged with increasing insistence to wear a headscarf as a sign of their Islamic identity and piety. The headscarf (normally called a *jilbab*, sometimes *krudung* or *tudung*) covers the hair completely and drapes over the shoulders. But the wearing of the *jilbab* with its close-fitting skullcap can cause problems. Women may develop dandruff or suffer hair loss, the scalp may become itchy and the hair may exude an unpleasant smell. Islamic books and magazines recommend frequent *kramas* to deal with these problems. One popular book, *Jilbab dan rambut sehat* (The headscarf and healthy hair) for example, tells readers that frequent washing of the hair with shampoo (at least once every three days, and every day if necessary) is 'absolutely essential, in fact an obligation (*kewajiban*), for women who wear the Islamic headscarf' (Ismiaulia and Solihah 1991:27). *Kramas* for Muslim women is not only a solution to a hair-health problem. It also helps them become more 'Islamic' by making possible the comfortable wearing of the *jilbab*. It is even argued that wearing the *jilbab* helps Muslim women protect their hair from dirt, thereby implementing Islamic injunctions on cleanliness (Ismiaulia and Solihah 1991:42).

Thus for Muslim women *kramas* is portrayed as component of public piety essential to the regulation of dress in a properly Islamic way. It is also of psycho-sexual importance, keeping beauteous but hidden the hair that is a symbol of female sexuality that should be seen only by a woman's *muhrim* (spouse and close family).

Even in the commercialized present with its ever encroaching pressure to adopt an Islamic persona in public, shampooing the hair can still connect an individual to the past and be a marker of Javanese identity.

Funeral customs are notoriously resistant to change and anecdotal evidence seems to suggest that in Javanese society ritual *kramas* of the deceased is still very much alive. In Java's local pilgrimage practices – a sub-culture that is burgeoning in a quite extraordinary way – ritual hair washing is still widely practiced as my experience at the Vanishing Place of King Joyoboyo suggests. The equally extraordinary burgeoning of the middle class wedding culture demands that many features of traditional weddings be 're-cycled' (albeit mostly in de-sacralized guise) and one of these is the *siraman* with its *kramas* component.

A number of manufacturers of shampoos market brands that use natural *merang* extract. These include the widely popular Sariayu and Mustika Ratu brands. Consumers who choose these *merang* shampoos probably do so because they see the word *merang* on the label as a marker (however degraded) of the authority of Javanese tradition and of Javanese identity. In a society in which foreign consumer items are highly valued, and Indonesian tradition can often be problematic or marginal, choosing *shampoo merang* may be one of the few ways left to them to say 'I choose Java' while at the same time being *moderen*.

Figure 2. Shampoo merang

REFERENCES

Douglas, Mary
1966   *Purity and danger*. London: Routledge & Kegan Paul.
Geertz, Clifford
1960   *The religion of Java*. Chicago and London: University of Chicago Press.
Hallpike, Christopher
1969   'Social hair', *Man* 4:256-64.
Hershman, P.
1974   'Hair, sex and dirt', *Man* 9:274-98.
Hiltebeitel, Alf and Barbara D. Miller (eds)
1998   *Hair; Its power and meaning in Asian cultures*. Foreword by Ganath Obeyesekere. Albany, NY: State University of New York Press.
Ismiaulia, Vidya and Diah Solihah
1991   *Jilbab dan rambut sehat*. Jakarta: Fikahati Aneska.
Koentjaraningrat
1985   *Javanese culture*. Singapore: Oxford University Press.
Leach, Edmund
1958   'Magical hair', *Journal of the Royal Anthropological Institute* 88:147-64.
Reid, Anthony
1988   *Southeast Asia in the age of commerce, 1450-1680; Vol. 1: The lands below the winds*. Chiang Mai: Silkworm Books.
Suwarto, Tok
2005   'Kalau orang Jawa berpuasa', *Pikiran Rakyat*, 17 October.
Tanojo, R.
1963   *Primbon Djawa petung kuna, tata tjara kasripahan*. Jogjakarta: Serodja.
Upacara padusan
1997   'Upacara padusan; Dudu laku spiritual maneh', *Panjebar Semangat* 6(8 February):15, 35.
Yudhistira, Aria W.
2007   'Rambut dan sejarah Indonesia', *Scribd*. http://www.scribd.com/doc/40248905/Rambut-Dan-Sejarah-Indonesia (accessed 19-7-2011).
Zoetmulder, P.J.
1982   *Old Javanese-English dictionary*. With the collaboration of S.O. Robson. 's-Gravenhage: Nijhoff. Two vols. [KITLV.]

7

Tropical spa cultures, eco-chic, and the complexities of new Asianism

Bart Barendregt

> Asia is like God. You cannot categorically deny or affirm its existence. No one knows where it begins, where it ends, or whether there is a way to define it.
> Goenawan Mohamad[1]

Western travellers, tourists and scholars have long perceived the 'Orient' as authentic, sensual and mysterious, and for many even today, Asia represents all that is lost to modern (Western) man. Such musings say more about the Western audience's longing for a sensual other expressed through a depiction of the East as a place of splendour, purity and its inhabitants' closeness to nature. However, more recently the Southeast Asian middle and upper classes themselves seem to have tapped into such stereotypes in order to retrieve an authentic life experience that, according to many, has been threatened by ongoing modernization, globalization and, most feared of all, Westernization. As an answer to these threats, over the last few years a regional culture has emerged that ironically uses the vocabulary, ideas and images of a lifestyle of health, beauty and spirituality that currently is so fashionable in the same West. In this contribution I focus on the most eye-catching manifestation of this 'New Asian' lifestyle, the tropical spa.

Spas are often traced to the thirteenth-century iron-bearing spring at the Wallonian town of Spa (Crismer 1989). Yet curative baths only become a trend in fifteenth-century Renaissance Europe when scholarly treatises devoted to the subject first appear and rudimentary spa directories were composed in England and

---

1 As quoted in Jong Won Lee 2006:2.

Italy.² By the mid seventeenth century it was an accepted habit for European elites to spend their time at mineral springs or at seaside resorts and eventually such resorts also provided Europe's newly developing bourgeoisie with leisure time away from industrial life (Mackaman 1998). The three – new rich, leisure, and spa – would from the nineteenth century onwards be even more closely knit together. As spas became commercially interesting, water from curative springs was bottled and exported as far as the United States. In 1826 a first American spa resort was opened up in Saratoga, New York, its name being derived from the word for 'medicine water' in Mohawk, the language of Native Indians who had settled the area (Corbett 2001:171). Within the context of the new American 'superspa' the Native American link was not only used to give credibility to the curative powers of the springs but was soon appropriated in tourism, a strategy that ever since has been widely used in the spa industry. In the late 1970s the first truly modern day spas appear, a process that was given impetus by the wellness revolution of the 1990s with its desire for slow living and an emphasis on bodily well-being. It was accompanied by a return to more craftsman-like practices and an appreciation of local products (Parkins and Craig 2006), and traditional and exotic prescriptions such as massage and Chinese medicine seem to fit this new bill. It is this renewed concept of the spa that attracted well-to-do visitors from Asia and in the early 1990s was also taken up by the first destination resorts in Thailand.³ Since then the spa industry is one of the fastest growing sectors in Southeast Asian travel and leisure, the spa even being used as a component in development strategies.⁴

---

2   These books included William Turner's *A book of the natures and properties of the baths of England* (1562), and two Venetian publications: Andrea Bacci's *De thermis* (1571) and Thomasso Guinta's *De balneis* (1553), which listed over 200 springs in Europe (Crebbin-Bailey, Harcup and Harrington 2005). Mackaman (1998) refers to nineteenth-century French directories and novels as a profitable industry serving both to promote and earn from spa tourism. For an early twentieth-century example, see Duguid (1968).
3   The development of the modern Asian spa market as a tourist phenomenon is hence relatively young, and starts with the opening of three major spas (including the Oriental and Chiva-Som) in Thailand in 1993 (Crebbin-Bailey, Harcup and Harrington 2005:30). These Asian spas focused especially on the art of massage, with limited use of mechanical equipment so as to distinguish them from ordinary beauty saloons. Spreading to major tourist resorts such as Phuket, Samui, and Bali, spas would soon become popular in the Southeast Asian hotel scene, but also as day spas in malls or shopping centers.
4   In South India, the states of Tamil Nadu, Karnataka and Kerala have, since the late 1990s, promoted themselves as health tourism destinations for both Westerners and visitors from well-off Asian economies (Hudson 2003:283). In Malaysia the promotion of spa resorts has similarly targeted the well-to-do in neighbouring countries.

7 Tropical spa cultures, eco-chic, and the complexities of new Asianism

Today, tropical spa is a term that refers to resorts, most of them located in Southeast Asia (hence the adjective 'tropical') where well-to-do tourists from both the East and West are pampered in luxurious, exotic and often 'mystical' settings.[5] Tropical spas offer a myriad of services including beauty, fitness, medicine and spiritual relief. Whereas most spas are open to both men and women, consumption of their practices seems highly gendered in nature and conditioned by the demands of industrial society (Hudson 2003:287): men are generally attracted by health and functionality of their bodies whereas women are more concerned with their appearance. However, in this contribution I am more interested in the different ways visitors from the East and West consume spas. I focus on the ways the tropical spa is attracting Western participants through guides, coffee table books and web directories, a method that historically has proven to be very successful. But the tropical spa phenomenon also serves to promote a New Asian lifestyle among the local well-to-do. It does so by emphasizing the spa as a tradition with local roots, and by using elements of local landscapes that visually stress Asianness. In various ways, this New Asianism is expressed through ideas of health, beauty and spirituality. Let us now turn to the first symptoms of this new Asian lifestyle.

RISE OF THE WELLNESS INDUSTRY OR EMERGENT REGIONALISM?

Early 2005 saw the publication of Erlinda Enriquez Panlilio and Felice Prudente Sta Maria's book *Slow food; Philippine culinary traditions*, which not coincidentally is dedicated to the founder of the Manila chapter of the International Wine and Food Society. The book offers a lush variety of Philippine foods under headings such as 'Pospas – my mother's legacy', 'The vanishing Tawilis of Lake Taal' and 'Christmas of my childhood', shading authentic dishes into the memories of a passing age. 'Today one wonders about the future of Philippine cooking', the introduction notes, 'Slow food ... traditional food ... food prepared from scratch with no shortcuts, using only the finest ingredients acquitted at the peak of their season, is a vital and valuable component of every Filipino's sense of self' (Panlilio and Prudente Sta Maria 2005:6-7).

Elsewhere, a Javanese businesswoman, Martha Tilaar, popularly known as the 'mother of natural based cosmetics', launched her

---

5 In a 2006 survey on most popular spa resorts by the UK based magazine *Traveller*, 6 out of the 10 most popular spas worldwide were located in Asia. See http://www.cntraveller.com/ReadersAwards/2006/Spas/ (accessed September 2006).

Dewi Sri line of body scrubs, which is now popularly advertised as 'the secret of the tropical Goddess'. Her website[6] explains that 'an old Indonesian folklore tells of an ancient remedy inspired by the Goddess of fertility and prosperity of rice fields and crop harvest. Her beautiful, healthy skin is the emanation of a timeless beauty ritual enhanced by traditional bathing. Based on this secret, a series of treatments was born.' Tilaar's recipes are believed to be based on the traditional ingredients used by the princesses of the palaces of Central Java, which only adds to the products' aura of mystery. These ancient secrets for beauty and health are now also available to ordinary women in both the East and the West.

Finally, moving eastward, the island of Bali was once called the Island of Gods but has since gradually become more of a sanctuary for those looking for self-actualization. Since the late 1990s it has been the Island of Tropical Spas as there are literally hundreds of spa resorts on the island, varying in size and facilities on offer. Here one can enjoy a traditional massage, aromatherapy, or simply relax, and afterwards enjoy an al fresco organic dinner while listening to traditional gamelan music. Slow food Filipino style, the ancient secrets of Javanese beauty, and in particular the Island of Tropical Spas: these are but few examples of the recent boom in Asian style eco-chic.[7] But, what do these products have in common and why are these and similar products suddenly so enormously popular throughout Southeast Asia?

Products that stress the local, the slow, and the natural are a current fad among the new wealthy of Southeast Asia's cities. The well-to-do often have come to consider consuming such products to be indispensable in dealing with the alienating effects of those difficult-to-handle, abstract processes of globalization, modernization and Westernization. While this remedy is very local in nature, I suspect that similar things can be found throughout the non-Western world, and argue that this model of consumption contrasts with its Western counterpart. For this reason the Southeast Asian middle and upper classes' current fascination with beauty, health, and all things natural can be seen as a distinct interpretation of global culture: an Asian

---

6 See http://www.dewisrispa.com/ (accessed September 2006).
7 The term ethnic chic as a development is traced to the 1990s when Euro-American populations started to desire clothing and items that were ethnically inspired. The term is now used to refer to the cultural production of formerly ethnic clothes that have moved into the mainstream fashion arenas internationally. Niessen, Leshkowich and Jones (2003), for example, signal the emergence of Indo chic; haute couture interpretations of Vietnamese peasant and elite clothing. From the world of fashion the terminology has spilt over into interior design. Here ethnic chic (or 'etnik chic') comes to stand for 'the use of carvings that are ethnically inspired and applied in the context of modern living houses' (Susilowati and Zi 2003:1).

response to the wellness industry of the West. Especially the nouveau riche, who until recently primarily defined themselves through their patterns of consumption, but who otherwise lack a shared identity, now seem to desire a more 'authentic' cultural experience. At the same time, the preference for natural, local, and more authentic products confronts us with a rupture, as the Southeast Asian middle class suddenly no longer seems solely obsessed with consuming the West and its 'symbols of modernity'. On the contrary, it is now modern and fashionable to read the 'Asian philosophies' of Deepak Chopra or to build a house based on the principles of Feng Shui or Vastu Sastra. Rather than fast food chains like McDonald's or Pizza Hut, the latest buzz word is slow food: one eats *nasi kampung* (village-style fried rice) in posh restaurants and drinks traditional and organically grown coffees at Starbucks or local equivalent of such classy coffee bars.

These practices, which I group together as Asian style eco-chic, are modish combinations of lifestyle politics, a dash of environmental awareness, and an urge to get back to the natural and authentic.[8] More than that, they are increasingly part of the identikit of the well-to-do in this part of the world. In mimicking the lifestyle and shopping practices of their equivalents in the West, they seem to demonstrate their cosmopolitan consciousness, combined with an appreciation of local (read: regional and Asian) culture. One of the ironies of such global flows is that as a result Asia rediscovers itself through the West!

What are we dealing with here? Cultural nostalgia, self-Orientalism, or some sort of elite cosmopolitanism? It surely is a cosmopolitan consciousness, which is then expressed in often patriotic ways: Philippine food as a sense of self, Dewi Sri as an ancient Javanese secret, or, as we will see, the tropical spa as 'Asia's botanic and cultural heritage'. In that case one could speak of cosmo-patriotism (see also Jurriëns and De Kloet 2007) a very rooted kind of cosmopolitanism. Being local in a globalizing world was long considered far from hip or modern, and thus locality had to be transformed and reinvented in new ways. Eco-chic Asian style offers such new opportunities for constructing community, and, as I will argue, it has therefore become part of an All-Asian renaissance and an elite lifestyle associated with it: New Asianism. A similar stress of a shared pan-Asian culture can elsewhere be found in fashion, cinema, science and not the

---

8 According to Tanqueray (2000), living an eco-friendly lifestyle has become chic. The dust jacket of her book *Eco-chic* states that 'not so long ago, environmental awareness was left almost exclusively to the experts or the eccentrics. However, now a more environmental friendly approach to life is something more and more people aspire to […]. No longer the domain of the "brown rice and sandals" brigade, eco-consciousness means knowing that you don't have to sacrifice taste or style to look after your body and the environment.'

least politics. However, Asian style eco-chic is the most visible of these manifestations and one that can be found in the everyday domain. It's in the ways the well-to-do dress, what they decide to eat, and more broadly in one's approach to life as such. For many Asianism has become a preferred lifestyle, though one that is full of contradictions, not least because it is one that most Asians can hardly afford; it is neither new nor solely based on the ancient secrets so often used in its advertisements; and it is a contradictory mixture of outright commercialism with a touch of instant spirituality. Importantly, it is neither fully Western inspired nor completely Asian. Apparently different audiences are consuming Asia in different ways and for different reasons as the case of tropical spa culture here will illustrate.

The tropical spa is the place where ideas of a cosmopolitan lifestyle, eco-chic and Asianism merge. Tropical spas are lavishly designed destination resorts where one can stay overnight and where visitors are offered an amalgam of beauty, health and spiritual practices. It is perhaps more appropriate to speak of tropical spa cultures rather than of a unitary phenomenon as they are a conglomeration of different sorts of newly invented or old, often profoundly romanticized traditions and therapies. The resorts, which today are primarily found in Southeast Asia (hence the adjective 'tropical'), are aimed at the wealthy Western and East Asian traveller but in many cases also at the local well-to-do. Although these groups might consume spa culture for various reasons as we will see below, tropical spas are seldom run either solely by Westerners or exclusively by Asians. These resorts are typically international ventures: the luxury resort Chiva Som, for instance, has a Thai manager and a Swiss hotel director, which counters the easy accusation that this is merely an imported foreign phenomenon. Moreover, in its outward appearance and in line with other forms of eco-chic, the tropical spa culture as a rule stresses the local, for example either indigenous practices or well-known traditions from neighboring Southeast Asian societies.

The past few years have seen an enormous boom in these tropical spas, and hundreds of them can be found in Bali alone. Bali, however, is but one of the many areas visited by the international leisure class that travels between similar resorts in Phuket, Kerala, Manila, or Singapore. Moreover, these spas have given rise to numerous derivative products, ranging from Martha Tilaar's Dewi Spa body scrubs, CDs with spa lounge music, and beautifully illustrated coffee table books that promote the new tropical spa culture as a New Asian life style that also can be enjoyed by the less wealthy. Before looking at such derivative products and the ways they spread spa culture beyond the resorts, we must first look at the ancient tradition of healing waters. It will help us understand the current popularity of tropical spas.

7 Tropical spa cultures, eco-chic, and the complexities of new Asianism

FROM HEALING WATER TO ASIAN BEAUTY

Although ironically the idea of the spa is a modern import from the West, Asian societies have long been familiar with the healing qualities of water, especially springs. One of the most famous examples is the Godavari River. Shelter to Rama and Sita in the Hindu epic *Ramayana*, it is believed to flow underground, invisible to the human eye. The river is said to be connected to underground basins, flowing into fountainheads or bowls supplying holy water to India's many temples. Holy purification water or *tirta* is also central to Balinese religion. The purification water is generally seen as a gift from the ancestral deities to their descendants, and almost each Balinese temple has its own source of water that is used to produce it. *Tirta* can help its consumers to remain conscious, free from sorcery and it can even save one from death (Ottino 2000). Hence, *tirta* is both vitalizing and purifying, albeit the latter tends nowadays to be stressed. In the aftermath of the growing worldwide popularity of the wellness industry and eco-chic, ideas of healing water are reinterpreted, both in the West and in Asia, with luxury spas becoming Asia's hottest trend of the 1990s.

Figure 1. Tirta Empul, Bali

Whereas nowadays Southeast Asia is a popular destination for spa and wellness tourism, water is also here no longer the only medication used. Nevertheless some spa resorts, like the Begawan Giri ('noble hermit of the mountain') and Mandara ('a reference to the mythology of the sacred centre in Hinduism'),[9] both located in Bali, are built next to what are respectively considered a sacred spring and the supposedly powerful confluence of two rivers. Emphasis also has slowly moved towards prevention rather than cures, putting beauty on an equal footing with health. A Los Angeles visitor summarizes the appeal of the Southeast Asian spa as follows:

> A must see for anyone who wants to witness paradise. I made my way up there [...] and found something so magical and beautiful that it was inspirational. I could not stop talking about it for days. The Asian Spas are so much more intoxicating and beautiful than the European Spas. The packaging of the products with natural fibers, banana leaves, lotus leaves, etc. is perfectly pleasing. They are politically correct and appealing ('Bali is becoming the Asian Spa Mecca, October 30, 1999').[10]

Tropical spas include Bali's pioneering Nusa Dua Spa, founded in 1994, where nowadays 26 therapists perform approximately 80 therapies a day. But they also include the 26 million US dollar Chiva-Som in the Gulf of Siam, a health resort that prides itself in blending well-being with exquisite luxury. One American visitor commented that:

> If you are looking for a relaxing spiritual cleanse coupled with a daily workout program, this is the place. I woke up to yoga, had 3 great tasting healthy meals and a massage each day. I couldn't ask for more. I felt the staff was extremely accomodating [sic] and paid close attention to little details (they even presented me with a basket of beautiful roses and a small cake on my birthday - that was truly a surprise!) The menu of spa services was excellent - my most memorable was an hour consultation with a monk and an hour with a hypnotherapist. I had my first Thai style massage there also.[11]

What we are dealing with here is simply a successful commercial practice that is targeted at the well-to-do, mostly Western tourists. The first part might be true, because like most life style practices,

---

9   A mythological mountain of Balinese Hinduism from which flow the waters of eternal youth.
10   From Amazon.com reviews of *The tropical spa*, see http://www.amazon.com/Tropical-Spa-Secrets-Health-Relaxation/dp/0794602622 (accessed September 2006).
11   Hua Hin: Chiva-Som Luxury Health Resort: 'Great stay at Chiva-Som', 10-9-2005: A TripAdvisor Member, Seattle

tropical spa culture has definite commercial aspects, explaining civilizations in terms of commodities and showing that what is so often despised by many Asians is Western liberalism and not the modernity of late capitalism. Regarding the last part of this criticism, however, not only the Western affluent make up the audience here, but also their Asian counterparts, although both categories of participants partake in spa culture for different reasons. Western, but also East Asian travellers visit spas as the resorts address the wish for an unpolluted, pure and very consumer-friendly version of the tropics. The local well-to-do, on the other hand, interestingly seem to frequent spas to pronounce and revalidate their own cultural roots. Different needs and tastes are also reflected in the sort of spa one visits. Whereas foreign travellers have a preference for spa destination resorts, where they can take a swim, enjoy a massage, while making the resort a background to their holidays, Javanese middle class members, as an illustration, seem to prefer so-called day spa salons. To them such spas are the place to prepare bride and groom for upcoming weddings, occasions that in this part of the world may take up to several days with the couple, for each episode, being donned in different clothing, make up, but also, and here the spa comes in again, being subjected to various ritual baths. Well-known spas, such as Martha Tilaar's salon Day Spa, offer so-called 'pre wedding packets' (*paket pengantin*). Such packets generally include services such as *mandi Ken Dedes* (a 3,5 hours treatment, including herbal baths, purification with scented smoke and the use of 'romantic' oils), facial treatment, and manicure. All of these services are offered at various occasions and to both bride and groom.[12] These services can be enjoyed at the spa compound but also back at home. The latter variant does obviously not differ much from the more traditional services offered by the *dukun pengantin* (traditional beautician for brides on Java) as described by Puntowati (1992).

In addition, many Javanese middle class women regularly visit nearby day spas, to have a traditional cream bath, or to enjoy aromatherapy and to them spas have become inherent to a modern though very genuine Asian lifestyle. In participating in spa culture, they have rediscovered treatments their grandmothers were fond of, but, by putting them in the context of an international spa culture, such therapies suddenly have become very modern and are no longer deemed backwards, village-like and therefore cheap. For these women (and to a lesser extent men) spa culture addresses various needs: it not only offers health, beauty and spiritual practices, a

---

12 Ken Dedes was the queen of Singosari and famed for her beauty. Legend has it that her bathing place was situated in Singosari, just outside of Malang. The local population believes that taking a bath at this spot would make one look young, charismatic and shiny (Suwardono 2007).

place where one in a relaxed atmosphere can meet with like-minded people, but it significantly also covers the need for social make up.

According to Benge (2003:15), it is exactly the focus on nature's abundance and her rich aromas that gives Asian beauty such an enormous worldwide appeal. In this it falls in line with eco-chic's fashionableness; 'while a deepening commitment to a kind of environmental consumerism now grips people in the West, it has been the mainstay of Asian culture until recent economic development'. Back to the basics, however contradictory this might sound, is therefore the 'new concept' of modern beauty. At present these spas, while focusing on traditional Asian beauty treatments, also include health therapies and ways to get back in touch with one's spirituality. Some spas, like the Banyan Tree spa in Pukhet, explicitly embrace Buddhist philosophy. Others only make vague references to any of the world's religions or promote themselves as karmic resorts that offer programs to de-stress or overcome trauma. In some societies spas more overtly address religious particularities. Responding to the emergence of an ever increasing Muslim middle class and its need to publicly express itself, Muslim day spas have become a lucrative niche in the market in Indonesia in places such as Jakarta, Yogyakarta and Palembang. Muslim salon spas exclusively target a female Muslim audience with services that are roughly similar to their more secular equivalents, but overall they promise a more serious and secluded atmosphere.[13]

In sum: Over time spas have come to emphasize leisure and wellness, and as a consequence spa culture has become a favorite destination for many, both in the West and in the East. Although spas are said not to be traditional to Asia, centuries of its health and beauty practices are being used and repackaged as the 'worldwide vogue for spiritual and mental, as well as physical, fitness has been at the core of Asian beauty custom since the beginning of time', as one handbook for spa aficionados notes (Benge 2003:11). Access to the spa resorts seems restricted to the happy few, for now. That said, there are other ways in which to share in the tremendously popular spa culture, ways that make an important contribution to the wider recognition of the spa ideals of beauty, health, and spirituality and, for that matter, New Asianism, of which it is increasingly becoming a part. To study the ways New Asianism as a lifestyle is gaining ground among affluent Southeast Asians it is informative

---

13 Combining the wellness industry with the religious is very much in line with the desecularization of other domains of public culture (Forbes and Mahan 2000). Illustrative of this phenomenon is a wide range of Christian health centres that today offer their services to a devout public, but also publications such as *Simply relevant* (2007:5), whose introduction reads 'Ok, so what's a Bible series got to do with a spa, you ask? Well this series is all about how we find refreshment in Jesus – how much he wants to renew and bless us. And what better metaphor for that than a spa?'

7 Tropical spa cultures, eco-chic, and the complexities of new Asianism

to have a closer look not only at the resorts, but also at the ways spa culture has been traditionally disseminated through public media.

SPAS MEDIATED, OR ASIA BROUGHT HOME

The tropical spa is in all respects a sanctuary for the senses: blending taste (spa cuisine ranging from after-massage snacks to Asian golden muesli), touch (a sensory spa journey consisting, for example, of a four hand massage) and smell (aroma therapy is one of the most popular treatments at tropical spas), thus breaking with the adage that our age is primarily a visual one. Still, the visual continues to matter, as it is instrumental in spreading spa culture's message beyond the resorts. Brochures, books and websites (see below) tell the story of an elegant fusing of indoor and outdoor spaces, the modern and the traditional, primitive (read: authentic) and the convenient mixing of, for example, five star amenities with a genuine local ambience. It is to these visual elements that I now turn.

Nowadays respected resorts have their private-label products, like the Spice Islands oils from *Esens* (available at the Nusa Dua Spa, Bali) or the *Dewi Sri* line of body scrubs with which to recreate the spa experience in your own home. One of the most eye-catching, or better ear-catching ways to do this has been the recent trend of repackaging otherwise traditional tunes as spa music.[14] Here, however, I will restrict myself to print magazines and coffee table books and the way they represent and disseminate tropical spa culture and associated eco-chic practices, as these are among the most important carriers of what is now fast becoming the trend of New Asianism. Without the authors possibly being aware, these books and magazines historically have their predecessors in the early spa publications of the sixteenth century, nineteenth-century guides and novels describing spa life in France (Mackaman 1998) or in-flight guides such as the 1960s Pan Am spa directory. Each in their way promoted spa tourism for a particular audience. Visiting any upmarket bookstore (or try Amazon.com) one will be struck by the literally thousands of titles that deal with the healing potential, the true power or *The holy order of water*. Titles include among others *SalonOvations; Day spa operations* (1996), *The spa encyclopedia* (2002), *Spa & wellness hotels* (2002), *Spa and salon alchemy* (2004) and *Spa &*

---

14 A good example is a CD that I bought two years ago in the Central Javanese town of Yogyakarta. This CD, which offers traditional *gendhing* music, was nothing new. Rather, it was a traditional recording that is now sold under the title 'Java relaxation and spa'. Another strategy is to record old tunes in a new age style, complete with bird song and other natural sounds, and sell it as 'Synbotanic aromatherapy spa music', as I found on a Chinese CD.

health club design (2005), all of which focus on a worldwide evolving spa culture. Many of these coffee table books are exclusively about Asian spas. They sometimes consider a particular national tradition, such as the *Japanese spa* (2005), or the *Thai spa book* (2002), but more often portray it as a regional all-Asian phenomenon, such as *Spa style Asia* (2003), or *Ultimate spa; Asia's best spas and spa treatments* (2006).

In this section I shall focus on two publications: Sophie Benge's best-selling *The tropical spa* published by Periplus in 2003,[15] and the internationally available glossy *AsianSpa* (2004-2006). Both are published in Asia. Benge is an expatriate who lived in Asia for seven years, while the editorial staff of *AsianSpa* is made up of both Western and Asian journalists. Again, neither publication seems to exclusively address a Western or Asian audience. Rather, they cater specifically to the urban middle or upper classes. As important to *The tropical spa* as its explanatory text, and in line with what is said above about stressing the visual, are the stunning photographs by Luca Invernizzi Tettoni.[16] *The tropical spa* is in fact a catalogue of some of the better-known Southeast Asian spas (although criteria for their selection are strikingly absent). The book also offers stress releasing therapies under witty titles like 'Rites of massage', 'Hair story' and 'Face value', thus giving the reader access to a holistic and uplifting life style. I will regularly quote from this book below, but let us first briefly look at *AsiaSpa*, the other publication.

AsiaSpa (not to be confused with the similarly named *SpaAsia* magazine) is one of the countless new life style magazines in Southeast Asia that increasingly act as 'missionaries of modernity' (Heryanto 1999). The bi-monthly magazine, which was first published in 2004, is now sold in Hong Kong, Singapore, Malaysia, Thailand, China, the Philippines and several other Asian Pacific countries. Like *The tropical spa*, *AsiaSpa* magazine clearly caters to the wealthy, as can be concluded from its advertisements for Hyatt resorts, expensive chocolate, and Aston Martin and Rolls Royce automobiles. The latter are items that are typically aimed at a male market and *AsiaSpa* in no way pretends to be a women's magazine, in spite of the orientation of some of the spas found in Southeast Asia today. The magazine's up-

---

15 Sophie Benge was formerly the deputy director of *Elle Decoration* magazine in Hong Kong. At present she lives in London where she works as a journalist and is a consultant in an integrated health centre for women. Periplus is also responsible for other wellness and do-it-yourself eco-chic books like *Jamu; The ancient art of herbal healing* and *A handbook of Chinese healing herbs*. Turtle and Archipelago Press similarly published spa books such as the *Thai spa book; Natural Asian way to health and beauty* (2003) and *Spa style Asia* (2003).
16 Tettoni is considered to be one of the best spa photographers in Asia. He also did the photography for books such as *Bali modern*, *Tropical Asian style* and *The ultimate spa* book as well as many spa portfolios for hotels and resorts throughout Asia.

market orientation is confirmed by its use of English, chosen in this case not so much because of its international (for example, Western) readership, but rather because this is the language of the new Asian middle class and therefore a marker of modernity and cosmopolitanism. The magazine is widely available in flight libraries, airport shops and in the lounges of various Asian airline companies, once again linking it with a wealthy leisure class and the modernity their lifestyle is generally associated with. Large segments of society thus seem excluded from the world of *AsiaSpa*, but it can be argued that, like other glossy magazines, its readership acts as a role model, displaying a middle class life style that is aspired to by many.[17]

Figure 2. *AsiaSpa* glossy

[17] This is proven by the recent attention spa culture has for example received in Indonesian newspapers and locally oriented and Indonesian language magazines such as Seri HomeSpa.

AsiaSpa magazine and its associated websites[18] are publications of the Hong Kong based AdKom group. Their editorial staffs are composed of Asians and Westerners, men and women. Most of the contributors to this and comparable magazines are people who are involved in the wellness industry as journalists, consultants or therapists. *AsiaSpa* magazine contains such regular features as SpaTalk, Urban Spa, Book Watch, Spa Finder and Dare to Dream, the latter being a section on the ultimate indulgence, unfolding people's wildest dreams of consumption. It also has special features, like articles on Angkor Wat revisited and, in the anniversary issue, an A to Z of Asian Therapies.

While to a large extent being advertisements for and by the industry, one cannot help noticing how superficial and shallow some of the modern day guides actually are. In their praise for a much romanticized mythical past everyone seems to have been healthier, more beautiful and noble then, and stereotypical images of spiritual traditions typically abound. Frequently such descriptions include clearly invented traditions and misrepresentations of the people who supposedly practiced them. In describing the Datai hotel on Langkawi Island in Malaysia, *The tropical spa*, for example, comments that 'with your third eye it is not hard to see a Dayak tribesman emerging from the trees to appear on the jetty of your spa suite. Stick to real vision and your visitor will likely be one of the many monkeys to whom this Malaysian slice of rainforest really belonged before the Datai (hotel) arrived.' (Benge 2003:40.) Nowhere is it explained that the Dayak people actually do not live in Langkawi, but on the relatively far off island of Borneo. Having said so, magazines and coffee table books will be referred to below as we consider the role they play in shaping a New Asian lifestyle by providing the new visualities and stressing alternative temporalities tropical spa culture has become known for.

SPA SCAPES: VISUALIZING THE PARADISE ASIA IS

An important aspect that is commonly stressed in spa culture is the way the spa is turned into part of a wider natural setting. Resorts are often located at very scenic spots and are carefully designed in accordance with the natural surroundings. The Tjampuhan Spa in Bali, for example, is housed in the former guest house of the royal prince of Ubud, that was once also home to international artists such as Spies

---

18 www.asiaspa.com and an all Indian version, www.asiaspaindia.com.

7 Tropical spa cultures, eco-chic, and the complexities of new Asianism

and Bonnet, and starting point of the Western inspired art movement Pita Maha.[19] Today, the resort offers open views of the river valley, 'with all buildings enjoying the natural insulation of traditional Balinese thatched roofs and surrounded by tropical greenery and flowers' (from its brochure). Massage rooms are located along the water, where the sacred Oos and Tjampuhan Rivers meet, and situated just opposite the 900 year old Gunung Lembah temple complex. Not seldom, and this is intentional, it is difficult to distinguish where the spa resort stops and nature is taking over. If such natural environment is not at hand, and many spas are nowadays found within larger Southeast Asian cities, such natural landscapes are artificially created. Summarized, this means that the spa can extend within nature, or that nature is simply invited in using such elements as natural or man-made caves, streams, or small bushes, but also organic materials, such as wood, stone and flowers. Again it is a tropical image that is constantly invoked, but one that is cautiously adapted to the needs and taste of the modern day urban visitor.[20] In any case, landscaping, e.g. adapting the resort to its direct surroundings, is an important process often undertaken by skilled architects and designers and inherent to the atmosphere that is thus created within the spa. By lack of other bodily experiences, and in absence of taste, smell and sounds, such visual cues are even more stressed in the magazines and coffee table books that represent tropical spa culture. It is through these visual cues as well that a shared Asian world seems to be drawn for both the Western as well as the local readership.

'The pictures are just so well taken, you feel like you want to go there' one reader of *The tropical spa* is quoted in an Internet review site. Indeed, some readers simply do so. A Singaporean girl tells that she bought the book in Bogor (Java) at the Novotel gift shop while on vacation. During this trip she visited the Chedi and the Mandara spas where 'foods are as portrayed in the book' (again, food is here merely reduced to a visual matter). Like a modern pilgrim she further visited the San Gria Spa and Resort in Lembang (Java) and the Dharmawangsa in Jakarta, concluding that: 'having had spa treatments in both the U.S. and Indonesia, I have to say that Asia can do it best!' Julia, a Malaysian woman from Kuala Lumpur, is similarly convinced:

---

19 Pita Maha (literally 'Grand Ancestors' and referring to the deity Brahma) was the art society in 1936 founded by local aristocrats and international artists. Pita Maha was successful in getting works by local artists into international art exhibitions (Clark 1993:23). Seemingly proud of this glorious past the staff of the hotel and spa prefer the old time spelling of *Tjampuhan* rather than its modern day equivalent *Campuhan* to refer to the river valley at which it is located.
20 In one case, in a Balinese spa, I found out that the management even prided itself in a weekly extermination of all insects and bugs, this by spraying the whole area covered by the resort.

One Day Spa Entrance

The Spa enjoys a lush river valley setting, centred on a unique grotto decorated with traditional carvings and stonework. Facilities include hot and cold whirlpool baths, sauna and steam rooms.
In-house guest - US$12   Outside guest - US$15

Spa Beauty Package

Enjoy the facilities of the Spa for one full day, including one of the traditional treatments available.
In-house guest - Single US$39/Couple US$71
Outside guest - Single US$49/Couple US$89

Spa Adventure Package

Before enjoying the facilities of the Spa, guests are invited to join an invigorating half-day trek through the peaceful riverside scenery and traditional villages. The walk begins in Payogan village, descending through valley to the holy temple of Pura Gunung Lebah in Tjampuhan.
In-house guest - Single US$50/Couple US$93

Spa Harmony Package

A full day to enjoy the facilities of the Spa, with the addition of your choice of one traditional spa treatment, plus a delicious, specially-prepared meal with beverages from the Spa Cafe.
In-house guest - Single US$55/Couple US$105

Traditional Balinese Massage

A full body treatment massage with Tjampuhan Valley aromatic oils, with a choice of Ratu Bidadari (Angel Queen) and Rajawangi oils (Royal Essence).
60 minutes - US$25

Traditional Mandi Lulur

The epitome of Balinese massage - detoxifying and stimulating herbal skin preparation flushes away tension, followed by a cooling yoghurt rub for Ph balance, with the final touches of a Bali flower bath and fresh pressed herbal tonic.
120 minutes - US$33

Traditional Balinese Boreh

Essence of the spice islands - clove, ginger, nutmeg and root of galangal ground together in a volcanic stone mortar - lightly applies a blood circulation and detoxifying scrub in preparation for a full body Swedish massage, complemented by sandalwood moisturizing.
120 minutes - US$33

Swedish Massage

Absorb the essences of Tjampuhan Valley aromatic oils while our Swedish technique massage therapist soothes and stimulates, stretches and re-aligns both body and spirit.
60 minutes - US$25

Acupressure Massage

Direct contact massage, from head to toe, providing overall body rejuvenation focusing on the breathing techniques essential to effective acupressure therapies.
60 minutes - US$25

Head/Neck/Shoulder Facial Massage

Stimulating and refreshing the upper body with Biokos toner and mask connecting face, skin, bones and nerves with your inner spirit.
60 minutes - US$30

Hotel Tjampuhan - Jalan Raya Campuhan - PO Box 198 - Ubud 80571 - Bali - Indonesia
Tel: (62 361) 975368 - Fax: (62 361) 975137
e-mail: tjampuhan@indo.net.id - homepage: http://www.indo.com/hotels/tjampuhan

Figure 3. Price list Tjampuhan Spa, Bali

7 Tropical spa cultures, eco-chic, and the complexities of new Asianism

Being Asian and proud of my heritage, I grew up watching my late grandmother prepare her own home-made facial products with natural herbs found in the forest. The resorts featured [in *The tropical spa*] offer travelers an incomparable and convenient setting for discovering the Asian secret to the ultimate relaxation and indulgence for the senses. A must have for all Spa lovers! (April 28, 2000).[21]

Needless to say, the spas do not always meet the visitors' expectations, Western or Asian, created by the books, magazines and websites. A German tourist who visited the Chiva-Som, one of Asia's most luxurious resorts in the Gulf of Siam, complained that:

In contradiction to the pictures you see on Chivasom's website this hotel is not located on a quiet beach! These pictures must be very old...The hotel is surrounded by high apartment buildings (up to 20 stories), the beach is very dirty (also directly in front of the hotel) and I personally didn't want to swim in the ocean after looking at all the garbage, dead jelly fish, and leftovers from the dogs and horses (August 19, 2005).[22]

However, *The tropical spa*, like *AsiaSpa* magazine and its equivalents, contains spectacular, visually stunning photographs, and in the tradition of coffee table books it could be argued that Benge's texts merely complement Tettone's photographs rather than the other way round. The text on the dust jacket of the similar *Spa Style Asia* (Lee and Lim 2003) does not exaggerate when it states that 'spa prices and services will appeal to destination-oriented travellers, while the extensive color shots of spa surroundings, both interior and exterior, offer plenty of ideas for homeowners who would create smaller versions of paradise'. Or, as the brochure of the Balinese Wibawa Spa reads: 'designed as a Healing Sanctuary it is situated *seemingly away from everything*'. Both the tropical spa and its representation here through books and magazines are therefore not so much trying to sell an outstanding reality but rather the dream of something of a different yet to be realized world, more beautiful and out of place and ordinary time. This touches upon the representative possibilities inherent in the spa's depiction of both Asian nature and culture and second the paradise-like qualities spa culture clearly wishes to invoke.

21 Both quoted from Amazon.com reviews of *The tropical spa*, see http://www.amazon.ca/Tropical-Spa-Secrets-Health-Rejuvenation/dp/9625932658 (accessed September 2006).
22 From http://www.tripadvisor.com, offering online reviews of among others Chiva Som Luxury Health resort (accessed September 2006).

Figure 4. Cover of *The tropical spa* by Sophie Benge

7 Tropical spa cultures, eco-chic, and the complexities of new Asianism

The tropical spa depicts a much-idealized world or at least a miniature version of it, where it is 'the mood of yesteryear [that] inspires the imagination and treatments somehow feel better in a truly authentic setting' (Benge 2003:67). Spa architecture reminds one of representations of the 'traditional' in World Expositions or in the invented traditions of modern day heritage displays, and it makes possible 'a world of images more real than real' (Hendry 2000:70). Whereas some tropical spas, such as the Oriental Spa in Bangkok, purposely invoke the somewhat decadent atmosphere of the colonial architecture of pre-Independence Asia, the Oriental palaces of former eras seem to be even more popular as a source of inspiration. Carved, painted double Majapahit doors are incorporated in some Indonesian spas evoking a princess's chamber, referring to a glorious and mysterious past. Finally, so-called chambers of 'ethnic chic' are added, again stressing the tropical or Asian aspect of the place.

In some cases whole 'traditional villages' have been recreated at a spa resort. An example is the Balinese Jimbaran Spa, where landscape designer Made Wijaya combined English Cotswold architecture with the ambience of Balinese village layout. In other Balinese spas, Benge (2003:33) adds, 'even that nostalgic image of maidens bathing naked at the water's edge is realized by the local village girls'.[23]

The spas, *The tropical spa* thus states, 'adopt an earthy ambiance in tune with the powerful landscape surrounding them'. In fact tropical spas are miniature landscapes, or one might say spa-scapes, which play with the nature-culture distinction and often substitute one for the other in fusing indoor and outdoor spaces. Among spa culture's top attractions are, for example, *al fresco* dining, eating organic food outdoors rather than at home and 'offering that all-Asian frisson of showering naked next to nature' (Benge 2003:43). Other spaces, too, have a supposed otherworldly quality, setting them apart from everyday life. This brings me to the second feature that spa-scapes seemingly share; its invocation of an Asian paradise.

The Nirwana Spa at the Meridien hotel in Bali, for example, is built on a much-contested site, although none of the spa books

---

23 Nowhere near the Tajampuhan spa did we ever, during our two week visit in 2006, run into the bathing girls. The image clearly seems to be given by colonial fantasies of an island of 'bare breasts'. This image dates at least to the twentieth-century photo albums that emphasized the physical beauty of Balinese bodies, especially nude Balinese women taking their bath (Picard 1996:28) and it illustrates how the breasts of Balinese women no doubt constituted a major attraction to the island during that time.

mention this. It is located next to the famous temple at Tanah Lot, which *The tropical spa* (Benge 2003:54) links to 'a 16th century Majapahit priest who suggested to local villagers that this was a sacred spot'. Similarly, *AsiaSpa* magazine's special feature for January 2005 speaks of Cambodian spas taking us 'into the mists of time to Angkor Wat whose spiritual ambiance is recreated within the surrounding resorts'.

'Creating your own paradise' is thus a very popular slogan on the dust jackets of spa books; 'whether you're a traveller seeking the ultimate spa, or a homeowner seeking ideas for reproducing paradise in your own backyard'. Paradise in this case seems to be nothing less than Asia itself, or at least a landscaped and much idealized version of the best it has to offer. Thus, the Divana Spa in Lang Suan, Bangkok, Thailand claims that 'On earth there is no heaven, but there are pieces of it', and such pieces are being shaped by ethnic chic, colonial style and the glory of palaces of former eras. The same advertisement also promises its audience a future twenty-first-century aristocracy, in 'unveil[ing] the royal secret of wellness', laying a link between spa culture and a new Asian royal life style that clearly deserves more attention.

SPA TIME I: TWENTY-FIRST CENTURY ROYAL LIFESTYLES

The pages of *Asia Spa* magazine of January 2005 contain a stylish black and white advertisement for the Intercontinental Spa in Hong Kong. A Eurasian woman is shown in profile, obviously enjoying the pleasure of water trickling down her nude body. The accompanying statement that 'For once, it's all about me' further intensifies this sensual and intimate atmosphere.

Indeed, 'spa' seems to be a 'mantra for the growing band of worshippers at the altar of self-preservation' as Benge (2003:9) also suggests. *AsiaSpa* magazine confirms that 'your spa experience is all about you – what you enjoy and what suits you'. These are not just empty slogans but are representative of the ways in which readers and wannabe visitors are encouraged to take time for self-actualization without having to be ashamed of the common association with hedonism. Not coincidentally, coffee table books always show individuals alone, in an isolated spa, clearly enjoying the supposed silence of what must really be a rather packed resort. Tropical spa culture thereby obviously endorses the cult of individualization. Parkin and Craig (2006:7, referring to the work of Beck and Beck-Gernsheim), describe

Figure 5. A spa advertisment

people's urge to increasingly construct their own biographies in contexts where traditional ways of life and identities are under pressure: 'appreciation of the knowledges', as they argue, 'customs, tastes and pleasures of previous times are becoming part of the plurality of life options to individuals in constructing their own life narratives.' But constructing one's own life narrative is the perquisite of the happy few, and Parkins and Craig (2006:13, quoting Giddens) add that nowadays 'access to means of self-actualization becomes itself one of the dominant focuses of class division'.

Indeed, the newly rich of Southeast Asia are constantly looking for new ways to acquire cultural capital by carefully selecting what to consume and which places to frequent, but also by adopting a particular life style or being generally obsessed with lifestyle itself. Ariel Heryanto (1999) argues that these new Asian affluent classes are trying to restyle themselves as a new aristocracy by partaking in specific cultural events, poetry readings or, for that matter, all things 'cultural'. A New Asian life style that is partly based on regular visits to spa resorts might in this sense not only be a means for self-preservation or self-actualization, but most of all for self-aristocratization. Not very surprisingly the link with aristocratic values is indeed often made in spa culture, portraying the new leisure elite as all too willingly identifying itself with former elites and vice versa. Thus Benge (2003:51) describes how both the Mandara Spa at the Ibah hotel in Bali, and the Tjampuhan and Pita Maha Private Villa Spa are the property of Balinese royal families. Elsewhere also other aristocratic families have transformed their former palaces into small spa resorts.

Similarly Benge (2003:15) describes how 'many of the natural treatments that are now commonly used throughout tropical Asian countries trace their origins to the palaces of Central Java.' Traditional *lulur*, a body polishing process using spices and yogurt, has reportedly been practiced in the palaces of Central Java since the seventeenth century. Martha Tilaar, the mother of natural cosmetics mentioned earlier, is reputed to use it as one of her ancient palace secrets that are now also available to the common woman in both the East and the West. Another example is Mooryati Soedibyo of Mustika Ratu, another famous Indonesian brand of natural cosmetics. Mustika Ratu's *jamu* (herbal medicine) and traditional cosmetics are based on recipes that originated in the Surakarta Hadiningrat royal palace, and President Director Soedibyo herself is a princess turned business-woman. The story told on the company's website is illustrative:

7 Tropical spa cultures, eco-chic, and the complexities of new Asianism

B.R.A. Mooryati Soedibyo was born in Surakarta, Central Java on January 5th, 1928. She is a princess that grew up inside the Surakarta Keraton (palace) under the watchful eyes of her grandparents. The aristocratic traditions of the keraton were a part of the princess' daily life from the very beginning. She was patient in her study of blending of ingredients to make Jamu and other preparations for health and beauty care, as well as giving careful attention to other traditional arts.

From her grandmother, B.R.A. Mooryati learned how certain plants could impart their restorative powers to those who use them in the proper fashion. This was typical of the kind of traditional wisdom that had long been known only to members of the keraton aristocracy. By the age of fifteen, the young princess had mastered the art of herbal making and making up faces. She used this knowledge in preparing the Bedhaya and Serimpi dancers for their performances at the Surakarta Keraton. At the same time, she was also trained in the Javanese art of body care-known as Ngadi Saliro Ngadi Busono as well as time-honored traditions of courtly ethics and manners.[24] B.R.A. Mooryati began a new chapter in her life in 1956. With her marriage that year, she left the charmed life at royal keraton and moved with her husband, Ir. Soedibyo Purbo Hadiningrat MSc., to the city of Medan in North Sumatra.

With this new life, came new opportunities. During her spare time, B.R.A. Mooryati began formulating her own Lulur (body scrub), an exfoliating masker designed to lighten the complexion. She also began to make Jamu according to traditional recipes. These she gave to the wives of her husband's colleagues. In 1978, Mustika Ratu's products began to be distributed to local stores through salons chosen to be the company's agents. The public became far more aware of the value of traditional health care and beauty products through magazine and advertising campaigns.[25]

Today, Mustika Ratu is an international bestseller, with its own spa resorts and a separate spa cosmetics line, 'enchanting the world with royal beauty'. Maybe, *AsiaSpa* (January 2005) magazine wonders, 'its time to consider your spa experience as a ritual rather than a luxury', a ritual that provides the New Asian well-to-do with the aristocratic values and cultural practices so eagerly desired. And there is more to that, as spa culture in many ways seems to contribute to a new Asian lifestyle that tries coming to terms with the fast pace of modernity without necessarily looking to the West.

---

24 Presumably this refers to beautifying one's appearance (*sariro*) and dress (*busono*) (Robson and Wibisono 2002:25).
25 See http://www.mustika-ratu.co.id/ (accessed September 2006).

| Bart Barendregt

SPA TIME II: ALTERNATIVE TEMPORALITIES

The tropical spa (Benge 2003:43) advertises the Jimbaran Spa in Bali as a resort 'maintaining its indigenous sense of the exotic; gamelan music, eastern aromas and a soul soothing atmosphere where time has no role to play'. Yet there seems to be an overall obsession with temporality in spa culture, as the process of taking time, the experience of time, but also past times, are stressed time and again. Using the splendor of ancient palace secrets, nostalgic nudes and a pre-modern Asia where life seemed simpler and more pure, spa owners seem consciously to evoke the past. Following MacCannell (1989: 8), one could argue that 'the final victory of modernity over other socio-cultural arrangements is not the disappearance of the non-modern world, but its artificial preservation and reconstruction in modern society.' In a similar vein, Benge (2003:135) seems to over-idealize a near but almost forgotten past in which nature is a place where times gone by can be retrieved. The book could be hinting at a way to cope with the uncertain future that many newly developing Asian countries face nowadays, but part of it might also point at a more general fear of modernity itself, particularly the directions it should locally take.

Eriksen (2001) has pointed out the acceleration, so typical of Western information society, which threatens to eliminate distance, space and time. While not a reality for most Southeast Asians, the new rich in Asia's cities surely will recognize much of what Eriksen describes. Similarly, they are unhealthily rushed and becoming victims of what he characterizes as the 'tyranny of the moment'. In the Western European context Eriksen asks for a re-appreciation of slow time, a temporal regime that differs radically from that fragmented rushed regime that regulates so much of our lives. We need to take charge of our own rhythmic changes to get the best from both worlds – to balance between 'the hyperactive, overfilled, accelerated temporality of the moment, and, ... a serene, cumulative, 'organic' temporality' (Eriksen 2001:164). In its most extreme forms spa culture, associated eco-chic practices and the New Asian lifestyle that spring from it, remind us of a similar critique of an ever-accelerating global culture. An attribution of positive value to certain kinds and uses of time seem to occur in spa culture, as it does in eco-chic generally: it is chic to be modern and to be modern is to be fast. At the same time it is very 'eco' to question this speed and to think of more conscious and sustainable modes of using time.

In spa culture ideally an effort is made, even while only temporarily, to get 'back in touch with nature and so with [your] spiritual souls, which have little role to play in day to day urban existence' (Benge 2003:15). Most tropical spas therefore employ a strict

7 Tropical spa cultures, eco-chic, and the complexities of new Asianism

Figure 6. Inside a Javanese spa

etiquette to ensure that their guests enjoy the promised peaceful sanctuary. This includes discouraging the avatars of global fast-life like mobile phones, pagers and other electronic devices. In describing the atmosphere at the Bali Hyatt's spa, *The tropical spa* (Benge 2003:47) summarizes it with 'like so many Javanese words, *leha-leha* says it all succinctly.[26] It says peace, relaxation, daydreaming, an empty mind and lying prostrate gazing at the sky'. Spa time in this perspective thus hints at timelessness, and the therapies are recommended as having been used for centuries by Javanese princesses as an elixir of youth, 'having been unchanged since Thailand's Ayutthaya period', or as one advertisement offering Kerala's 500-year old *ayurveda* system says, 'your trip to eternal youth'.[27] 'Taking time' is yet another often used expression that explains spa culture's advocating of a slower if not different

---

26 The Javanese words here presumably refer to Old Javanese that for long was the language of literature and learning in Bali. *Léha-léha*, means to do at one's leisure, or *dolce far niente* (Stevens and Schmidgall-Tellings 2004:569).

27 *Ayurveda* is an ancient Indian system of holistic health care that according to some (Crebbin-Bailey, Harcup and Harrington 2005) dates back to 5000 BCE. It provides, as they argue 'the foundation for a lot of therapies practiced in spas today'.

temporality.[28] Taking time, for example, in such sanctuaries of spiritual silence as the tranquil room, the quiet room, or in the absolute void of the flotation tank, where half an hour's relaxation is equivalent to eight hours of sleep. These are the places where, as Benge (2003:27) puts it, 'the sound is waves, the view is seashore, the smell is spicy and the mood is thick with calm'.

Spa time means retreating into the self, and by getting attuned with the surrounding spa-scapes the inner landscape should be explored. Spa time is offered here as an alternative temporality, an articulation of the present and one's presence therein (Parkins and Craig 2006). The visit to the spa thus promises an instant experience of spirituality that is so difficult to come by in modern life. It is an inner beauty, but achieved at the speed of an extreme make over from the inside out.

Comparable to lifestyles based on New Age or Slow Living, spa time therefore does not so much offer a complete break with modernity, nor a continuous parallel temporality, isolated from the rest of global culture, but rather is its obverse. By slowing down just temporarily as long as a visit or a holiday to a resort may take, it helps one to recharge and to cope with the speediness of everyday life. Or as *AsiaSpa* magazine of January 2005 puts it, 'Being able to get away from the outside world, retreat inside and relish some well-deserved time out is vital for our physical, mental and spiritual health'. Significantly many spa brochures, books and magazines promise an explicitly modern experience, advertising urban spas where you can 'maintain your equilibrium in the city'. *The tropical spa* shows people enjoying a hot stone massage while overlooking Shanghai's skyline, and the Thai therapists of the Oriental Spa are said to live as 'Buddhists in the urban tumult of Bangkok' seeking to 'understand the nature of tranquility' (Benge 2003:61).

Spa culture, from resorts, to books, websites and other forms of advertising, excels in a reflexive negotiation on using the pleasures of previous times in the present, at times also projecting utopian possibilities, 'in the sense of a longing for a different, and better way of living, a reconciliation of thought and life, desire and the real, in a manner that critiques the status quo without projecting a full-blown image of what future society should look like' (Parkins and Craig 2006:8). Spa culture might serve here as a key to a new age, a new age with Asianism as its preferred life style.

---

28 It is obvious that in reality this does not always seem to work. During our own holidays in a Balinese spa resort, for example, my wife was struck by the careful attention constantly being paid by employees to a clock that was centrally positioned in the main treatment room. The clock constantly seemed to remind her of common time that was ticking on outside and that eventually would signal the end of the treatment.

7 Tropical spa cultures, eco-chic, and the complexities of new Asianism

THE SPA AS SOURCE OF A FUTURE ASIA – SOME CONCLUSIONS

Resort companies increasingly seem to realize the potential of Asianness, praising the attention that natural health and beauty have traditionally received in local societies.[29] Besides the revaluing of local traditions this also leads to newly created identities. One of these is cosmopolitan in character. The book *Spa style Asia* (Lee and Lim 2003) uses the term cosmopolitan to refer to 'a kaleidoscope of international cures' consisting of such therapies and treatments as *lomi lomi* (Hawaiian massage), Swedish massage and the like. These are by no means associated with their original localities nor are they seen as exclusively Western. Rather, they are global and are thereby rendered less threatening to Asian culture. The latest and most hip therapies are, moreover, advertised as being New Asian, or again, to quote the *Spa Style Asia* guide, 'Asia's paradigms revamped'. Whereas 'Cosmopolitan focuses on international treatments which are offered by Asian spas (e.g. Western therapies domesticated) [...], New Asianism is devoted to traditional Asian treatments updated with a modern twist' (Lee and Lim 2003:71), or, as *The tropical spa* puts it, the spa is a concept 'as old as the hill it springs from, rewritten for the contemporary scene'. Many of the therapies variously known as Asian Approach, Oriental philosophy, or more aptly here, New Asian, are therefore based on traditional oriental healing systems 'that have been practiced throughout history'. *Watsu*, or water *shiatsu*, for example, is a Japanese form of massage re-invented in America but further developed as an aquatic body therapy for tropical waters by the Breathing Space Company of Singapore. The Java wrap, as offered by *The tropical spa* (Benge 2003:94), is yet another example of 'a global beauty phenomenon waiting to happen: an age-old process for a new age answer to slimming'.

Rather than focusing solely on local traditions, globalization has thus triggered a newly emergent regionalism in which the idea of Asia is used as a counter to the take on modernity and globalized fast life that the West is known for. As I have sketched here, eco-chic and most notably the latest trend of tropical spa culture is

---

29 Although not yet part of spa advertising there is indeed a long tradition of praising beauty and seeing it as a quality with which heavenly beings are endowed and attributing king and rulers with a similar beautiful appearance. Malay *hikayat* proved the king to be a worthwhile and legitimate ruler due to his strength and extraordinary beauty (Hadijah Rahmat 2001:83). The protagonist of another classical tale, Prapanca's king in the *Desawarnana*, is described by Taylor (2004:94) as very attractive to women. When he passed by in royal procession, the narrator says, 'some village women rushed so fast to see the king that their breast-cloths fell off'. Ugliness and sicknesses on the other hand were often symptomatic of a disturbed relation between the ruler and his realm (Jordaan and De Josselin de Jong 1985).

importantly contributing to the lifestyle industry New Asianism is steadily becoming. In the process spa culture seems to have gained different meanings to different groups of visitors. Western but also East Asian visitors praise spa resorts for their paradise-like qualities and their consumer friendly approach in representing the tropics/ Asia, complete with its beauty, health and to a lesser extent spiritual practices. However, locally spa culture is at the same time contributing to a new pan Asian lifestyle that is eagerly consumed by the Southeast Asian new rich who are looking for the shared values they were lacking hitherto. New Asianism is therefore typically a process that occurs at the interface where cultures meet, and the tropical spa is its successful shop window. To quote Leo Ching (2000:257), 'Asianism no longer represents the kind of transcendental otherness required to produce a practical identity and tension between the East and the West. Today, "Asia" itself is neither a misrepresentation of the Orientalist nor the collective representation of the anti-imperialists. "Asia" has become a market, and "Asianness" has become a commodity circulating globally through late capitalism.'

But why the spa as the popular choice in celebrating this new Asianism, why health and beauty, practices that so often are associated with the Western evils of individualism and the cult of hedonism?

One explanation of the spa's popularity as a source for Asian identity construction might be the assumption that the spa is merely popular culture and leisure activity and therefore a 'soft' cultural form that is relatively innocent. At the same time, culturally it seems far more effective than the often-politicized Asian values debate[30] of the mid-1990s or today's economic approach of ASEAN and similar organizations. In the aftermath of such top down approaches, as Chua Beng Huat (2003) suggests, a genuine reinvention of Asian cultural identity is now being undertaken, not only by governments but also by intellectuals, artists and commercial enterprises. New Asianism has thus far led to new approaches in filmmaking, fashion and media regionalism.[31] In this process

---

30 'Asian values' is these days usually associated with the leaders of East and Southeast Asian nations, its most prominent advocates being the former Prime Minister of Malaysia, Mahathir, and Senior Minister Lee Kuan Yew of Singapore. Asia has a unique set of values that sets it apart from the West. These values include a stress on the community rather than the individual, the privileging of order and harmony over personal freedom, refusal to separate religion from other spheres of life, an insistence on hard work, respect for political leadership, and an emphasis on family loyalty (Milner 2000).

31 On Sony's media regionalism and other forms of Asianism, see, for example, Iwabuchi 1999. On Singapore pop star Dick Lee's Asian music, see Wee 1996. At the same time the new Pan Asian culture of manga, pokèmon and J-Pop (Japanese pop culture) is predominantly East Asian in character, leading to assertions of neo-colonialism (Thomas 2004:178).

7 Tropical spa cultures, eco-chic, and the complexities of new Asianism

an Othering of the West takes place by stressing the uniqueness of being Asian, a feature that is also clearly present in the mediations of tropical spa culture we are considering here. As such, Sophie Benge's *The tropical spa* (2003:99) characterizes Asian people as more intuitive, stating that 'low touch Western society keeps tactile expression behind closed doors, while Indonesians touch all the time [...] they carry compassion in their hands'. Elsewhere Benge (2003:11) notes: 'In Indonesia, the birthplace of many tropical health and beauty secrets, there is an ancient Javanese expression; *rupasampat whaya bhiantara*. It roughly translates as 'the balance between inner and outer beauty, between that which is visible and that which is within and it is the parable by which women in this part of the world live without even thinking of it'. Which brings me to a second possible explanation.

Significantly it is mostly women who are participating in spa culture and therefore mostly depicted in the mediations of spas as well. In their *Re-orienting fashion*, Niessen, Leshkowich and Jones (2003) allude to the construction of the feminine in Asia as the bearer and wearer of national tradition. In the spa publications, however, it is not so much a national as a pan-Asian identity that is stressed by the women portrayed. The photographs in *The tropical spa* and other coffee table books and magazines like *AsiaSpa* mainly show women, both as visitors and as therapists. These women are rarely recognizably Western. Most often it is Asian women of indeterminate nationality who are featured in the photographs. According to Steve Kemper's study (2001) on advertising in Sri Lanka and Malaysia, they may be called pan-Asian models. Kemper notes that during the heydays of the New Economic Policy, in the 1980s and early 1990s, advertising in multicultural Malaysia was not to privilege any single ethnic group (Malay, Chinese, or Indian), lifestyle, or profession. Advertising agencies therefore promoted an all-Malaysian identity by recruiting pan-Asian models whose origins are often complicated but who are mostly of Eurasian descent.[32] Away from a Malaysian context also in other Southeast Asian societies Eurasian or mestizo women continue to set the beauty standard (Rafael 1995), leaving those dark of skin to

---

32   The models resemble a neutral, unmarked race of Southeast Asians. To the Asian audience, moreover, the models are attractive as they resemble Western Hollywood stars but are also a bit like the Asians themselves. As for the here referred to Malaysian ideal, obviously much has changed since the demise of the New Economic policy. With the emergence of more orthodox Islamic powers, especially in the Malaysian state of Kelantan, new beauty ideals are promoted publicly, and in outdoor advertisements women are now suitably covered up with a veil (Ismail 2004; Wong 2007). Strikingly, many of these Muslim advertisements continue to depict very 'white' women.

take their recourse to whitening cream or other measures. Ideally, women are a bit of the East meeting a bit of the West and the 'pan-Asian models' depicted in the coffee table books therefore seem to again highlight the complexities and contradictions present in new Asianism.

Lastly, the popularity of spa culture as the carrier of New Asianism might be explained with reference to the long tradition of adopting ideas on beauty, health and spirituality in the Asian countries under study, but also the neighboring East Asian societies. Many of these ideas have been exchanged for centuries and could to a certain extent be regarded as cosmopolitanism *avant la lettre*, but also as an early form of a pan-Asian culture. They are an easily recognized hybrid that, again due to its outward innocence, can serve perfectly as the foundation of an imagined regional community.

The question remains to what extent Asianism as a lifestyle and its associated practices of eco-chic and tropical spa culture will remain a minority cosmopolitanism, a new form of exclusion that helps the consuming classes to define what is hip and modern. Will it eventually trickle down to the now-excluded masses? If it does it might well be incorporated as some sort of new ecology that, next to pride in local produce and its being used as a basis for identity, might also stress the much needed sustainability and environmental consciousness that still seems to be lacking in many parts of Southeast Asia.

For now, the wellness industry, eco-chic and the tropical spa cultures seem to be involved in constructing a possible new post-national imagery in which life style and the leisure industry increasingly play a role. Here the new Asia is presented as collectively facing the West, a collectivity in which race, religion and nation become mere nuances in an overall taste that is Asia. The New Asia is in many aspects still an idealized Asian landscape, a dream of identity in a time when all identities seem increasingly to be under pressure. Above all, New Asianism is a way to reflect on a possible near future, a future that *The tropical spa* (Benge 2003:111) posits as a break with 'a time, not so long ago, when the notion of beauty was literally skin deep...[but now] not anymore. Recent decades of materialism have given way to a caring millennium and new approach to beauty that stems from within.'

REFERENCES

Benge, Sophie
2003 *The tropical spa; Asian secrets of health, beauty and relaxation.* Singapore: Periplus.

Clark, John
1993 *Modernity in Asian art.* Broadway, NSW: Wild Peony. [University of Sydney, East Asian Series 7.]

Ching, Leo
2000 'Globalizing the regional, regionalizing the global; Mass culture and Asianism in the age of late capital', *Public Culture* 12-1:233-57.

Chua Beng Huat
2003 *Life is not complete without shopping; Consumption culture in Singapore.* Singapore: Singapore University Press.

Corbett, T.
2001 *The making of American resorts; Saratoga Springs, Ballston Spa, Lake George.* New Brunswick, NJ: Rutgers University Press.

Crebbin-Bailey, Jane, John Harcup and John Harrington
2005 *The spa book; The official guide to spa therapy.* Australia: Thomson.

Crismer, L.M.
1989 *The original Spa waters of Belgium.* Spa: Monopole.

Duguid, J.
1968 *Pleasures of the spa; Pan Am's guide to the great health resorts of the world.* New York: Macmillan.

Eriksen, Thomas Hylland
2001 *Tyranny of the moment; Fast and slow time in the information age.* London: Pluto Press.Forbes, Bruce David and Jeffrey H. Mahan (eds)
2000 *Religion and popular culture in America.* Berkeley, CA: University of California Press.

Hadijah Rahmat
2001 *In search of modernity; A study of the concepts of literature, authorship, and notions of self in 'traditional' Malay literature.* Kuala Lumpur: Akademi Pengajian Melayu, Universiti Malaya.

Hendry, Joy
2000 *The Orient strikes back; A global view of cultural display.* Oxford: Berg. [Materializing Culture.]

Heryanto, Ariel
1999 'The years of living luxuriously', in: Michael Pinches (ed.), *Culture and privilege in capitalist Asia*, pp. 159-87. London and New York: Routledge. [The New Rich in Asia Series.]

Hudson, Simon (ed.)
2003 *Sport and adventure tourism.* New York: Haworth Hospitality Press.

Ismail, Rose
2004 'Women and Islam in Malaysia', *Kyoto Review of Southeast Asia.* http://kyotoreview.cseas.kyoto-u.ac.jp/issue/issue4/ (accessed 14-4-2011).

Iwabuchi, Koichi
1999 'Return to Asia; Japan in Asian audiovisual markets', in: Kosaku Yoshino (ed.), *Consuming ethnicity and nationalism; Asian experiences.* Honolulu: University of Hawai'i Press.

Jong Won Lee
2006 'An introduction', in: Urvashi Butalia et al. (eds), *The community of Asia; Concept or reality.* Pasig City: Anvil.

Jordaan, R.E. and P.E. de Josselin de Jong
1985 'Sickness as a metaphor in Indonesian political myths', *Bijdragen tot de Taal-, Land- en Volkenkunde* 141:253-74.

Jurriëns, Edwin and Jeroen de Kloet
2007 *Cosmopatriot; On distant belongings and close encounters.* Amsterdam: Rodopi. [Thamyris Intersecting: Place, Sex, and Race 16.]

Kemper, Steve
2001 *Buying and believing; Sri Lankan advertising and consumers in a transnational world.* Chicago: University of Chicago Press.

MacCannell, D.
1989 *The tourist.* New York: Schochen Books.

Mackaman, Douglas Peter
1998 *Leisure settings; Bourgeois culture, medicine, and the spa in modern France.* Chicago: University of Chicago Press.

Milner, Anthony
2000 'What happened to "Asian values"?', in: Gerald Segal and David S.G. Goodman (eds), *Towards recovery in Pacific Asia*, pp. 56-68. London/New York: Routledge. [ESRC Pacific Asia Programme.]

Niessen, Sandra, Ann Marie Leshkowich and Carla Jones (eds)
2003 *Re-orienting fashion; The globalization of Asian dress.* Oxford: Berg. [Dress, Body, Culture.]

Ottino, Arlette
2000 *The universe within; A Balinese village through its ritual practices.* Paris: Karthala.
Panlilio, Erlinda Enriquez and Felice Prudente Sta María
2005 *Slow food; Philippine culinary traditions.* Pasig City: Anvil.
Parkins, Wendy and Geoffrey Craig
2006 *Slow living.* Oxford: Berg.
Picard, Michel
1996 *Bali; Cultural tourism and touristic culture.* Translated by Diana Darling. Singapore: Archipelago. [Originally published as *Bali; Tourisme culturel et culture touristique.* Paris: L'Harmattan, 1992.]
Puntowati, S.W.
1992 'The *dukun pengantin*; Mediator at the Javanese wedding ceremony', in: Sita van Bemmelen (ed.), *Women and mediation in Indonesia*, pp. 187-201. Leiden: KITLV Press. [Verhandelingen 152.]
Rafael, Vicente L.
1995 'Taglish, or the phantom power of the lingua franca', *Public Culture* 8:101-26.
Robson, Stuart and Singgih Wibisono
2002 *Javanese-English dictionary.* With the assistance of Yacintha Kurniasih. Hong Kong: Periplus.
Simply relevant
2007 *Simply relevant heartSpa; Relational bible series for women.* N.p.: Group Publishing.
Stevens, Alan M. and A.Ed. Schmidgall-Tellings
2004 *A comprehensive Indonesian-English dictionary.* Revised edition. Athens, OH: Ohio University Press. [In association with the American Indonesian Chamber of Commerce.] [Originally published as *Contemporary Indonesian-English dictionary*, 1981.]
Susilowati and A. Zi
2003 *Sentuhan etnik.* Jakarta: Gramedia Pustaka Utama. [Seri Rumah Gaya.]
Suwardono
2007 'Identifikasi Ken Dêdês dalam arca perwujudan sebagai Dewi Prajñaparamita; Tinjauan filsafat religi dan ikonografi', *Berkala Arkeologi* 27-1:127-54.
Tanqueray, Rebecca
2000 *Eco-chic; Organic living.* London: Carlton Books.

Taylor, Jean Gelman
2004   *Indonesia; Peoples and histories.* New Haven, CT: Yale University Press.
Thomas, Mandy
2004   'East Asian cultural traces in post-socialist Vietnam', in: Koichi Iwabuchi, Stephen Muecke and Mandy Thomas, *Rogue flows; Trans-Asian cultural traffic,* pp. 177-96. Hong Kong: Hong Kong University Press.
Wee, C.J.W.L.
1996   'Staging the new Asia; Singapore's Dick Lee, pop music, and a counter-modernity', *Public Culture* 8-3:489-511.
Wong, L.
2007   'Market cultures, the middle classes and Islam; consuming the market?', *Consumption, Markets and Culture* 10-4:451-80.

Contributors

Bart Barendregt is an anthropologist who lectures at the Institute of Social and Cultural Studies, Leiden University in the Netherlands. Presently he is coordinating a four-year research project (Articulation of Modernity) funded by the Netherlands Organisation for Scientific Research (NWO) that deals with popular music, modernity and social change in Southeast Asia. As a senior researcher he is as well affiliated to the NWO project, The Future is Elsewhere; Towards a Comparative History of Digital Futurities, in which he is looking at Islamic ideas of information society, halal software and appropriation and localization of digital technology in an overt religious context. He has done extensive fieldwork in Java, Sumatra, and Malaysia and has published on performing art, new and mobile media and popular culture.

Marieke Bloembergen is a research fellow at the Royal Netherlands Institute of Southeast Asian and Caribbean Studies (KITLV). She publishes on policing and security in the Netherlands Indies and on (post)colonial imagination, memory and heritage formation in the Netherlands and Indonesia. She is author of *De geschiedenis van de politie in Nederlands-Indië; Uit zorg en angst* (2009) and *Colonial spectacles; The Netherlands and the Netherlands Indies at the World Exhibitions, 1880-1931* (2006). At the moment she is conducting a research project on archaeological sites and the dynamics of heritage formation in colonial and postcolonial Indonesia, in local, trans-Asian and international perspectives.

Kees van Dijk was a researcher at the Royal Netherlands Institute of Southeast Asian and Caribbean Studies (KITLV) from 1968 to 2007. He holds a chair as Professor of the history of Islam in Indonesia at Leiden University since 1985. Among his publications are *A country in despair; Indonesia between 1997 and 2000* (2001) and *The Netherlands Indies and the Great War, 1914-1918* (2007).

David Henley is professor of Indonesia Studies at the Leiden University Institute for Area Studies (LIAS). Since 1993 he has been a researcher at the Royal Netherlands Institute of Southeast Asian and Caribbean Studies (KITLV). He is the author (with Peter Boomgaard) of *Credit and debt in Indonesia, 1860-1930; From peonage to pawnshop, from kongsi to cooperative* (2009) and *Fertility, food and fever: Population, economy and environment in North and Central Sulawesi, 1600-1930* (2005).

Mary Somers Heidhues taught in universities in Germany and the USA. She has written about Chinese in Southeast Asia, most recently *Golddiggers, farmers, and traders in the 'Chinese' districts of West Kalimantan, Indonesia* (2003 and, in Indonesian, 2008) and is a contributor to the *Encyclopedia of global migration* (forthcoming).

Jean Gelman Taylor teaches Southeast Asian and Indonesian history at the University of New South Wales in Sydney, Australia. Her publications include *The social world of Batavia* (1978, second edition 2009), *Indonesia; Peoples and histories* (2003), and articles on the social history of colonialism.

George Quinn is Adjunct Professor and Visiting Fellow in the College of Asia and the Pacific, Australian National University. He is author of *The novel in Javanese* (1991), *The learner's dictionary of today's Indonesian* (2001) and, most recently, several short studies on pilgrimage to holy shrines in Java and Madura.

Index

Abé, Yoshio 61, 67
Aceh 7, 50, 52, 65, 71-2, 117
Adiwijaya, Sultan 151
Adriani, N. 98
advertisements 1, 18-20, 26, 117-20, 154, 164, 187
Ageng Serang, Nyi 151
Algiers 24
Ambon 48, 64
Anthony, Saint 6
Anti-Revolutionaire Partij (ARP) 140
Ariès, Philippe 43
Arnold, David 41
Arya Penangsang 151
Athanasius, Saint 6

Bali 53, 131, 138, 160, 162, 164-6, 169, 172, 174, 177, 180, 182-3
Bandung 49, 57
Banggai 97-8, 105
Bangka 63, 68, 73-7, 80-8
Bangkok 67-8, 177-8, 184
Banten 86
Barratt, Thomas J. 18
Batavia 12, 29, 44, 55, 69-70, 83, 85-6, 127, 129-32, 134-8, 141-2
bathing 1, 7, 12, 26, 29, 41-6, 55-6, 96, 102, 106, 162
 – bathhouses 6-7, 11, 45, 55
 – bathing places 7, 50, 147-53, 165, 167
 – bathing/washing rituals 56-7, 147-51, 155, 167
 – soldiers and 12
 – Turkish bath 10
Beecher, Henry Ward 24
Beecher Stowe, Harriet 24
Belitung 80-1, 83, 87
Bellamy, George C. 17-8, 27
Benge, Sophie 168, 170, 175-8, 180, 182, 184, 187
beriberi viii-ix, 61-84, 87-9, 97
 – epidemic proportions of 63
 – immunity to 69
 – Japanese army and 66
 – orphans and 69
 – Philippine militia and 68-9
 – prisoners and 69
 – Roman armies and 63
 – soldiers in the Netherlands Indies and 64-5, 71, 81
 – students and 69
 – treatment for 67
Best, Thomas 7
Bima *see* Wrekudara
bin Abdul Kadir, Abdullah 8
Biow, Douglas 44
Blinyu 84-5, 87
blowing the nose 45, 56
body 27, 30, 42, 45, 66, 74-5, 97, 119, 153, 178
 – beauty and xi

Index

—body care viii, 163, 181
—body/bodily odour/smells 5, 11, 44, 117, 120
—body therapy 185
—cleanliness of xii, 31
—cleaning/washing of the 5, 7, 9, 11, 23, 43, 45-7, 56, 106, 150
—'colonization' of 41
—concepts of 42
—smells 7-11, 22, 44, 117
—filthy body 5-6, 23
—body polishing/scrubs (*lulur*) 162, 164, 169, 180-1
—bodily hygiene xi, 5, 9, 42-5
—bodily functions 46
—bodily pleasure 117
—bodily training 129
—bodily well-being 160
—bodily experiences 173
Böck, William Edward 133-5
Boer War 20
Boers 20
Bogor 15, 73, 78, 81-3, 87, 173
Bonnet, Rudolf 173
Bontius, Gerardus 64
Boomgaard, Peter 41
Boyolali 150, 153
Brighton 10
British India 30
Bruni, Leonardo 9
Buddhism 168
Buol 109
Burma 18

Campuhan, River 173
Carpenter, Kenneth J. 61, 66
Cephas, Kassian 51
Ceribon 86

Ceylon 17
childbirth 109-10
China 11, 24-5, 45, 75, 78, 80-3, 86, 88-9, 170
Ching, Leo 186
Chiva-Som 160, 164, 166, 175
cholera 97-9, 109
Chopra, Deepak 163
Christelijke Staatspartij (CSP) 130-1, 137, 140, 142
Christianity 1, 5-6, 13-6, 22-4, 44, 168
Chua Beng Huat 186
Cirebon 7
Clarkson, Jeremy 31
class 9, 16-7, 43-7, 56, 123
cleanliness viii-ix, xii, 14, 41
—as embodiment of civilization 18
—as mark of social honour 44
—as metaphor x, 117-43
—as social construct 43
—as virtue 17-8, 22
—bathing and 106
—class and 46
—clothing and 110
—colonial policing and 117, 123
—concepts of vii-ix, 9, 11, 16, 31, 41, 44, 56, 63, 70, 96
—cooking and 110
—definition of 31
—Dutch concern for 42
—Dutch doucumentation of 41-2
—Dutch housewife and 26
—Dutch obsession with 8
—epidemics/diseases and vii-ix, 61, 74, 81
—flush toilets and 4, 45
—godliness and 18, 22-4, 44
—housing and 109

–lack of 96, 111
–personal 11, 14, 17, 24, 44, 95
–pleasure and 50
–political cleanliness viii
–pride and 42
–propagating vii
–public cleanliness 95
–race and 46
–regulations and viii
–repulsion to 6
–self-respect and 44
–servants and 50
–shame and 42
–shared understanding of 42
–social distinction and 44
–status and 44
–studies of/on viii, 11, 41
–superiority and viii-ix, 17, 20, 28-9, 31
–Western 26
–Westerners as standard bearers of xi
clothes
 –airing of 8
 –changing of 5, 20, 29, 42, 46, 51-2
 –underwear 5, 14, 29, 44
 –washing of ix, 5, 18, 26-9, 44-7, 55
 – *see also* footwear
Cockayne, Emily 7
Collis, Maurice 15
Colombo 17
Colijn, H. 131
Coolhaas, W.Ph. 139
Corbin, Alain 9, 44
cosmetics 155, 161-2, 164, 169, 180-1, 188
Craig, Geoffrey 178, 180

culture 29, 186
 –appreciation of local 12-3
 –Asian culture 168, 175, 185
 –destruction of 3
 –developments in material 42
 –dislike of other vii
 –distancing from other 15
 –global culture 162, 182, 184
 –homosexual subculture 117, 132, 155
 –maintaining Dutch culture 46
 –nature-culture distinction 177
 –pan-Asian culture 163, 186, 188
 –popular culture 186
 –public culture 168
 –regional/local culture 159, 163
 –soap and indigenous culture 111
 –turning away from the culture of Islam 24
 –Western civilization superior to other 15, 96
Curtin, Philip 41

Dalrymple, William 12
Dead Sea 23
defecating 3-4, 31, 46-7, 105-6 *see also* toilet
Dekker, P. 129, 131, 137
Depok 66
Dewi Sri 152
diet *see* nutrition
Diponegoro 151
dirty environment 4, 9-10, 75, 96, 103-5
Djojohadikusumo, Margono 41
Donggala 102
Drupadi 152
Dursasana 152

eating manners 46, 56
eco-chic Asian style 162-9, 182, 185-6
Eisenhower, Dwight D. 24
Elias, Norbert 11, 45
England 1, 8, 15, 42, 45, 159
Erasmus 8, 45
Eriksen, Thomas Hylland 182
Evangelicals 13-6, 24
Eijkman, Christiaan 61-2, 70-1, 73, 81, 84, 87
Eyndthoven, W.G. van 132-4, 136, 142

farting 8, 11
fasting month 150-1, 154
Fievez de Malines van Ginkel, H. 131, 136-7
Fiji 12-3
Finland 5
Flecker, James Elroy 23
Florence 9
Fonvizin, Denis 9
footwear x, 110
France 6, 8-9, 17, 22, 42, 169
Francis of Assisi, Saint 6
funeral rites 56-7, 155

Ganesha 147
Garvey, Ellen Gruber 26, 30
George V, King 10
Geraerts, H.A.I. 133-6
German New Guinea 22
Germany vii, 17, 22, 140, 194
Gerstäcker, Friedrich 12, 16
Gilray, James 3
Goa 7
Godavari River 165
Gorontalo 24, 95, 102

Graafland, Nicolaas 24, 96, 110
Great Britain 8, 10, 12, 16, 22, 30, 111
Grijns, G. 73, 87

Haan, F. de 12
Hadiningrat, Soedibyo Purbo 181
Hague, The 46
hair xi, 5, 7, 10, 14, 20, 47, 147-8, 150-5
Hamengkubuwono I, Sultan 7
Hamengkubuwono VII, Sultan 51
Hastings, Warren 15
headdress 154-5
Headrick, Daniel 41
health x, 6-7, 17, 46, 64, 95, 108-9, 161, 164, 166, 184-6
– authorities vii
– bathing and 11-2
– colonial health policy measures x, 46
– health implications 95
– health inspections 81
– health services 66
– health problems 70-1
– health conditions/situation x, 80, 82, 95-6, 102, 107
– lifestyle and 159
– promotion of vii, 75
– public health 41, 95, 111
– health treatments xi
– secrets for 162, 187
– spa culture and 167-8, 188
– tourism and 160
– upper classes' fascination for 162
Heerklotz, Dedo 81
Herport, Albrecht 63
Heryanto, Ariel 180

Hickson, Sydney 103, 105, 109
Hikayat Abdullah 8
Hinduism 165-6
Hobhouse, Emily 20
Hoetink, B. 87-8
Holland 45-7, 52, 55
Hollandia 22
holy places 147-8, 153-4, 165-6, 178
homosexuality 117-43
Hong Kong 170, 172, 178
Hoogeveen, Eva van 42
houses 47, 55, 75, 96, 102-9
 – bathrooms and 46, 55
 – cleanliness in 109
 – cosiness and 47
 – crowded conditions in 105, 111
 – development of house design 41, 95, 163
 – disinfection of 41
 – Dutch house 47, 56
 – Dutch housewives viii, 8, 26, 42
 – filthy houses ix, 17, 27
 – for the sick 82, 84
 – household 42-3, 45, 55, 108, 134
 – Indonesian house 51
 – keeping houses viii, 31
 – neglected housing 75
 – on piles 96, 103, 105
 – rubbish in front of 8
 – sweeping in front of 8
 – swidden houses 102, 104
household goods 8, 27, 42, 150
Hulshoff Pol, D.J. 73, 87
hygiene x, 10-1, 22, 46, 56, 67, 97, 102, 107, 121, 123, 142
 – concepts of 8, 62, 70, 96
 – German Hygiene Museum vii
 – hygiene conditions 95-6
 – hygiene habits/practices 44, 46-7
 – improvement of 99, 111
 – indigenous hygiene 110
 – lack of ix, 22-3, 31, 64, 88, 98
 – personal hygiene viii, 4, 11, 31, 42, 50-1, 56, 95, 105, 110-1
 – physical hygiene viii, xi, 5, 9, 14
 – promotion of vii, 11, 22, 24, 106
 – public hygiene viii, 95, 110, 127
 – standards of 23, 50

Ibn Saud, King 4
India 3, 7-14, 17, 30, 160, 183
Indochina 22, 27
Indo-Europeans 15-6, 29-30, 47, 187-8
Indramayu 86
Ireland 5, 22
Islam 6, 23, 44, 56, 147-55, 168
Italy 5, 9, 20, 42, 44, 46, 160

Jakarta 168, 173
jamu 170, 180-1
Japan 63, 68-9
Jasanoff, Maya 12
Java xi, 15-6, 30, 50-1, 67, 70, 73, 85-7, 110, 138, 147, 152-3, 167, 173
 – Central 150, 153, 162, 180-1
 – East 135, 147, 153
 – West 71
Jebus 80
Jennings, George 3-4
Jennissen 81
Jepara 151
Jerome, Saint 6
Joana 86
Jones, Carla 162, 187

Index

Jones, William 15
Jongh, de 87
Jordan, River 23
Joyoboyo 147-8
Judaism 6, 23, 44
Julianus, J.C. 135
Jumprit 153

Kalinyamat, Ratu 151
Karanganyar 150
Karaton 103
Karnataka 160
Kartasura 150, 153
Kediri 147
Kemper, Steve 187
Ken Dedes 167
Kerala 160, 164
Kerkhof, Gosse 128
Khouw Kim An 86
Kingsley, Charles 22
Kipling, Rudyard 18
Klaten 150
Koch, Robert 73
Koentjaraningrat 148, 150
Koetaradja 52
Kotta Goenoengan 52
kramas 148-55
Kroeëng Daroe 52
Kruyt, Alb.C. 98
Kuala Lumpur 173
Kuala Selangor 17

Labre, Benedictus 6
Lampung 48
landscape 24, 54, 172-8
Langkawi Island 172
Lebanon 23
Lee Kuan Yew 186

Leent, F.J. van 65, 70
Lembang 173
Leshkowich, Ann Marie 162, 187
Levuka 12
Lindman, L. 75
Linnaeus, Carl 7
Linschoten, Jan Huygen van 7
London 3-4, 10, 73
Lucknow 14
lulur see body polishing/scrubs
Lynch, William Francis 23

MacCannell, D. 182
McClintock, Anne 26
MacDonald, Robert H. 29
Mackaman, Douglas Peter 160
McKeown, Thomas 111
McLaughlin, Terrence 43-4
Mahomed, Sake Dean 10
Malacca viii, 8, 15
Malang 167
malaria 88, 96-9, 108
Malaya 17, 30, 69, 139-40
Malaysia 160, 170, 172, 186-7, 193
Malcolm, Howard 18, 27
Manado 108, 110
Manchester 45
Manderson, Lenore 41
Manila 18, 161, 164
Marcella, H. 135-7, 139, 142
marriage ceremonies 56-7, 148,
    150, 155, 167
Matthes, B.F. 24
Medan 133-5, 181
medical science ix-x, 41, 61-6,
    69-74, 88-9
Melania, Saint 6
Mentok 75, 80, 83, 87

200

miasma 67, 72-5, 81
Middle East 23-4
Minahasa x, 24, 95-7, 99, 101, 105, 109-10
miners, tin 74-87
Minto, Earl of 15
missionaries 1, 13-5, 23-4, 110
Molinari, Gustave de 22
Monplaisir, Hortense de 31
Muhammad, Prophet 23
Mustika Ratu 155, 180-1

nakedness 5, 11, 51-2, 177
Nanusa 103
Nationaal-Socialistische Beweging (NSB) 140
Netherlands 8-9, 11, 16, 29, 31, 42, 56, 122, 129, 131-2, 139-40, 193
Netherlands Indies 16, 22, 26, 29-30, 46, 62-4, 66, 69-71, 73, 80, 86, 117, 121-23, 127-9, 131-3, 136, 138-40, 142-3, 193
New Asian lifestyle 159, 161, 163-4, 168-9, 172, 178, 180-2, 185-6, 188
New Asianism 161, 163, 168-9, 185-6, 188
New Guinea 105
Ngawi 54
Niessen, Sandra 162, 187
Nieuwenhuys, Rob 46, 56
Notker of St Gall 5
Nusa Dua Spa 166
nutrition 62, 65-77, 81, 87, 111
Nyagumbo, Maurice 20
Nyi Ageng Serang 151

Odol mouthwash vii
Oesman 134-5

Oos, River 173
Orange Free State 20
Oren, Michael B. 23
Owen, Norman 41

Pacific islands 1, 12-3
Palembang 49, 85-6, 168
Palu Valley 98, 102, 105
Panarukan 86
Pangkal Pinang 80, 82, 84
Parakan 153
Paris 4
Parkins, Wendy 178, 180
Parra, T.M. de la 136-8, 142
Pasteur, Louis 73
Pekelharing, C.A. 71-3, 83-4
Peling 97, 105
Peltzer, W.H.H. 133
Philippines 18, 69, 170
Phuket 160, 164, 168
plague 7
police x, 117-29
 – as civilizing force 122, 124, 127, 129, 132
 – campaign against homosexuals by x-xi, 121, 135-9, 141-3
 – corruption of 137
 – investigation methods 121, 132-6, 138, 140
 – police academy Sukabumi 124, 127, 129, 133-5
 – police association 124, 128, 130
 – police authorities and homosexual relationships 129-31, 137-8
 – police handbook 124
 – police journals 117, 124, 128, 130
 – police reforms 123

Index

– policy towards homosexual police officers 129, 131
– political policing 124, 127, 136-8
– self-image of 124
– violence of 124, 129
Poso 103, 106-7
Poso, Lake 108
press 121, 130-1, 141
privacy 43, 46-55
Probolinggo 75
prostitution 128
Prudente Sta Maria, Felice 161
public space 43-7, 51-2, 55
Purol 117-8

race 17-22, 26-9, 41, 43, 46, 88-9, 95-6, 123
Raffles, Olivia Mariamne 15-6
Raffles, Thomas Stamford 14-5
Rama V, King 3
Rangoon 67-8, 81, 87
Reid, Anthony 50, 151
Riau-Lingga 85
rice 61, 67-9, 73, 76, 81, 84-8, 138, 152
Ries, L.A. 141
Roosevelt, Franklin Delano 4
Roosevelt, Theodore 23
Russia 5
Russo-Japanese War 66

Sadono 152
Said, Edward W. 54
Saigon 67-8, 86
saints 5-6
Sake Dean Mahomed 10
Salle, Saint Jean-Baptiste de la 6
Samui 160

Sangir Islands 96, 98, 102
sanitary measures 4, 56, 71-2, 105-11
Saratoga 160
sauna 5-6, 10
Schama, Simon viii, 8, 42-3, 55
Scheube, B. 64
scurvy 67
Semarang 127
Senopati, Panembahan 154
servants 17, 50-1
sewerage 55, 110
shampoo xi, 10, 111, 147-8, 150, 154-5
– *banyu landha* 148-52
Sharif, Jafar 14
Siam 3, 68, 73, 81
– Gulf of 166, 175
Singapore 70, 75, 78, 81-3, 85-6, 164, 170, 185-6
Singosari 167
skin disease 97-9, 105, 110
slow food/living 161-3, 183-5
Smith, Virginia 6, 45, 56
Soedibyo, Mooryati 180-1
Soedirohoesoedoe, Wahidin 51
soap ix-x, 1-5, 11-3, 16-20, 22-8, 110-1, 117, 147-8
– Lifebuoy 117, 119-20, 129, 142
– Pears' 1, 18-9, 24-5, 28, 30
– Schichts Seifen 21
– Sunlight 26-7
Soedibyo, B.R.A. Mooryati 181
Sontag, Susan 89
Spa 159
spa 159-60, 165, 173
– eco-chic and 162-5, 168-70, 182, 185, 188

202

–spa architecture 172, 177
–spa cosmetics 181
–spa cuisine 169
–spa music 164, 169
–spa publications 164, 169-78, 184-8
–spa tourism 160, 166, 169
–tropical spa 159, 161, 163-4, 166, 169, 175, 177, 182. 186
–tropical spa culture 164, 167, 169, 172-3, 178, 185, 187-8
Spies, Walter 131, 172
spitting 45
Sri Lanka 187
Starkenborgh Stachouwer, A.W.L. Tjarda van 130-1, 139, 142
Steller, E. 96, 102
Stephens, John Lloyd 23
Straits Settlements 30, 81, 83
streets 8-9, 42
Suez 46
Sukabumi 124, 127, 129, 133-4
Sulawesi
 –Central 95, 97-8, 103-4, 106-10
 –North x, 24, 95, 99, 110
 –South 24
Suleimanov, Gabdulvakhid 29
Sungaiselan 80
Surabaya 85, 127, 131, 137
swimming 6, 46-7, 52
Szreter, Simon 111

Tagulandang 102
Takaki, Kanehiro 65, 69-70
Talaud Islands 98, 102-3, 105, 109
Taman Ledok 7
Taman Sari 7
Tamil Nadu 160

Tanjung Pandan 81, 86
Tanqueray, Rebecca 163
Taveuni Island 13
Taylor, Jean Gelman ix, 12, 185
Taylor, Lou 44
Tegal 86
Tentena 108
Tettoni, Luca Invernizzi 170
Thackeray, William Makepeace 10
Thailand 11, 160, 170, 178, 183
Thames 4
Thamrin, Mohammad Husni 122, 141
Thorn, William 16
Tilaar, Martha 161, 164, 167, 180
Tillema, H.F. viii, 106
Tirto Kamandanu 147
To Wana 104
Togian 102
toilets 3-4, 31, 42, 45, 55,
Tondano 97, 109
toothbrush 45
trade in women and children 128
Twain, Mark 23

United States 18, 20, 24, 68-9, 160
Ural Mountains 29
Urquhart, David 10

vice scandal 117, 129-43
Vietnam 22
Vigarello, Georges 44
Vonk, G. 131
Vorderman A. 73, 87

water
 –access to x, 13, 55, 99, 102, 107, 110

– boiling of 84, 109
– healing qualities of xi, 45, 152, 160, 164-8
– shortage of 99, 102
– use of 5, 44, 56, 84, 96, 102
Wellesley, Marquis of 15
wellness industry 160-72
Wesley, John 23
Wijaya, Made 177
Wilberforce, William 14
William IV, King 10
Winkler, C. 71

Wonogiri 150
Woodard, David 102
World War I 22
World War II 24, 45
worms 84, 97, 110
Wrekudara 152
Wright, Lawrence 44-5

Yogyakarta 7, 50-1, 168-9

Zentgraaff, H.C. 131
Zimbabwe 20

www.ingramcontent.com/pod-product-compliance
Lightning Source LLC
Chambersburg PA
CBHW050634300426
44112CB00012B/1788